The Concept of Non-International Armed Conflict in International Humanitarian Law

Anthony Cullen advances an argument for a particular approach to the interpretation of non-international armed conflict in international humanitarian law. Part I examines the origins of the 'armed conflict' concept and its development as the lower threshold for the application of international humanitarian law. Here, the meaning of the term is traced from its use in the Hague Regulations to the present day. Part II focuses on a number of contemporary developments which have affected the scope of non-international armed conflict. The case law of the International Criminal Tribunal for the former Yugoslavia has been especially influential, and the definition of non-international armed conflict provided by this institution is examined in detail. It is argued that this concept represents the most authoritative definition of threshold and that, despite differences in interpretation, there exist reasons to interpret an identical threshold of application in the Rome Statute.

ANTHONY CULLEN is a researcher on the joint British Red Cross and International Committee of the Red Cross (ICRC) project to update the collection of practice underlying the ICRC's Study on Customary International Humanitarian Law. He is also a Research Fellow at the Lauterpacht Centre for International Law and a Visiting Fellow at Wolfson College, University of Cambridge.

CAMBRIDGE STUDIES IN INTERNATIONAL AND COMPARATIVE LAW

Established in 1946, this series produces high-quality scholarship in the fields of public and private international law and comparative law. Although these are distinct legal sub-disciplines, developments since 1946 confirm their interrelation.

Comparative law is increasingly used as a tool in the making of law at national, regional and international levels. Private international law is now often affected by international conventions, and the issues faced by classical conflicts rules are frequently dealt with by substantive harmonisation of law under international auspices. Mixed international arbitrations, especially those involving state economic activity, raise mixed questions of public and private international law, while in many fields (such as the protection of human rights and democratic standards, investment guarantees and international criminal law) international and national systems interact. National constitutional arrangements relating to 'foreign affairs', and to the implementation of international norms, are a focus of attention.

The Board welcomes works of a theoretical or interdisciplinary character, and those focusing on the new approaches to international or comparative law or conflicts of law. Studies of particular institutions or problems are equally welcome, as are translations of the best work published in other languages.

A list of books in the series can be found at the end of this volume.

The Concept of Non-International Armed Conflict in International Humanitarian Law

Anthony Cullen

CAMBRIDGE
UNIVERSITY PRESS

CAMBRIDGE UNIVERSITY PRESS
Cambridge, New York, Melbourne, Madrid, Cape Town,
Singapore, São Paulo, Delhi, Tokyo, Mexico City

Cambridge University Press
The Edinburgh Building, Cambridge CB2 8RU, UK

Published in the United States of America by
Cambridge University Press, New York

www.cambridge.org
Information on this title: www.cambridge.org/9780521760485

First published 2010

A catalogue record for this publication is available from the British Library

ISBN 978-0-521-76048-5 Hardback

Contents

Acknowledgements

This work would not have been completed without the help and guidance of Professor William Schabas, Director of the Irish Centre for Human Rights, National University of Ireland, Galway. For his thorough and very patient supervision, I am greatly indebted.

Thanks are due also to a number of individuals who have read and commented on parts of this study. These include Ruby Carmen, Andrew Clapham, Rose Cullen, Aoife Daly, Shane Darcy, Paul Downes, Roja Fazaeli, Michael Kearney, Donncha McDermott, Ray Murphy, Marko Divac Öberg and A. P. V. Rogers.

I am grateful to the Irish Research Council for the Humanities and Social Sciences for funding received in the form of a research scholarship.

Abbreviations

ABiH	Army of Bosnia and Herzegovina
AJIL	American Journal of International Law
ARK	Autonomous Region of Krajina
ASU	Active Service Unit
BH	Republic of Bosnia-Herzegovina
BRITBAT	UNPROFOR British Battalion
BYBIL	British Yearbook of International Law
CBOZ	Central Bosnia Operative Zone
ECHR	European Convention on Human Rights
ECMM	European Commission Monitoring Mission
EJIL	European Journal of International Law
EU	European Union
FRY	Federal Republic of Yugoslavia [Serbia and Montenegro]
HDZ	Croatian Democratic Community; Croat Democratic Union
HOS	Croatian Defence Forces
HV	Army of the Republic of Croatia
HVO	Croatian Defence Council
HZHB	Croatian Community of Herceg-Bosna
ICC	International Criminal Court
ICCPR	International Covenant on Civil and Political Rights
ICJ	International Court of Justice
ICRC	International Committee of the Red Cross
ICTR	International Criminal Tribunal for Rwanda
ICTY	International Criminal Tribunal for the former Yugoslavia
ILC	International Law Commission
ILM	International Law Materials
IRRC	International Review of the Red Cross

IYBHR	Israel Yearbook on Human Rights
JACL	Journal of Armed Conflict Law
JCSL	Journal of Conflict & Security Law
JNA	Yugoslav People's Army
KLA	Kosovo Liberation Army
NYUL Rev	New York University Law Review
SC	Security Council [United Nations]
SCOR	Security Council Official Records
SDA	Muslim Party of Democratic Action
SDS	Serb Democratic Party
SIS	HVO Security and Information Service
SUP	Serbian Secretariat of Internal Affairs
TO	Bosnian Territorial Defence
UN	United Nations
UNCHR	UN Commission on Human Rights
UNESCO	United Nations Educational, Scientific and Cultural Organization
UNGA	UN General Assembly
UNPROFOR	United Nations Protection Force
UNTS	United Nations Treaty Series
VJ	Army of the FRY
VRS	Army of Republika Srpska

Introduction

The objective of this study is twofold. First, it seeks to highlight misconceptions surrounding the concept of non-international armed conflict in international humanitarian law. Second, it advances an argument refining interpretation of the lower threshold of non-international armed conflict. Although the majority of armed conflicts that have occurred since the Second World War may be characterised as non-international, research on the application of international humanitarian law to such situations has been sparse. Substantive scholarship in this area has been discouraged by a number of factors. The extremely complex and highly politicised nature of non-international armed conflict tends to provide an especially difficult subject area for research. Also, many scholars have argued that the distinction between internal and international armed conflict is an unhelpful, artificial one which should ultimately be dispensed with.[1] Contending that the same body of law should apply to all situations of armed conflict, irrespective of their characterisation as either internal or international, publicists have argued against continuing use of the distinction in international humanitarian law.[2] This has, understandably, lessened interest in research on the characterisation of armed conflict. Irrespective of one's position on the merit of the distinction, its recent codification in the Rome Statute of the International Criminal Court provides for the continued classification of armed conflict as either international or non-international. Given the frequency of non-international armed conflict, and problems surrounding the application of international

[1] See, for example, Crawford, 'Unequal before the Law'.
[2] See Stewart, 'Towards a Single Definition', McDonald, 'Eleventh Annual Waldemar A. Solf Lecture'.

humanitarian law in such situations, the lack of scholarship on the subject is regrettable.

As a starting point for the analysis of the concept of non-international armed conflict, Chapter 1 focuses on how the application of international humanitarian norms to such situations had evolved prior to the formulation of the Geneva Conventions of 1949. This chapter examines the characterisation of situations using the concepts of rebellion, insurgency and belligerency in traditional international law. As precursor to the regime established by the Geneva Conventions, recognition of belligerency required the application of the 'laws of war' to situations of internal conflict. The threshold for the recognition of belligerency was that of civil war.

Chapter 2 examines Article 3 common to the four Geneva Conventions of 1949 and its impact as a development of international humanitarian law. The drafting history of this provision is explored in depth to highlight the intended scope of the term 'armed conflict not of an international character'. As the first substantive provision of international humanitarian law specific to situations of non-international armed conflict, attention is drawn to the import of common Article 3 as a development of this body of law. The Commentary on this provision provided by the International Committee of the Red Cross (ICRC) is also probed to investigate its consistency with the intentions of those who drafted common Article 3.

Chapter 3 looks at changes in the concept of non-international armed conflict resulting from the 1977 Protocols Additional to the Geneva Conventions of 1949. Additional Protocol I expands the scope of international armed conflict to include wars of national liberation, while Additional Protocol II creates a new category of non-international armed conflict. The *travaux préparatoires* of both instruments is examined to highlight the basis for these developments of international humanitarian law. While the distinctions introduced by the Additional Protocols are significant, it is argued that they do not affect the lower threshold for the application of international humanitarian law to situations of non-international armed conflict.

Chapter 4 examines the threshold distinguishing situations of non-international armed conflict from situations of internal disturbances and tensions in light of recent developments. The objective is to clarify the terms of its application under international humanitarian law. An argument will be advanced in support of a particular approach to the application of this threshold in the characterisation of non-international armed conflict. The definition of non-international armed conflict provided in the case law of the International Criminal Tribunal for the former Yugoslavia (ICTY) will form a central tenet of this argument. The interpretation of this definition will focus on two aspects of non-international armed conflict: the intensity of hostilities and the organisation of armed groups. The temporal and geographical scope of non-international armed conflict will also be examined. The application of international humanitarian law to hostilities between non-state armed groups is furthermore discussed as a recent development affecting the scope of non-international armed conflict.

Chapter 5 examines possible lines of interpretation applicable to non-international armed conflict in the Rome Statute of the International Criminal Court and in doing so sets out an argument for an understanding of the threshold contained in Article 8(2)(f) as one equivalent to that of Article 3 common to the four Geneva Conventions of 1949. The drafting history of the Rome Statute is explored in this chapter and provisions relating to war crimes committed in non-international armed conflict are analysed in light of guidance on interpretation provided by the Vienna Convention on the Law of Treaties.

Chapter 6 concludes the study with a summary of recommendations on the interpretation of non-international armed conflict. Attention is drawn to state practice on the complementarity of international humanitarian law and international human rights law. It is argued that as the interpretation of non-international armed conflict evolves, it is important that an approach is employed which is guided by the object and purpose of international humanitarian law. This approach must proceed with a view to providing the best possible legal framework for the implementation of this body of law. If the role of international humanitarian law in situations of armed conflict is misconstrued, its utility is undermined. It is essential therefore that the concept of non-international armed conflict be interpreted in terms consistent with the object and purpose of this body of law, which concerns the protection of victims of armed conflict.

Overall, this study seeks to remedy some of the confusion that exists surrounding distinctions that are used to differentiate non-international armed conflict. It presents an approach to the interpretation of important distinctions which define the concept of the non-international armed conflict in international humanitaran law. In doing so, an attempt is made to develop a framework for the characterisation of armed conflict. It is hoped, in adopting this approach, that the analysis may prove useful in determining the applicability of international humanitarian law to situations of non-international armed conflict.

PART I • ORIGINS OF THE NON-INTERNATIONAL ARMED CONFLICT CONCEPT AND ITS DEVELOPMENT IN INTERNATIONAL HUMANITARIAN LAW

1 The application of international humanitarian norms to internal conflict prior to the Geneva Conventions of 1949

In appreciating the significance of recent developments affecting the scope of non-international armed conflict in international humanitarian law, it is important to view the current concept in the context of its historical evolution. Notable influences on the development of the contemporary legal regime for situations of non-international armed conflict are the concepts of belligerency, insurgency and rebellion in traditional international law (the body of law that preceded the regime established by the Geneva Conventions of 1949).[1] These will be explored in this chapter as a means of illustrating the origins of legal concern for adherence to international humanitarian norms in situations of non-international armed conflict. In doing so, changes in the scope of international regulation to the conduct of hostilities will be highlighted.

1.1 The practice of recognition and the application of humanitarian norms in traditional international law

The relevance of traditional international law to the concept of non-international armed conflict is an area that is frequently overlooked.[2] However, as the succeeding analysis will show, it merits scrutiny not

This chapter was developed from an earlier publication: Cullen, 'Key Developments', 65.

[1] The term 'traditional international law' is that which is generally used by commentators when referring to the laws of war prior to 1949. It was also employed in this way by the Appeals Chamber of the ICTY. See *Prosecutor* v. *Tadić*, Decision on the Defence Motion for Interlocutory Appeal on Jurisdiction, 2 October 1995, Case No. IT-94-1-AR72, para. 96.

[2] This occurs mainly for two reasons. First, international instruments such as the Geneva Conventions of 1949 (Geneva Convention for the Amelioration of the Conditions of the Wounded and Sick in Armed Forces in the Field, 12 August 1949,

only as the predecessor of the current legal regime governing situations of non-international armed conflict, but also as the starting point for international concern over adherence to humanitarian standards in such situations. The issue of recognition in traditional international law is studied in this chapter as a means of investigating the application of international humanitarian norms to the conduct of hostilities prior to the formulation of the Geneva Conventions of 1949. The purpose of doing so is to indicate the origins of the contemporary concept of non-international armed conflict in traditional international law. Three discernible stages in the development of internal conflict are examined: rebellion, insurgency and belligerency. Particular attention is paid to the grounds for recognising the application of international humanitarian norms in the second and third stages. In doing so, the scope of protection provided in traditional international law is shown to be limited to situations where the belligerency of insurgents is recognised.

1.2 The non-application of the laws of war to situations of rebellion

The concept of rebellion in traditional international law refers to situations of short-lived insurrection against the authority of a state.[3] In

6 UST 3114, 75 UNTS 31; Geneva Convention for the Amelioration of the Conditions of the Wounded and Sick and Shipwrecked Members of Armed Forces at Sea, 12 August 1949, 6 UST 3217, 75 UNTS 85; Geneva Convention Relative to the Treatment of Prisoners of War, 12 August 1949, 6 UST 3316, 75 UNTS 135; Geneva Convention Relative to the Protection of Civilian Persons in Time of War, 12 August 1949, 6 UST 3516, 75 UNTS 287), the Additional Protocols of 1977 (Protocol Additional to the Geneva Conventions of 12 August 1949, and Relating to the Protection of Victims of International Armed Conflicts (Additional Protocol I), 1125 UNTS 3, 1977; Protocol Additional to the Geneva Conventions of 12 August 1949 and Relating to the Protection of Victims of Non-International Armed Conflicts (Additional Protocol II), 1125 UNTS 609, 1977) and the Rome Statute of the International Criminal Court of 1998 (37 ILM 999, 1998), have overtaken this body of law in their provisions relating to non-international armed conflict. Second, the doctrine of belligerency, utilised in traditional international law for the recognition of internal armed conflict, has fallen into disuse and is now considered obsolete. For further reading on the concept of belligerency in traditional international law, see Garner, 'Recognition of Belligerency', 106; Lootsteen, 'Concept of Belligerency', 109; Menon, 'Recognition of Belligerency', Menon, *Law of Recognition*, pp. 109–37; O'Rourke, 'Recognition of Belligerency', 398; Schindler, 'State of War', in Cassese (ed.), *New Humanitarian Law* at p. 3.

[3] See Falk, 'Janus Tormented', in Rosenau (ed.), *International Aspects*, pp. 197–9. Heather A. Wilson defines rebellion as 'a sporadic challenge to the legitimate government'. *International Law*, p. 23.

part because of their brevity, situations of rebellion were considered to be completely beyond the remit of international humanitarian concern.[4] Rebels challenging the *de jure* government during a rebellion were afforded no protection under traditional international law. According to Richard A. Falk, a situation of rebellion was to be understood as 'a sporadic challenge to the legitimate government, whereas insurgency and belligerency are intended to apply to situations of sustained conflict'.[5] He has stated that situations qualify as rebellion 'if the faction seeking to seize the power of the state seems susceptible to rapid suppression by normal procedures of internal security'.[6] Lothar Kotzsch has supported a similar position, stating that 'domestic violence is called rebellion or upheaval so long as there is sufficient evidence that the police force of the parent state will reduce the seditious party to respect the municipal legal order'.[7]

In traditional international law a situation of rebellion may thus be characterised as a short-lived, sporadic threat to the authority of a state. Such situations may manifest themselves as a 'violent protest involving a single issue ... or an uprising that is so rapidly suppressed as to warrant no acknowledgement of its existence on an external level'.[8] According to the International Criminal Tribunal for the former Yugoslavia (ICTY), the lack of provision in traditional international law relating to situations of rebellion was partially because of the fact that states preferred to regard it as 'coming within the purview of national criminal law and, by the same token, to exclude any possible intrusion by other States into their own domestic jurisdiction'.[9] Falk commented that in situations of rebellion:

> external help to the rebels constitutes illegal intervention. Furthermore, the incumbent government can demand that foreign states accept the inconvenience of domestic regulations designed to suppress rebellion, such as the closing of ports or interference with normal commerce ... There is also the duty to prevent domestic territory from being used as an organising base for hostile activities overseas ... Thus if an internal war is a 'rebellion', foreign states are forbidden to help the rebels and are permitted to help the incumbent, whereas the incumbent is entitled to impose domestic restrictions upon commerce and normal alien activity in order to suppress the rebellion.[10]

[4] Dhokalia, 'Civil Wars', at 224. [5] Falk, 'Janus Tormented', p. 99.
[6] *Ibid.* [7] Kotzsch, *Concept of War*, p. 230.
[8] Falk, 'Janus Tormented', p. 197. [9] *Tadić*, Case No. IT-94-1-AR72, para. 96.
[10] Falk, 'Janus Tormented', p. 198.

The conduct of participants in situations of rebellion did not fall within the remit of traditional international law. Such situations were considered purely a matter for the domestic authorities of the state concerned. Hence, Heather A. Wilson states that where a rebellion takes place

> the rebels have no rights or duties in international law. A third State might recognize that a rebellion exists, but under traditional international law a rebellion within the borders of a sovereign State is the exclusive concern of that State. Rebels may be punished under municipal law and there is no obligation to treat them as prisoners of war ... Because rebels have no legal rights, and may not legitimately be assisted by outside powers, traditional international law clearly favours the established government in the case of rebellion, regardless of the cause for which the rebels are fighting.[11]

The absence of legal rights for insurgents in situations of rebellion helped to ensure non-interference in the internal affairs of sovereign states. While arguably not to the advantage of securing justice for those involved in rebellion, this lack of international regulation effectively strengthened the position of governments wishing to deal swiftly with dissent. When a government would fail in its efforts to suppress rebellion, the status of the conflict would shift to one of insurgency. As the section that follows shows, this shift in status allowed for the possibility of insurgent recognition, providing a window for the application of international humanitarian norms.

1.3 The concept of insurgency

When a rebellion survives suppression, it duly changes in status to a situation of insurgency.[12] The concept of insurgency in traditional international law is, however, ambiguous in the sense that its broad parameters are ill-defined. Falk has described it as a 'catch-all designation', holding that '[o]n a factual level, almost all that can be said about insurgency is that it is supposed to constitute more sustained and substantial

[11] Wilson, *International Law*, pp. 23–4.

[12] According to Erik Castrén, '[r]ecognition of insurgency means acknowledgement of the existence of an armed revolt of grave character and the incapacity, at least temporarily, of the lawful government to maintain public order and exercise authority over all parts of the national territory'. *Civil War*, p. 212. For further reading on the concept of insurgency in traditional international law, see Wilson, 'Insurgency', 46; O'Brien, '*Jus in bello*', 193; Menon, 'Recognition of Belligerency', in Menon, *Law of Recognition*, pp. 109–37.

intrastate violence than is encountered if the internal war is treated as a "rebellion" '.[13] Heather A. Wilson has noted that

> there seems to be general agreement that recognition of insurgency is recognition of a 'factual relation' or acknowledgement of the fact that an internal war exists. Beyond that, there is little explanation of the characteristics of the 'fact'. There are no requirements for the degree of intensity of violence, the extent of control over territory, the establishment of a quasi-governmental authority, or the conduct of operations in accordance with any humanitarian principles which would indicate recognition of insurgency is appropriate. Indeed, the only criterion for recognition, if one could call it that, is necessity.[14]

Recognition of insurgency occurs out of necessity when the interests either of the *de jure* government or a third state are affected by the conflict, requiring the establishment of relations with the insurgent party. This vague criterion of necessity referred to by Wilson alleviates much of the ambiguity surrounding the concept of insurgency in traditional international law. As the conditions are not clearly defined, the legal situation arising from such acts of recognition differs in each case.[15] In regard to objective grounds for the recognition of insurgency, Hersch Lauterpacht has stated that

> any attempt to lay down the conditions of recognition of insurgency leads itself to misunderstanding. Recognition of insurgency creates a factual relation in the meaning that legal rights and duties as between insurgents and outside States exist only in so far as they are expressly conceded and agreed upon for reasons of convenience, of humanity, or of economic interest.[16]

Although the legal effects of recognition differ according to each situation of insurgency, generally it may be taken as 'an indication that the recognizing state regards the insurgents as legal contestants, and not as mere lawbreakers'.[17] As noted by Lauterpacht, recognition of insurgency is linked to the desire of foreign states 'to put their relations with the insurgents on a regular, although clearly provisional, basis'.[18]

[13] Falk, 'Janus Tormented', p. 199. [14] Wilson, *International Law,* p. 24.

[15] According to Erik Castrén, 'recognition of insurgency includes as one of its principle elements the grant [sic] of certain rights [which vary] according to whether recognition has been received from the lawful Government or from a third State. It is thus impossible to define in advance the legal situation consequent on recognition of insurgency.' *Civil War,* p. 212.

[16] Lauterpacht, *Recognition,* pp. 276–7.

[17] Higgins, 'Internal War', in Black and Falk, *International Legal Order,* p. 88. See also Lauterpacht, *Recognition,* p. 270.

[18] Lauterpacht, *Recognition,* p. 270.

The indeterminate scope of insurgency allows for the concept's manipulation by states wishing to define their relationship with insurgents. Third states may recognise the existence of insurgency without explicitly declaring an allegiance or adopting a position of neutrality towards the conflict.[19] An act recognising the existence of belligerency would infer an obligation to refrain from offering assistance to either party.[20] In contrast, the recognition of insurgency may be utilised to tailor the position of the state according to its interests, avoiding the risks involved in explicitly joining the conflict and also the restrictions on behaviour resulting from neutrality. On this point, Falk has written that the recognition of insurgency

> serves as a partial internationalisation of the conflict, without bringing the state of belligerency into being. This permits third states to participate in an internal war without finding themselves 'at war', which would be the consequence of intervention on either side once the internal war had been identified as a state of belligerency. Interventionary participation in an insurgency may arouse protest and hostile response, but it does not involve the hazards and inconveniences that arise if a state of war is established with one or the other factions.[21]

The concept's indeterminate range of efficacy allows states the greatest measure of flexibility in defining their relationships with insurgents.[22] As an international acknowledgement of the existence of conflict by a third state, the recognition of insurgency leaves it 'substantially free to control the consequences of this acknowledgment'.[23] Possible motives for the recognition of insurgency are illustrated by Lauterpacht. He has stated that '[i]t may prove expedient to enter into contact with insurgent authorities with a view to protecting national interest in the territory occupied by them, to regularizing political and commercial intercourse with them, and to interceding with them in order to ensure a measure of humane conduct of hostilities'.[24] It is important to recognise here that the concept of

[19] Recognition of insurgency was first employed by the US government in relation to the Cuban Civil War of 1868–78. See Castrén, *Civil War*, pp. 46–7.

[20] See section 2.4. [21] Falk, 'Janus Tormented', p. 200.

[22] Falk states that

> [i]n general, the status of insurgency is a flexible instrument for the formulation of claims and tolerances by third states. If it is used to protect economic and private interests of nationals and to acknowledge political facts arising from partial successes by insurgents in an internal war, then it can adjust relative rights and duties without amounting to a mode of illegal intervention in internal affairs. (*Ibid.*, p. 202.)

[23] *Ibid.*, p. 199. [24] Lauterpacht, *Recognition*, p. 270.

insurgency in traditional international law does not necessitate the application of humanitarian norms. Unless explicitly conceded, the *de jure* government would not have been obligated to adhere to such norms.[25] Any legal protection available to insurgents would have had to come only from the provisions of municipal law unless the application of humanitarian standards was specifically provided for in the act of recognition.

International law has now evolved to require the application of the law of armed conflict in all situations of insurgency.[26] In contrast to the position of traditional international law, existence of insurgency is now recognised as triggering the applicability of international humanitarian law. The ICTY Appeals Chamber in the *Tadić* Jurisdiction Decision summarises succinctly four reasons for the historical extension of international humanitarian law to cover situations of insurgency:

> First, civil wars have become more frequent, not only because technological progress has made it easier for groups of individuals to have access to weaponry but also on account of increasing tension, whether ideological, inter-ethnic or economic; as a consequence the international community can no longer turn a blind eye to the legal regime of such wars. Secondly, internal armed conflicts have become more and more cruel and protracted, involving the whole population of the State where they occur: the all-out resort to armed violence has taken on such a magnitude that the difference with international wars has increasingly dwindled ... Thirdly, the large-scale nature of civil strife, coupled with the increasing interdependence of States in the world community, has made it more and more difficult for third States to remain aloof: the economic, political and ideological interests of third States have brought about direct or indirect involvement of third States in this category of conflict, thereby requiring that international law take greater account of their legal regime in order to prevent, as much as possible, adverse spill-over effects. Fourthly, the impetuous development and propagation in the international community of human rights doctrines, particularly after the adoption of the Universal Declaration of Human Rights in 1948, has brought about significant changes in international law, notably in the approach to problems besetting the world community. A State-sovereignty-oriented approach has been gradually supplanted by a human-being-oriented approach. Gradually the maxim of Roman law *hominum causa omne jus constitutum est* (all law is created for the benefit of human beings) has gained a firm foothold in the international community as well.[27]

[25] Castrén, *Civil War*, pp. 207–23.
[26] For the lower threshold for the application of international humanitarian law to situations of non-international armed conflict, see Chapter 4.
[27] *Tadić*, Case No. IT-94-1-AR72, para. 97.

This development of international humanitarian law strengthens the protection available to the victims of non-international armed conflict. It is noteworthy that prior to the Geneva Conventions of 1949, the only form of internal conflict deemed to necessitate unequivocally the application of laws of war was one involving a state of belligerency or civil war. The section that follows examines the concept of belligerency, enquiring into its range of efficacy and thus also into the conditions necessitating the application of humanitarian norms.

1.4 The recognition of belligerency and the application of international humanitarian norms in civil war

The distinction in traditional international law between insurgency and belligerency is referred to in the *Tadić* Jurisdiction Decision made by the ICTY.[28] It states that the 'dichotomy was clearly sovereignty-oriented and reflected the traditional configuration of the international community, based on the coexistence of sovereign States more inclined to look after their own interests than community concerns or humanitarian demands'.[29] The distinction marked a line necessitating the application of international humanitarian norms in situations of internal conflict. In traditional international law, the recognition of belligerency demands that in all circumstances the laws of war be adhered to. As mentioned in the previous section, the humanitarian norms contained in this body of law could also have been applied to situations of insurgency, but only when specifically provided for in the act of recognition. Thus, Lauterpacht has stated that '[t]he difference between the status of belligerency and that of insurgency in relation to foreign States may best be expressed in the form of the proposition that belligerency is a relation giving rise to definite rights and obligations, while insurgency is not'.[30]

1.4.1 The practice of belligerent recognition

An early example of how the doctrine of belligerency was employed is provided in the case of *The Santissima Trinidad and The St. Sander* (1822) where the Supreme Court of the United States referred to recognition by its government of a state of civil war between Spain and its colonies.

[28] *Ibid.*, paras. 96 and 97. [29] *Ibid.*, para. 96.
[30] Lauterpacht, *Recognition*, p. 270.

The government of the United States has recognized the existence of a civil war between Spain and her colonies, and had avowed a determination to remain neutral between the parties and to allow to each the rights of asylum and hospitality and intercourse. Each party is, therefore, deemed by us a belligerent nation having, so far as concerns us, the sovereign rights of war, and entitled to be respected in the exercise of those rights. We cannot interfere to the prejudice of either belligerent without making ourselves a party to the contest, and departing from the posture of neutrality. All captures made by each must be considered as having the same validity and all immunities which may be claimed by the public ships in our ports, under the law of nations, such must be considered as equally the right of each; and as such, must be recognized by our courts of justice, until Congress shall prescribe a different rule. This is the doctrine heretofore asserted by this court, and we see no reason to depart from it.[31]

Forty years after the *Santissima Trinidad* case, the Supreme Court of the United States rendered its decision known as the *Prizes Cases* (1862) dealing with the capture of four neutral vessels, which had allegedly violated a blockade during the American Civil War. In its decision, the Court elaborated an interpretation of the threshold required for the recognition of belligerency:

Insurrection against a government may or may not culminate in an organized rebellion, but a civil war always begins by insurrection against the lawful authority of the Government. A civil war is never solemnly declared; it becomes such by its accidents – the number, power, and organization of the persons who originate and carry it on. When the party in rebellion occupy and hold in a hostile manner a certain portion of territory; have declared their independence; have cast off their allegiance; have organized armies; have commenced hostilities against their former sovereign, the world acknowledges them as belligerents, and the contest a *war.*[32]

In order for a civil war to be recognised as such, the situation must possess the material characteristics of conventional warfare between two sovereign states. Regarding grounds for the recognition of belligerency in civil war, the Supreme Court of the United States stated that '[t]he true test of its existence, as found in the writings of the sages of the common law, may be thus summarily stated: "When the regular course of justice is interrupted by revolt, rebellion, or insurrection, so

[31] As cited in Oglesby, *Internal War*, p. 11.

[32] *The Brig Amy Warwick; The Schooner Crenshaw; The Barque Hiawatha; The Schooner Brilliante* (1862) 2 *Black* 635, at 666–7. Reprinted in Brown Scott (ed.), *Prize Cases*, pp. 1413–60, at p. 1436. Emphasis in original.

that the Courts of Justice cannot be kept open, civil war exists and hostilities may be prosecuted on the same footing as if those opposing the Government were foreign enemies invading the land" '.[33]

In the case of *Williams* v. *Bruffy* (1877) the Court referred again to the conditions that underlie recognition of belligerency: 'When a rebellion becomes organized, and attains such proportions as to be able to put a formidable military force in the field, it is usual for the established government to concede to it some belligerent rights.'[34] The Court emphasised that:

> This concession is made in the interests of humanity, to prevent the cruelties which would inevitably follow mutual reprisals and retaliations. But belligerent rights, as the terms import, are rights which exist only during war; and to what extent they shall be accorded to insurgents depends upon the considerations of justice, humanity, and policy controlling the government ... The concession made to the Confederate government in its military character was shown in the treatment of captives as prisoners of war, the exchange of prisoners, the recognition of flags of truce, the release of officers on parole, and other arrangements having a tendency to mitigate the evils of the contest. The concession placed its soldiers and military officers in its service on the footing of those engaged in lawful war, and exempted them from liability for acts of legitimate warfare.[35]

Similar to international war, the conduct of hostilities in civil war was thus acknowledged as a situation to which norms of international law, the 'law of nations', would be applicable.[36] Recognition of the applicability of the laws and customs of war was, however, dependent on the situation reaching the threshold of belligerency. De facto recognition of this could occur if the authorities of the state in question interacted with insurgents using practices similar to those generally employed with an external enemy in international war, allowing for prisoner exchanges, flags of truce, and so on. Recognition of belligerency could furthermore be implicitly bestowed by a declaration of neutrality by a state whose interests are affected by the situation. Referring to the case of *Santissima Trinidad*, the Court in the *Prize Cases* held that '[i]t is not necessary that the independence of the revolted province or State be acknowledged in order to constitute it a party belligerent in a war according to the law of nations. Foreign nations acknowledge it as war

[33] *Ibid.*, at p. 1437.

[34] US Supreme Court, *Williams* v. *Bruffy* (1877), 96 US 176, at 186.

[35] *Ibid.*, at 187.

[36] The terms 'law of armed conflict' and 'international humanitarian law' are not used here, as the phraseology did not exist at the time.

by a declaration of neutrality. The condition of neutrality cannot exist unless there be two belligerent parties.'[37]

The threshold that allowed for an act of recognition by a neutral state was fundamentally determined by two factors: the magnitude of the conflict and its effect on the interests of the state in question. According to the judgment of the US Supreme Court in *United States* v. *The Three Friends*, a case concerning the seizure of a steamboat bound for Cuba to assist insurgents in their struggle against Spain in 1896: 'Belligerency is recognized when a political struggle has attained a certain magnitude, and affects the interests of the recognizing power ... it belongs to the political department to determine when belligerency shall be recognized, and its action must be accepted according to the terms and intention expressed.'[38]

Recognition of belligerency was thus generally conceived of as an inherently political act. It was a matter that concerned first and foremost the executive of a state and could not therefore be determined by a court of law without the court conforming to the position adopted by its government. Nevertheless, recognition of belligerency was a matter to be determined by the facts of a situation. According to an opinion issued by British Law Officers in 1867, the question of recognising the belligerent status of those engaged in hostilities turned on whether the situation resembled one of 'war': 'It is always a question of fact to be determined by the Government of the Neutral State, whether the Insurrection has or has not assumed the dimensions of War, and whether the legitimate interests of the Neutral State do or do not require that she should claim from both parties the performance towards her of the obligations incident to the *Status* of a belligerent; – according equally to both parties in return, and recognition of that *status*.'[39]

The recognition of belligerency could thus only be conferred by a state once the conflict had reached a certain threshold of intensity manifesting a situation similar to that of a war between states. Belligerent status was in this way understood as a question of fact presupposing the existence of a de facto governmental authority in conflict with that of a *de jure* government:

[37] Brown Scott (ed.), *Prize Cases*, at p. 1438.

[38] US Supreme Court, *United States* v. *The Three Friends et al.* (1897) 166 US 1, at 63.

[39] Opinion of Law Officers of the Crown (Karslake, Selwyn and Phillimore) Great Britain, 14 August 1867. Reprinted in Pfankuchen, *Documentary Textbook*, p. 135. Emphasis in original.

This statement of fact cannot in our opinion be established by the mere assertion of a number of persons styling themselves 'Provisional Government': many other circumstances must obviously be required before a Neutral State can be justified in recognising, as Belligerents, persons in insurrection against the Government of a State with whom she is on terms of Amity. Amongst these considerations the length of time during which the contest has existed, the number, order, and discipline of the rebel forces; their subordination to a *de facto* existing Government, capable of maintaining International relations with Foreign States; the acts of the Government against whom the Rebels are in arms – both with respect to the Rebels themselves, and to Foreign States, – must obviously find place.[40]

1.4.2 *The legal personality of belligerents in civil war*

The main advantage of recognising the belligerency of parties to a civil war for a neutral state was that it would allow for protection of national interests. Bestowing a peculiar kind of international legal personality on insurgent authorities, this act of recognition enabled very directly a change in status. According to Roscoe Oglesby, '[a] *de facto* insurgent government recognized as a belligerent has international standing. Foreign nations and their citizens who suffer injuries at the hands of the insurgents can bring their claims directly to the *de facto* government, for now responsibility for its conduct and for its tortuous acts no longer reside with the parent government, but with the entity newly clothed with international personality.'[41]

Prior to the adoption of the Geneva Conventions of 1949, any legal obligation to ensure a minimum standard of humane treatment for the victims of an internal conflict was essentially a matter of exclusive domestic concern. The Commentary of the International Committee of the Red Cross (ICRC) on the Additional Protocols of 1977 states that '[p]ositive law has very largely abstained from laying down rules governing non-international armed conflict. According to traditional doctrine, states were the only sovereign entities considered to be the subjects of international law; thus the laws of war which were conceived to govern international relations, were not applicable to internal conflicts.'[42]

This, of course, has now changed with the codification of international humanitarian law relating to situations of non-international armed

[40] *Ibid.*, pp. 135–6. [41] Oglesby, *Internal War*, p. 78.
[42] Pilloud *et al.*, *Commentary*, p. 1320.

conflict.[43] Prior to this codification, international law required that the belligerency of parties to an internal conflict be afforded either formal or tacit recognition before obligations under the laws of war could be said to exist. According to Lindsay Moir: '[a]n examination of some major internal conflicts of the nineteenth and early twentieth centuries shows that, in those cases where the laws of war were accepted and applied by opposing forces, some form of recognition of belligerency has invariably taken place. In contrast, where recognition of belligerency was not afforded by the government, the laws of war tended not to be applied, leading to barbaric conduct by both sides.'[44]

1.4.3 Conditions determining belligerent recognition

The recognition of belligerency was the only institution in traditional international law that necessitated the application of laws of war to situations of internal conflict. In order for the existence of belligerency to be recognised, certain conditions needed to be fulfilled. Hersch Lauterpacht listed the following four criteria for the recognition of belligerency:

> first, there must exist within the State an armed conflict of a general (as distinguished from a purely local) character; secondly, the insurgents must occupy and administer a substantial portion of national territory; thirdly, they must conduct the hostilities in accordance with the rules of war and through organised armed forces acting under a responsible authority; fourthly, there must exist circumstances which make it necessary for outside States to define their attitude by means of recognition of belligerency.[45]

The first condition refers to the scale of hostilities and required that the character of the conflict is similar to that of an international war.[46] The second condition, stating that the insurgent force must 'occupy and administer a substantial portion of national territory', demanded the existence of a quasi-governmental authority controlled by insurgents. The third condition necessitated insurgent adherence to laws governing the conduct of hostilities, ensuring respect for humanitarian norms. The fourth condition listed by Lauterpacht, requiring the act of recognition to be a diplomatic necessity, is included so that it was not 'open to abuse for the purpose of a gratuitous manifestation of sympathy with

[43] See section 2.2 for an analysis of Article 3 common to the four Geneva Conventions of 1949.

[44] Moir, *Internal Armed Conflict*, p. 345.

[45] Lauterpacht, *Recognition*, p. 176.

[46] Falk, 'Janus Tormented', p. 203.

the cause of the insurgents'.[47] Without defining its position in relation to the situation, an act of recognition performed by a third state could be deemed 'a premature and unfriendly act'.[48]

When recognised as belligerents, parties to an internal conflict were, under traditional international law, to be treated in essentially the same way as states at war. The obligation to ensure respect for the humanitarian norms was equally binding on both insurgents and the authorities of the *de jure* government.[49] Falk stated that

> [i]nternational law treats an internal war with the status of belligerency as essentially identical to a war between sovereign states. This also means that an interventionary participation on behalf of either the incumbent or the insurgent is an act of war against the other. That is, as with a truly international war, a state is given the formal option of joining with one of the belligerents against the other or of remaining impartial.[50]

With recognition of belligerency, insurgents acquired the same rights and duties as a party to an international war. If recognition was bestowed by a third state, the government of that state would have been required to act as a neutral until the conflict's cessation. While neutral states were not permitted to offer assistance to insurgents, the benefits of third-state neutrality for the insurgent party would have been manifold, including the right to obtain credit abroad, the maintenance of blockades and the use of foreign ports.[51] By recognising the belligerency of parties to an internal conflict, neutral states also obligated the application of humanitarian norms by both insurgents and the armed forces of the *de jure* government.

1.4.4 Problems in the interpretation of belligerency

As a doctrine necessitating adherence to international humanitarian norms, the recognition of belligerency extended the law governing

[47] Oppenheim and Lauterpacht, *International Law*, p. 198.

[48] Dhokalia, 'Civil Wars', at 227.

[49] D. Khairallah states that '[t]he laws of war then become applicable to both parties in the conflict, not only with regard to the conduct of hostilities, but also for all other war activities, such as the care for the sick and wounded, prisoners of war, etc'. *Insurrection*, in Wilson, *International Law*, p. 37.

[50] Falk, 'Janus Tormented', p. 203. Similarly, James E. Bond states: 'Once the rebels had achieved the status of belligerents ... they had become in effect a *de facto* state; as a state they were entitled to all the incidents of that privileged status, one of which was being accorded the benefits of the laws of war.' *Rules*, p. 51.

[51] Falk, 'Janus Tormented', p. 205.

situations of international war to internal conflicts. The application of the humanitarian standards provided for by traditional international law was, however, contingent not only on a conflict meeting the criteria mentioned above, but also on the willingness of states to recognise it as such. There appears to have been little consensus among scholars as to whether the recognition of belligerency constituted a duty when certain objective conditions were fulfilled or whether it was fundamentally a matter of discretion for state authorities.[52] Falk argued that if the four conditions provided by Lauterpacht were fulfilled, it would be 'intervention to refuse recognition of insurgency as belligerency'.[53] An alternative view was expressed by David A. Elder, describing the recognition of belligerency as 'an act of unfettered political discretion'.[54] Other areas of controversy surrounding the recognition of belligerency included the extent of territorial control required, the question of what constitutes a 'responsible authority' and the nature of circumstances deemed to necessitate the act of recognition for third states.[55]

1.4.5 *The substitution of 'armed conflict' for 'war'*

Another factor that contributed to the contemporary disuse of the belligerency doctrine was the use of the term 'armed conflict' in the drafting of the Geneva Conventions of 1949. The term is used only twice in each of the Geneva Conventions: once in the first paragraph of common Article 2 and once in the first paragraph of common Article 3. However, as these clauses define the scope of application for each Convention, the interpretation of what constitutes an armed conflict is a point of critical importance in determining the relevance of this body of law to particular situations. The term 'armed conflict' was employed by the drafters of the Geneva Conventions in these clauses to help to avoid problems of recognition not only in regard to situations of civil war, but also in regard to international armed conflict. As noted in the ICRC Commentary on Article 2 common to the four the Geneva Conventions:

> It fills the gap left in the earlier Conventions, and deprives the belligerents of the pretexts they might in theory invoke for evasion of their obligations. There is no longer any need for a formal declaration of war, or for recognition of the state of war, as preliminaries to the application of the Convention. The Convention becomes applicable as from the actual opening of hostilities. The

[52] Castrén, *Civil War*, pp. 173–7. [53] Falk, 'Janus Tormented', p. 206.
[54] Elder, 'Historical Background', at 39.
[55] Castrén, *Civil War*, pp. 177–84.

existence of armed conflict between two or more Contracting Parties brings it automatically into operation.[56]

As the concept of belligerency in traditional international law was very much equated with that of 'war', it was of less relevance when the issue concerned the interpretation of 'armed conflict'. While the Geneva Conventions do contain references to 'belligerents', the words 'belligerency' and 'belligerence' are used nowhere in the text of these instruments. The significance of this as a point of departure from traditional international law will be explored further in Chapter 2.

1.4.6 The decline of belligerency as a doctrine of international law

Given its high threshold of application, and the many grey areas that exist in the conditions for recognition, traditional international law was clearly inadequate as the legal regime governing situations of non-international armed conflict.[57] In practice the doctrine of recognition has served more to support the interests of states than to prioritise adherence to humanitarian norms.[58] The current total disuse of the belligerency doctrine arguably resulted from states resorting to the more flexible concept of insurgency. For many commentators, the non-recognition of the Spanish Civil War as a situation of belligerency by neighbouring states demonstrated the demise of the concept.[59] By recognising a situation as one of insurgency, states avoided the restrictions on behaviour incurred by recognition of belligerency, allowing a greater degree of flexibility in defining relations with insurgents.

Irrespective of whether recognition of belligerency was to be regarded as a duty or as a matter of pure discretion, it is important to acknowledge that the act placed obligations on each party to ensure respect for humanitarian norms and thus, despite its inadequacies, represents an important starting point for the development of international laws governing the situations of non-international armed conflict.[60] Although the scope of belligerency is narrowed by its high

[56] Commentary on Convention (I), Pictet (ed.), *Commentary I*, p. 31.
[57] Noted by Falk, 'Janus Tormented', p. 191.
[58] See generally Menon, *Law of Recognition*.
[59] See, for example, Gomulkiewicz, 'International Law', 43.
[60] See Lootsteen, 'Concept of Belligerency', at 114.

threshold of application, its employment nevertheless represented a shift in state practice, eroding the impermeability of state sovereignty in international law.

1.5 Concluding observations

While the recognition of belligerency in civil war was undertaken on the basis of a situation assuming the dimensions of an international war, it nonetheless characterises a starting point for the application of international law in cases of internal conflict. As such, it represents the origins of legal concern for adherence to international humanitarian norms in situations of non-international armed conflict.

As previously illustrated, the existence of insurgency was not viewed as necessitating the application of laws of war in traditional international law. It was only through the recognition of belligerency, either by the *de jure* government or by a third state, that parties to an internal conflict were categorically obligated to comply with the laws of war. According to the UK Ministry of Defence *Manual of the Law of Armed Conflict*:

> In the past, the application of the law of armed conflict in non-international armed conflict was largely dependent on 'recognition of belligerence'. The law of armed conflict, or parts of it, could be brought into effect if a government recognized the belligerent status of an insurgent faction opposing it, or if foreign states recognized the belligerent status of that faction. The doctrine has declined to the point where recognition of belligerency is almost unknown today.[61]

The strict criteria governing the recognition of belligerency, together with its high threshold of application, were considerations in the drafting of common Article 3. The chapter that follows examines the significance of this provision as the first codification of international law specific to all situations of non-international armed conflict.

[61] UK Ministry of Defence, *Manual*, p. 382.

2 Article 3 common to the four Geneva Conventions of 1949 and the threshold of non-international armed conflict in international humanitarian law

Prior to the formulation of the four Geneva Conventions of 1949, there existed no substantive provision of international humanitarian law specific to situations of non-international armed conflict. The 'Marten's clause', a provision situated in the preamble of the Hague Regulations of 1907, stipulated that in cases not included in the Regulations 'the inhabitants and the belligerents remain under the protection and the rule of the principles of the law of nations, as they result from the usages established among civilized peoples, from the laws of humanity, and the dictates of the public conscience'.[1] While this provision clearly covered situations of internal conflict, it is a provision of a general nature and not specific to situations of non-international armed conflict. Article 3 common to the four Geneva Conventions of 1949 was the first provision of its kind to deal specifically with humanitarian protection in situations of non-international armed conflict:

In the case of armed conflict not of an international character occurring in the territory of one of the High Contracting Parties, each Party to the conflict shall be bound to apply, as a minimum, the following provisions:

1. Persons taking no active part in the hostilities, including members of armed forces who have laid down their arms and those placed hors de combat by sickness, wounds, detention, or any other cause, shall in all circumstances be treated humanely, without any adverse distinction

[1] Convention (IV) respecting the Laws and Customs of War on Land and its annex: Regulation concerning the Laws and Customs of War on Land, 3 Martens Nouveau Recueil (ser. 3) 461, 187 Consol. TS 227, entered into force 26 January 1910. For a commentary on significance of the Martens clause, see Meron, *Humanization*, pp. 16–29. For an early commentary on the Hague Regulations of 1907, see Erskine Holland, *Law of War*.

founded on race, colour, religion or faith, sex, birth or wealth, or any other similar criteria.

To this end, the following acts are and shall remain prohibited at any time and in any place whatsoever with respect to the above-mentioned persons:

(a) Violence to life and person, in particular murder of all kinds, mutilation, cruel treatment and torture;
(b) Taking of hostages;
(c) Outrages upon personal dignity, in particular humiliating and degrading treatment;
(d) The passing of sentences and the carrying out of executions without previous judgment pronounced by a regularly constituted court, affording all the judicial guarantees which are recognized as indispensable by civilized peoples.

2. The wounded and sick shall be collected and cared for.
An impartial humanitarian body, such as the International Committee of the Red Cross, may offer its services to the Parties to the conflict.
The Parties to the conflict should further endeavour to bring into force, by means of special agreements, all or part of the other provisions of the present Convention.
The application of the preceding provisions shall not affect the legal status of the Parties to the conflict.[2]

Under the legal regime contemporary to the formulation of common Article 3, the application of international humanitarian law to a situation of non-international armed conflict depended upon it being fundamentally akin to an international armed conflict. The adoption of common Article 3, which extended the reach of international humanitarian law to 'armed conflicts not of an international character', provided the basis of a shift in this position.[3] This chapter explores the threshold of application intended by the drafters of the Geneva Conventions for situations of non-international armed conflict. In doing so, the *travaux préparatoires* (preparatory work) of the Geneva Conventions is examined in detail. The Commentary of the International Committee of the Red Cross (ICRC) is also examined to assess its interpretation of 'armed conflict not of an international character'. It is argued that the Commentary accurately reflects the intentions of those who drafted common Article 3. However, as the drafters of this provision understood

[2] Roberts and Guelff, *Documents*, p. 302.

[3] According to the UK Ministry of Defence, '[u]ntil 1949, armed conflicts which were not of an international character were regarded as being governed exclusively by the domestic law of the state in which they occurred'. *Manual*, p. 31.

'armed conflict not of an international character' in terms equivalent to civil war, it is held that the Commentary is of little relevance to the contemporary threshold for the application of international humanitarian law to situations of non-international armed conflict.

2.1 The drafting history of common Article 3

The concept of non-international armed conflict that has emerged from the text of common Article 3 differs significantly from that assumed by state practice in traditional international law. As illustrated in the previous chapter, recognition of belligerency was generally conceived as a prerequisite for the mandatory application of international humanitarian norms under traditional international law.[4] The body of international law governing the conduct of hostilities was only deemed applicable in situations of 'war'. The term 'armed conflict' was used instead of 'war' in the Geneva Conventions of 1949 to provide a broader basis for the application of international humanitarian law and in doing so to avoid arguments arising with respect to the legal definition of war.

At the time of the drafting of the Geneva Conventions, the legal meaning of 'armed conflict' was undefined. The term had been used before in the Hague Regulations of 1899 and 1907, but not in the context of a substantive provision relating to the field of application for either instrument.[5] The ICRC Commentary on the first Geneva Convention of 1949 highlighted the uncertain meaning of armed conflict:

> It remains to ascertain what is meant by 'armed conflict'. The substitution of this much more general expression for the word 'war' was deliberate. One

[4] As noted by Roberts and Guelff, '[t]he laws of war, as embodied in customary international law, were regarded as applicable in a civil war if the government of the state in which an insurrection existed, or a third state, chose to recognize the belligerent status of the insurgent group and thereby acknowledge the law's application. In addition, absent recognition of belligerency, there were instances in which the law was treated by parties in a civil war, or by third parties, as being applicable.' *Documents*, p. 481.

[5] Both instruments include preambular references to 'seeking means to preserve peace and prevent armed conflicts among nations'. Convention (II) with Respect to the Laws and Customs of War on Land and its annex: Regulation concerning the Laws and Customs of War on Land, 26 Martens Nouveau Recueil (ser. 2) 949, 187 Consol. TS 429, entered into force 4 September 1900, preambular para. 1. Convention (IV), 187 Consol. TS 227, preambular para. 1. The *travaux préparatoires* of these instruments provide no indication of discussions relating to the meaning of 'armed conflict'. See Brown Scott, *Proceedings*.

may argue almost endlessly about the legal definition of 'war'. A State can always pretend, when it commits a hostile act against another State, that it is not making war, but merely engaging in a police action, or acting in legitimate self-defence. The expression 'armed conflict' makes such arguments less easy.[6]

While the extension of the applicability of humanitarian principles to situations of 'civil war' had been raised on a number of occasions by the ICRC, the initiative to expand the scope of legal protection available did not bear fruit until the XVIIth International Red Cross Conference at Stockholm in August 1948. This Conference approved four draft Conventions to be used as a basis for discussion at the Diplomatic Conference in Geneva from 21 April until 12 August 1949. These early drafts of the Geneva Conventions stipulated their applicability to all situations of armed conflict, including non-international armed conflict. Article 2 common to the four draft Conventions (hereinafter draft Article 2) formulated by the Stockholm Conference outlined their field of application:

In addition to the stipulations which shall be implemented in peacetime, the present Convention shall apply to all cases of declared war or any other armed conflict which may arise between two or more of the High Contracting Parties, even if the state of war is not recognized by one of them.

The Convention shall also apply to all cases of partial or total occupation of the territory of a High Contracting Party, even if the said occupation meets with no armed resistance.

If one of the Powers in conflict is not party to the present Convention, the Powers who are party thereto shall notwithstanding be bound by it in their mutual relations.

In all cases of armed conflict not of an international character which may occur in the territory of one or more of the High Contracting Parties, each of the adversaries shall be bound to implement the provisions of the present Convention. The Convention shall be applicable in these circumstances, whatever the legal status of the Parties to the conflict and without prejudice thereto.[7]

The last paragraph of draft Article 2 stipulates the full application of the Conventions to situations of non-international armed conflict taking place in the territory of a High Contracting Party. The term 'armed conflict not of an international character' had never been used in an

[6] Pictet (ed.), *Commentary I*, p. 32.

[7] *Final Record*, vol. I, 'Text of Draft International Conventions for the Protection of War Victims as Approved by the XVIIth International Red Cross Conference at Stockholm in August 1948 (Taken as the Basis for Discussion at the Diplomatic Conference)', p. 47.

instrument of international law prior to 1949. The use of this phrase at the Diplomatic Conference that drafted the Geneva Conventions resulted in an extended debate on the applicability of the Conventions to situations of non-international armed conflict. The content of this debate illuminates how 'armed conflict not of an international character' was understood by drafters of common Article 3.

2.1.1 Interpretation of 'armed conflict not of an international character' at the Geneva Conference of 1949

The notion of including a provision specific to non-international armed conflict was a contentious one for delegates at the Diplomatic Conference. The potential for the encroachment on state sovereignty was well recognised and led many states to oppose the inclusion of a provision relating to situations 'not of an international character'. From the outset, the process of securing of a provision relating to non-international armed conflict was an awkward one. The issue was first discussed by the Joint Committee, which was established by the Plenary Assembly to examine articles common to all four Conventions.[8] Divergences of opinion immediately became apparent.

The Joint Committee was composed of delegates from all states present at the Diplomatic Conference. The first item discussed by the Committee was draft Article 2. Its fourth paragraph, providing for the application of the Conventions 'in all cases of armed conflict not of an international character', received mixed reviews from delegates. For some, the idea that the Conventions would apply in their entirety to armed conflicts taking place within the borders of a sovereign state was excessive. Albert Lamarle of the French delegation criticised the drafters of the article for placing the rights of individuals above those of states:

> The Conference at Stockholm had been mainly concerned with the protection of the rights of the individual; but it was also necessary not to lose sight of the rights of the States. It [is] impossible to carry the protection of individuals to the point of sacrificing the rights of States. In order to protect the rights of the State the French delegation would like to propose an amendment making it impossible for forms of disorder, anarchy or brigandage to claim protection under the Convention.[9]

[8] *Final Record*, vol. II-A, Minutes of Plenary Meetings, 4th Meeting, 25 April 1949, pp. 21–4.

[9] *Final Record*, vol. II-B, Summary Records of the Joint Committee, 1st Meeting, 26 April 1949, p. 10.

The amendment proposed by the French delegation was to include a definition of the non-state armed forces that would be deemed to qualify as an adversary according to how the term is used in draft Article 2. The following text was put forward as an alternative to the fourth paragraph of draft Article 2: 'In all cases of armed conflict not of an international character which may occur on the territory of one or more High Contracting Parties, each of the Parties to the conflict shall be bound to implement the provisions of the present Convention, if the adverse Party possesses an organized military force, an authority responsible for its acts acting within a defined territory and having the means of observing and enforcing the Convention.'[10]

The French proposal was supported by Spain,[11] Italy[12] and Monaco.[13] Speaking on behalf of the Spanish government, the Marquis of Villalobar stated that '[t]he Conventions should only be applied in cases where the legal government [is] obliged to have recourse to the regular military forces against insurgents militarily organized and in possession of a part of the national territory'.[14] The consul of the Italian delegation, Adolfo Maresca, said that Italy would be disposed to support the French amendment and added the suggestion that it 'might be accompanied by a recommendation stipulating that the humanitarian principles which are the essence of the Conventions should guide the conduct of States'.[15] De Geouffre de la Pradelle of the Monaco delegation also voiced support for the proposal, remarking that if the amendment was used, the Article 'would not frighten the supporters of sovereignty of the State'.[16]

Victor Dimitriu, representing Romania, however, expressed opposition to the French proposal: 'Humanitarian considerations should prevent the Conference from introducing restrictions in the text, the whole object of which was to extend the protection of the Convention to the greatest possible number of persons. The amendment of the French Delegation seem[s] redundant, since paragraph 4 provided for the application of the Convention, subject to its observance by the opposing party.'[17]

[10] *Final Record*, vol. III, Amendment proposed by France, 26 April 1949, Annex 12, p. 27.
[11] *Final Record*, vol. II-B, Summary Records, 1st Meeting, p. 11.
[12] *Final Record*, vol. II-B, Summary Records of the Joint Committee, 2nd Meeting, 27 April 1949, p. 13.
[13] *Ibid.*, p. 14. [14] *Final Record*, vol. II-B, Summary Records, 1st Meeting, p. 11.
[15] *Final Record*, vol. II-B, Summary Records, 2nd Meeting, p. 13.
[16] *Ibid.*, p. 14. [17] *Final Record*, vol. II-B, Summary Records, 1st Meeting, p. 11.

The delegation of the USSR also opposed the French amendment. Speaking on behalf of the Union of Soviet Socialist Republics, General Slavin stated that '[i]f the French proposal were followed, there would be a danger of one party declaring, without proof, that the other party was not in a position to ensure order, and thus of justifying any violation of the basic humanitarian principles of the Conventions'.[18]

Both Russian and Romanian delegations expressed their support for retaining the original text of paragraph 4 of draft Article 2. The rationale was to extend the application of international humanitarian law uniformly to all situations of armed conflict, irrespective of their intensity or characterisation as international or non-international. The problem with the French proposal was that it set a high threshold for the application of international humanitarian norms by including conditions for the recognition of an adversary. According to Claude Pilloud of the ICRC:

> Application of the Conventions, either totally or partially, had even been achieved in situations which did not exactly correspond to the definition given in the French proposal. Therefore, if limitations were to be included in paragraph 4 ... there should likewise be introduced a clause stipulating that the present provisions would not prevent the voluntary application of the Conventions by Parties to a conflict which did not correspond to the definition given in this paragraph.[19]

It was argued that the proposal would not only narrow the applicability of the Conventions, but that it would also complicate the application of the law with preliminary enquiries as to whether certain conditions had been fulfilled. The most practical and straightforward approach would be for the Conventions to be uniformly applicable in all forms of armed conflict. While clearly not without merit, this position represented a radical departure from contemporary international law and was not supported by the majority of delegates.

The United Kingdom's Head of Delegation, Robert Craigie, spoke strongly against the adoption of draft Article 2, stating that it would 'strike at the root of national sovereignty and endanger national security'.[20] Holding that the application of the Conventions should be limited to situations of 'war', Craigie expressed concern that the

[18] *Final Record*, vol. II-B, Summary Records, 2nd Meeting, p. 14.

[19] *Final Record*, vol. II-B, Summary Records of Special Committee of the Joint Committee, 3rd Meeting, 9 May 1949, p. 43.

[20] *Final Record*, vol. II-B, Summary Records, 1st Meeting, p. 10.

provision would affect the legal status of insurgents that were not considered subjects of international law: 'In the United Kingdom Delegation's view, paragraph 4 of Article 2 [is] a source of difficulties, not only because the Conventions would be applicable to situations which were not war, but because the application of the Conventions would appear to give the status of belligerents to insurgents, whose right to wage war could not be recognized.'[21]

The United States' Head of Delegation, Leland Harrison, expressed a position similar to that of the United Kingdom, asserting that '[t]he United States of America [does] not consider that it could bind itself to observe the provisions of the Convention except in the case of war as understood in international law'.[22] Positing his government's interpretation of international law, Harrison made the following statement:

[T]he Convention should be applicable only where the parent government had extended recognition to the rebels or where those conditions obtained which would warrant in recognizing the belligerency of the rebels whether or not such recognition was accorded by the Power on which they depend in this latter eventuality. The application of this Convention could not be regarded as recognition of belligerency by any party thereto. The conditions which should obtain before the Convention would be applicable to an armed conflict within a State, party to the Convention, might be briefly stated as follows:

(1) The insurgents must have an organization purporting to have the characteristics of a State.
(2) The insurgent civil authority must exercise *de facto* authority over persons within a determinate territory.
(3) The armed forces must act under the direction of an organized civil authority and be prepared to observe the ordinary laws of war.
(4) The insurgent civil authorities must agree to be bound by the provisions of the Convention.[23]

Given its lack of specificity regarding the meaning of 'armed conflict not of an international character', paragraph 4 of draft Article 2 was unacceptable to the United States. The criteria stipulated in the statement of Harrison provided an interpretation of the material conditions warranting recognition of belligerency and thus the application of international humanitarian law.[24] While the French proposal had implicitly included the conditions by qualifying the kind of 'adverse Party' which would bring

[21] *Ibid.* [22] *Final Record*, vol. II-B, Summary Records, 1st Meeting, p. 11.
[23] *Final Record*, vol. II-B, Summary Records, 2nd Meeting, p. 12.
[24] See Bond, *Rules*, pp. 52–3.

into force the Conventions, the American delegate felt it was necessary to state more unequivocally the four criteria required for the application of international humanitarian norms by international law.

Colonel W.R. Hodgson, Head of the Australian delegation, posited an alternative set of criteria to that of the United States, setting a much more restrictive standard for the application of the Conventions to situations of non-international armed conflict:

> [T]he Convention should apply when an armed conflict [becomes] a full-scale war and when there [is] an organized form of Government which effectively control[s] definite portions of the national territory and the inhabitants therein.
>
> To distinguish between the aforementioned state of affairs and local uprisings, the principles of the present Convention should be applied to the Parties to the conflict, provided:
>
> (1) the *de jure* government had recognized the insurgents as belligerents, or;
> (2) the *de jure* government had claimed for itself the right of belligerent, and;
> (3) the *de jure* government had accorded the insurgents recognition as belligerents for the purposes only of the present Conventions;
> (4) that the dispute had been admitted to the Agenda of the Security Council or the General Assembly of the United Nations as being a threat to international peace, a breach of the peace, or an act of aggression.[25]

The Australian proposal interpreted the use of the term 'armed conflict' in the Conventions as being synonymous with 'war' in traditional international law.[26] The threshold for the application of international

[25] *Final Record*, vol. II-B, Summary Records, 2nd Meeting, p. 15. The text of the Australian amendment as recorded in the *Final Record* of the Diplomatic Conference:

> In the case of civil war in any part of the home or colonial territory of a Contracting Party the present Convention (or if this goes too far, 'The Principles of the present Convention') shall be applied between the Parties to the conflict, provided:
>
> (1) that the *de jure* Government has recognized the insurgents as belligerents; or
> (2) that the *de jure* Government has claimed for itself the rights of a belligerent; or
> (3) that the *de jure* Government has accorded the insurgents recognition as belligerents for the purposes only of the present Convention; or
> (4) that the dispute has been admitted to the Agenda of the Security Council of the General Assembly of the United Nations as being a threat to international peace, a breach of the peace, or an act of aggression.

Final Record, vol. III, Amendment proposed by Australia, 4 May 1949, Annex 11, p. 27.

[26] According to the Seventh Report drawn up by the Special Committee of the Joint Committee, the Australian delegation suggested that 'the expression

humanitarian norms in situations of non-international armed conflict was thus derived from that which was required by the doctrine of belligerency in traditional international law. The final condition listed in the Australian proposal was, however, distinct from the conditions required for the recognition of belligerency and may be interpreted as an attempt to include an additional threshold for the application of international humanitarian law.

Michel Pesmazoglou of the Greek delegation voiced further criticism of paragraph 4 of Article 2 and pointed to potential difficulties that could arise with its application in conjunction with the Prisoners of War Convention. He also questioned how it would affect the doctrine of belligerency in international law. It was contended that, if adopted, the draft Article could

> prevent rebels from being charged with crimes under common law committed before their arrest, and they would automatically be granted a pardon at the end of disturbances. Furthermore, they could claim the protection of a Protecting Power. The possibility of such protection might incite political opponents to take up arms against a legitimate government. In the Conventions it [is] necessary to distinguish between the humanitarian and the legal principles. The recognition of belligerency entailed certain rights; but who would be competent to recognize belligerency in the case of civil war?[27]

The question raised by the Greek delegate was one that embodied many of the concerns voiced by previous speakers. The scope of paragraph 4 of Article 2 was too broad for the majority of those present and needed to be restricted. As a means of rectifying this, Pesmazoglou proposed a motion providing grounds for the application of the Conventions in the case of civil war. The Conventions would be deemed applicable if the belligerency of parties was recognised 'individually by the majority of countries represented in the [United Nations Security] Council'.[28] Like the proposal of the Australian delegation, the Greek initiative set a higher threshold for the application of international humanitarian law than that assumed by the doctrine of belligerency.

Expressing support for the doctrine of belligerency as a means of determining the application of international humanitarian law, the Deputy

"non-international armed conflict" should not be used, but be replaced by the terms "civil war in any part of the home or colonial territory of a Contracting Party" '. *Final Record*, vol. II-B, Seventh Report drawn up by the Special Committee of the Joint Committee, 16 July 1949, p. 121.

[27] *Final Record*, vol. II-B, Summary Records, 1st Meeting, pp. 10–11.

[28] *Final Record*, vol. II-B, Summary Records of the Joint Committee, 3rd Meeting, p. 16.

Head of the Canadian delegation, Max Wershof, stated in firm terms his government's opposition to the use of paragraph 4 of draft article 2:

> [B]efore saying that a civil war [is] of the kind in which the Convention should be applied, the test should be: recognition of belligerency of the rebels by the lawful Government. Except in the instance of a civil war of that kind, the Canadian Delegation were not in favour of the provisions contained in paragraph 4, Article 2.[29]

On the question of the recognition of belligerency, Frede Castberg of Norway expressed an opinion differing from the majority. Viewing the application of the international humanitarian law in the absence of recognition as progressive, Castberg adopted a position in support of draft Article 2:

> It is a step forward in international law to say explicitly that, even if war was not recognized, the rules concerning the conduct of war should be applied. As to civil war, the term 'armed conflict' should not be interpreted as meaning 'individual conflict', or 'uprising'. Civil war [is] a form of conflict resembling international war, but taking place inside the territory of a State. It [is] not a conflict between a number of individuals ... As for belligerency, when belligerency was recognized in an internal conflict, serious legal consequences were entailed; but it [is] to be hoped that the Conference would agree that purely humanitarian rules should be applied in armed conflicts independently of any recognition of belligerency.[30]

Despite its significant departure from contemporary thought in 1949, the position of the Norwegian delegation regarding the issue of recognition was to prevail at the Diplomatic Conference. The comments of the French, British, American, Australian, Greek and Canadian delegations reflect the conventional view of traditional international law, that the obligation to apply international humanitarian norms only occurs through the recognition of belligerency. In addition to Norway, the USSR and Romania, support for draft Article 2 was also voiced by the representatives of Mexico, Denmark and Hungary. Each expressed a position against any restriction on the scope of the Conventions, arguing for the inclusion of non-international armed conflict on the grounds of humanitarian considerations.

The divergent views expressed by delegates during the first two meetings of the Joint Committee made it clear that a compromise formula was needed to secure a provision relating to non-international armed

[29] *Final Record*, vol. II-B, Summary Records, 2nd Meeting, p. 13.
[30] *Final Record*, vol. II-B, Summary Records, 1st Meeting, p. 11.

conflict. The Head of the Swiss delegation, Plinio Bolla, proposed the nomination of a small Sub-Committee 'to deal with the definition of what was meant by armed conflict'.[31] The group would also be responsible for drafting a text which would reconcile the different points of view expressed by delegates.[32] Bolla's proposal was accepted by the Chairman who suggested that the Sub-Committee be composed of delegates from Australia, the United States of America, France, Greece, Italy, Monaco, Norway, the United Kingdom, Switzerland, and the Union of Soviet Socialist Republics.[33] The suggested composition was unanimously approved by delegates on 29 April 1949;[34] the Special Committee was formed, and had its first meeting on 4 May 1949.

The bulk of formal discussion at the Diplomatic Conference on the formulation of a provision relating to non-international armed conflict took place within the Special Committee of the Joint Committee. Debate on the issue spanned eleven weeks and was concluded without agreement on which approach to take.[35] Despite this lack of consensus, the record of the debate in the Special Committee provides an invaluable source of evidence concerning how non-international armed conflict was understood by the drafters of the Geneva Conventions.

Initially intended to clarify the meaning of 'armed conflict not of an international character', the work of the Special Committee was expanded to include examination of other issues referred to it by the Joint Committee. While a diverse range of provisions was transferred to the Special Committee, none consumed as much of its time as the formulation of a text pertaining to non-international armed conflict.[36] The majority of proposals considered for the text of this provision contained conditions for the application of the Conventions. These conditions were included as a way of defining the scope of non-international armed conflict. According to the Seventh Report drawn up by the Special Committee of the Joint Committee, all proposals stipulating conditions for the application of international humanitarian law to armed conflicts not of an international character reflected

[31] *Final Record*, vol. II-B, Summary Records, 2nd Meeting, p. 15. [32] *Ibid.*

[33] Representatives of Burma and Uruguay joined the membership of the Special Committee after the Seventh Meeting of the Joint Committee on 17 May 1949. *Final Record*, vol. II-B, Summary Records of the Joint Committee, 7th Meeting, 17 May 1949, p. 26.

[34] *Final Record*, vol. II-B, Summary Records, 3rd Meeting, p. 16.

[35] From 3 May until 12 July 1949.

[36] The issue of a provision relating to armed conflict not of an international character was discussed at no less than twenty meetings of the Special Committee.

the idea 'that it would be dangerous to weaken the State when confronted by movements caused by disorder, anarchy and banditry, by compelling it to apply to them, in addition to its peacetime legislation, Conventions which were intended for use in a state of declared or undeclared war'.[37]

Delegations in favour of the original Stockholm text did not consider it either necessary or helpful to include conditions for the application of the Conventions in non-international armed conflict. The Seventh Report of the Special Committee states that those in favour of this text understood 'armed conflict not of an international character' to presuppose 'an armed conflict resembling an international war in dimensions, and did not include a mere strife between the forces of the State and one or several groups of persons (uprisings, etc.)'.[38] This point illuminates how the scope of non-international armed conflict was conceived by delegates in favour of broadening the applicability of the Conventions. The use of the term 'armed conflict not of an international character' was thus understood to refer to situations of civil war, i.e., non-international armed conflict reaching the threshold of intensity associated with contemporaneous conventional international warfare.

At the fourth meeting of the Special Committee, it became clear that that Stockholm text would not receive the support needed for it to be adopted at the Conference. The Chairman proposed a vote and the provision was abandoned.[39] Considered 'too wide in scope',[40] the Stockholm text was set aside so that delegates could 'define more clearly the cases of armed conflict not of an international character to which the Conventions should apply'.[41] To this end, Colonel Hodgson of the Australian delegation proposed the formation of a Working Party made up of the United States,

[37] *Final Record*, vol. II-B, Seventh Report, p. 121. [38] *Ibid.*

[39] As chairman of the Special Committee of the Joint Committee, Plinio Bolla of Switzerland suggested that the Committee 'pronounce either in favour of the Stockholm text, or of a new text which would define more clearly the cases of armed conflict not of an international character'. *Final Record*, vol. II-B, Summary Records of the Special Committee of the Joint Committee, 4th Meeting, 11 May 1949, p. 45. The Summary Records state: 'By 10 votes for, 1 against, and 1 abstention, the Committee was of the opinion to abandon the Stockholm text and to define more clearly the cases of armed conflict not of an international character to which the Conventions should apply.' *Final Record*, vol. II-B, Summary Records, 4th Meeting, p. 45.

[40] *Final Record*, vol. II-B, Seventh Report drawn up by the Special Committee of the Joint Committee, 16 July 1949, p. 121.

[41] *Final Record*, vol. II-B, Summary Records, 4th Meeting, p. 45.

France and Australia to work out a compromise formula that would take into account the different views expressed by delegates. The Chairman's suggestion to include a Norwegian representative was approved. After four meetings, the Working Party had drawn up a proposal demarcating the conditions for the application of the Conventions to situations of armed conflict not of an international character. The proposal was presented to the Special Committee and then amended to take into account views expressed by the delegates. The following provision was then issued by the Working Party as new draft Article 2A:

(1) In the case of armed conflict not of an international character occurring in the territory of one of the High Contracting Parties, each Party to the conflict shall be bound to apply the provisions of the present Convention, provided:
   (a) that the *de jure* Government has recognized the status of belligerency of the adverse party, even for the sole purposes of the application of the present Convention or
   (b) that the adverse party possesses an organized civil authority exercising de facto governmental functions over the population of a determinate portion of the national territory, an organized military force under the direction of the above civil authority, and the means of enforcing the Convention and the other laws and customs of war; application of the Convention in these circumstances shall in no wise [*sic*] depend on the legal status of the Parties to the conflict.

(2) This obligation presupposes, furthermore, that the adverse party likewise recognizes its obligation in the conflict at issue to comply with the present Convention and the other laws and customs of war.

(3) The provisions relating to the Protecting Powers shall, however, not be applicable, except in the instance of special agreement between the Parties to the conflict. In the absence of such agreement, an impartial humanitarian body, such as the International Committee of the Red Cross, may offer its services to the Parties to the conflict.

(4) In the case of armed conflict not of an international character occurring in the territory of one of the High Contracting Parties, but which does not fulfil the conditions as set out above, the Parties to the conflict should endeavour to bring into force, by means of special agreements, all or part of the provisions of the present Convention, and in all circumstances shall act in accordance with the underlying humanitarian principles of the present Convention.

(5) In all cases foreseen in the foregoing provisions, total or partial application of the present Convention shall not affect the legal status of the Parties to the conflict.[42]

[42] *Final Record*, vol. II-B, Seventh Report, 16 July 1949, Annex B, p. 125.

According to the ICRC Commentary on common Article 3, the above proposal of the Working Party (which includes amendments put forward by delegates), 'represents a fair summary of the different trends of opinion at the Diplomatic Conference'.[43] Nevertheless, the concern of the ICRC representative at the Special Committee was that 'the rigid conditions laid down in the Working Party's document would result in interminable discussions between the Parties to the conflict, before it were decided that the Conventions could be applied'.[44] The position of the ICRC had been consistent on the matter since the original proposal produced by the Working Party (the unamended version of the above text) had been shared with delegates. Claude Pilloud, the Chief of the ICRC Legal Division, stated the following at the fifth meeting of the Special Committee:

> The text drawn up by the Working Party could never have been applied in any recent case of civil war. It therefore did not represent a progress with regard to the present situation. Moreover, it would often be difficult to determine which was the legal government, since each Party to the conflict would pretend to be the legal government.[45]

Despite the efforts of the Working Party to incorporate amendments suggested by delegates, the deadlock on reaching an agreement continued. The above draft of Article 2A was rejected with seven delegations voting against the text and three abstaining.[46] No delegation voted in favour. According to the Seventh Report drawn up by the Special Committee:

> The main objections to the second Draft of the Working Party were that the sub-division of non-international conflicts into two categories would raise interminable discussions at the beginning of each civil, colonial, or other war as to whether the conditions for full application of the Conventions had been met in a specific case; that in reality such a decision was left to the discretion of the *de jure* government; and that the conditions in question would very seldom be fulfilled.[47]

The issue of the application of the Conventions being left to the discretion of the *de jure* government, and the problem of the conditions

[43] Pictet (ed.), *Commentary I*, p. 45.

[44] *Final Record*, vol. II-B, Summary Records of the Special Committee of the Joint Committee, 24th Meeting, 15 June 1949, p. 79.

[45] *Final Record*, vol. II-B, Summary Records of the Special Committee of the Joint Committee, 5th Meeting, 16 May 1949, pp. 47–8.

[46] *Ibid.* [47] *Final Record*, vol. II-B, Seventh Report, 16 July 1949, p. 123.

stipulated in this draft of Article 2A being fulfilled, is echoed in the ICRC Commentary on common Article 3:

There was no provision for any kind of judicial authority to decide whether the conditions stipulated were fulfilled, or not. In practice they would rarely all be fulfilled. In short, the application of the Conventions, and consequently the greater or lesser degree of cruelty of the hostilities, would depend solely on the whim of the *de jure* Government.[48]

In response to the failure of the draft drawn up by the Working Party, a second Working Group was formed consisting of delegates from France, Italy, Monaco, the United Kingdom and the USSR.[49] The task of this Working Party was to examine the French proposal to apply the humanitarian rules contained in the preamble of the Civilians Convention to armed conflicts not of an international character.[50] Instead of limiting the cases of non-international armed conflict to which the Conventions would apply, the approach now was to restrict the provisions of the Conventions that would apply in such situations.

The initial product of the second Working Party was the text of a provision setting out a list of minimum humanitarian rules to be adhered to in all situations of non-international armed conflict:

Paragraph 1. – In the case of armed conflict not of an international character occurring in the territory of one of the High Contracting Parties, each Party to the conflict shall be bound to apply, as a minimum, the following provisions:

(1) Persons taking no active part in the hostilities, and those placed hors de combat by sickness, wounds, captivity or any other cause, shall be treated humanely in all circumstances and without any discrimination.
To this end, the following acts are and shall remain prohibited with respect to the above-mentioned persons:
(a) violence to life and person, in particular murder of all kinds, mutilation, cruel treatment and torture;
(b) taking of hostages;
(c) outrages upon personal dignity, in particular, humiliating and degrading treatment;
(d) the passing of sentences and the carrying out of executions without previous judgment pronounced by a regularly constituted court, affording all the judicial guarantees which are recognized as indispensable by civilized peoples.

[48] Pictet (ed.), *Commentary I*, p. 46.
[49] *Final Record*, vol. II-B, Summary Records, 24th Meeting, p. 79.
[50] *Ibid.*, pp. 78–9.

(2) The wounded and sick shall be collected and cared for.
(3) No adverse discrimination shall be practised on the basis of differences of race, colour, religion or faith, sex, birth or wealth.

Paragraph 2. – An impartial humanitarian body, such as the International Committee of the Red Cross, may offer its services to the Parties to the conflict.

Paragraph 3. – The Parties to the conflict should further endeavour to bring into force, by means of special agreements, all or part of the other provisions of the present Convention.

Paragraph 4. – The application of the preceding provisions shall not affect the legal status of the Parties to the conflict.[51]

As the conditions determining the existence of 'armed conflict not of an international character' were not included in the above provision, the problems that had faced the Special Committee in limiting explicitly the scope of applicability were avoided. However, like the other proposals that had been considered, the text of the second Working Party did not receive the support required for it to be submitted to the Joint Committee as the amended form of Article 2, paragraph 4. Since none of the proposals examined by the Special Committee were supported by the majority of its members, the solution was to submit each of the proposals for the consideration of the Joint Committee. The Chairman of the Joint Committee, Maurice Bourquin of Belgium, called a vote on each proposal to see which draft would rally the largest number of votes.[52] The proposal that received the most support (a text based on the draft of the second Working Party) was then put to a final vote. It was adopted by 21 votes to 6, with 14 abstentions.[53]

France, Greece, Italy, the United Kingdom, Switzerland and Uruguay were among those who supported the text adopted by the Joint Committee. Given the positions previously expressed by France, Greece and the United Kingdom, it can either be assumed that these delegations underwent a radical change in perspective, or that the recognition of belligerency, either formal or tacit, came to be considered an unexpressed implicit condition for the application of the Conventions to conflicts not of an international character. The Report drawn up by the Joint Committee and presented to the Plenary Assembly interprets

[51] *Final Record*, vol. II-B, Seventh Report, 16 July 1949, Annex D, pp. 125–6.
[52] *Final Record*, vol. II-B, Summary Records of the Joint Committee, 11th Meeting, 19 July 1949, p. 35.
[53] *Final Record*, vol. II-B, Summary Records of the Joint Committee, 12th Meeting, 19 July 1949, p. 37.

the term 'armed conflict not of an international character' as having the same meaning as 'civil war'.[54] In explaining what was understood by 'armed conflict not of an international character', the report states that '[i]t was clear that this refers to civil war'.[55] This Report of the Joint Committee will be discussed further in the section that follows. It is referred to here only to highlight that the terms 'civil war' and 'armed conflict not of an international character' were understood as possessing equivalent thresholds. This is significant, as the concept of civil war presupposes the existence of hostilities of a scale and duration similar to that of an international conflict. Situations falling short of this level of intensity would not merit the recognition of belligerency and hence would not qualify for application of international humanitarian law.

Although some delegations favoured a more flexible and expansive approach to the application of international humanitarian norms, it appears that none contested or objected to the use of the term 'civil war' as synonymous with 'armed conflict not of an international character'. The scope of the latter at the Diplomatic Conference would thus clearly have been considered identical to that of the former. If the report of the Joint Committee to the Plenary Assembly is accurate in its description of delegates' views, then it appears that there was broad agreement that the threshold required for the application of international humanitarian law would be similar to that traditionally assumed for the recognition of belligerency. It appears that the concerns of some delegations who had previously supported a reference to the recognition of belligerency were alleviated by how well established the doctrine was in international law as a means of determining applicability of international humanitarian norms. It was clear that the prevailing standard for determining the existence of civil war was the recognition of belligerency. As the term 'armed conflict not of an international character' had a meaning synonymous with 'civil war', the same test would be used for determining the applicability of the Conventions in such situations.

2.1.2 Report of the Joint Committee to the Plenary Assembly of the Diplomatic Conference

The Report of the Joint Committee, drawn up by Colonel Claude du Pasquier of Switzerland, was presented to the Plenary Assembly

[54] *Final Record*, vol. II-B, Report drawn up by the Joint Committee and presented to the Plenary Assembly, p. 129.

[55] *Ibid.*

prior to the assembly's consideration of articles common to the four Conventions.[56] The Report merits attention here for its outline of the debate on the application of the Conventions to situations of non-international armed conflict.[57] Although the Report of the Joint Committee might appear only to restate what was said during discussions on the application of the Conventions to non-international armed conflict, its content is of much greater significance for two reasons. First, the Joint Committee had the same membership as that of the Plenary Assembly, including delegates from every state that participated in the Conference. As the Report of the Joint Committee was unanimously adopted by its members,[58] the content of this document was therefore approved by all states present at the Conference. Second, the Report represents the conclusion of work that spanned fifteen weeks, including twenty-three meetings where the matter of non-international armed conflict was discussed. As a submission to the Plenary Assembly, its content thus carries considerable weight.

On the concept of 'armed conflict not of an international character', the views of delegates are summarised in the Report of the Joint Committee as follows:

> It was clear that this referred to civil war, and not to a mere riot or disturbances caused by bandits. States could not be obliged as soon as a rebellion arose within their frontiers, to consider the rebels as regular belligerents to whose benefit the Conventions had to be applied. But at what point should the suppression of the rising be regarded as a civil war? What criterion should be adopted?[59]

As illustrated earlier, these are questions for which the Joint Committee had no answers. The issue of defining 'armed conflict not of an international character' had proved too problematic. Because differentiation of such situations according to formal or material criteria could not be agreed, references to conditions for the application of the Conventions were omitted. The problem of distinguishing situations of non-international armed conflict from ones that did not meet the

[56] For the final Plenary debate on Article 2A, see: *Final Record*, vol. II-B, Minutes of 18th Plenary Meeting, 28 July 1949, pp. 325–30; and *Final Record*, vol. II-B, Minutes of 19th Plenary Meeting, 29 July 1949, pp. 331–9.

[57] *Final Record*, vol. II-B, Report, p. 129.

[58] *Final Record*, vol. II-B, Summary Records of the Joint Committee, 13th Meeting, 25 July 1949, p. 39.

[59] *Final Record*, vol. II-B, Report, p. 129.

required threshold was thus ultimately avoided by focusing on the issue of minimum humanitarian standards:

> [I]n view of the enormous practical difficulties to which these differentiations would have given rise, and the very thorny problems presented by the application to civil war of Conventions drawn up for international war, an attempt was made to find another principle which might provide a solution, and it was proposed to restrict the obligations of the legitimate government and the rebel authority to the most obvious and imperious rules of the Conventions, that is, to humanitarian duties as a whole [...]
>
> The Draft of the second Working Party, whether in its first form or in the form as amended by the Special Committee, abandons the idea of applying the Conventions as a whole and also of defining the objective conditions which would make it obligatory. It repeats the wording of the Stockholm text: 'conflict not of an international character' and lays down a minimum of humanitarian rules which both parties are bound to respect.[60]

The Report's use of the term 'civil war' when referring to 'armed conflict not of an international character' is particularly significant. It implies a threshold for the application of Conventions similar to that required for the recognition of belligerency. Although the text of a provision relating to non-international armed conflict was approved by the Joint Committee, debate on the issue continued in the Plenary Assembly of the Diplomatic Conference. The section that follows examines the final stage of the debate leading up to the adoption of Article 2A by the Diplomatic Conference.

2.1.3 *Plenary debate on the application of the Conventions to armed conflicts not of an international character*

The Plenary Assembly debate on Article 2A, while brief in comparison to that of the Joint Committee, was no less vigorous.[61] The issue of extending the applicability of the Conventions to situations of non-international armed conflict was discussed during the eighteenth and nineteenth meetings of the Assembly, on 28 and 29 July 1949. The records of these meetings provide an overview of the different views expressed at the Conference and illustrate some of the positions that

[60] *Ibid.*

[61] Speaking on behalf of the Soviet delegation, Platon Morosov remarked that '[n]o other issue has given rise to such a long discussion and to such a detailed and exhaustive study as the question of the extension of the Convention[s] to war victims of conflicts not of an international character'. *Final Record*, vol. II-B, Minutes of 18th Plenary Meeting, 28 July 1949, p. 325.

came into conflict at different stages. The Asian bloc, represented by Burma, was completely opposed to the inclusion of a provision pertaining to non-international armed conflict. The Soviet bloc, represented by the USSR, maintained that the humanitarian protection provided by Article 2A was too limited. The USSR wanted the Conventions to apply without restriction to situations of non-international armed conflict.[62] As a compromise, the USSR put forward a proposal to broaden the number of provisions applicable to situations of non-international armed conflict. As an alternative to Article 2A, Platon Morosov, Deputy Head of the Soviet delegation, proposed the following wording: 'In cases of armed conflict not of an international character, each of the Parties to the conflict shall be bound to implement all the provisions of the Convention, which ensure that protected persons shall be treated in accordance with humane principles.'[63] This proposal was aimed at broadening the humanitarian protection provided by the Conventions in times of non-international armed conflict.[64]

The representative of Burma, General Tun Hla Oung, put forward a motion for the deletion of Article 2A on behalf of the Asian bloc. While doing so, he spoke at length against the adoption of Article 2A,[65] describing the provision as 'an encouragement and incentive to [...] insurgents'.[66] Oung concluded his speech by stating that '[Article 2A's]

[62] Platon Morosov, Deputy Head of the Soviet delegation, maintained that the humanitarian protection provided by Article 2A was too restrictive. He asserted its adoption to be 'tantamount to denying the necessity of applying, in cases of conflict of a non-international character, a large number of important provisions in the Draft Conventions drawn up by our Conference'. Given that Article 2A allowed for the Conventions to be applied in full to situations of non-international armed conflict, the Soviet delegate appears to have overstated the issue. The second last paragraph of Article 2A stated: 'The Parties to the conflict should further endeavour to bring into force, by means of special agreements, all or part of the other provisions of the present Convention.' *Final Record*, vol. II-B, Seventh Report, 16 July 1949, Annex E, p. 126.

[63] *Final Record*, vol. II-B, Minutes, 28 July 1949, p. 326. Representatives of Romania and Czechoslovakia voiced support for the Soviet amendment. It was nevertheless rejected by the Conference (11 delegates voting in favour, 20 against and 7 abstaining) in favour of the Article 2A text submitted by the delegations of France, Greece, Italy, the UK, Switzerland and Uruguay. *Final Record*, vol. II-B, Minutes of 19th Plenary Meeting, 29 July 1949, p. 339.

[64] Morosov stated that '[i]n contrast to the text of Article 2A, which restricts the application of the Convention, the proposal submitted by the Soviet Delegation is based on the necessity of giving effect to many important provisions of the Conventions, in order to ensure the protection of war victims in the case of conflicts of a non-international character'. *Final Record*, vol. II-B, Minutes, 28 July 1949, p. 327.

[65] *Ibid.*, pp. 327–30. [66] *Ibid.*, p. 330.

inclusion is especially harmful and beyond the scope of our conference. The Article ... is an incentive to armed conflicts and I propose the complete deletion of any extension of the Conventions to civil war and insurgency.'[67]

The views expressed by the representatives of USSR and Burma are indicative of the broad spectrum of opinion that the Diplomatic Conference had to accommodate. Other difficulties with the text of Article 2A were raised by the representatives of Denmark and the United Kingdom. Speaking on behalf of the Danish delegation, Georg Cohn expressed concern about the use of the term 'Parties to the conflict' instead of 'belligerents'. He explained:

> [W]e are no longer dealing with humanitarian duties only but with the whole subject matter of the four Conventions, not only as regards the mutual relations between the Parties, but also as regards the relations between the Parties to the conflict and those which are not Parties to it. We must recognize that all these 'Parties to the conflict,' however small and insignificant they may be (for example, a gang of ordinary criminals engaged in armed conflict), will have the benefit of all the rights recognized by the Convention ... To give an example: a small gang of criminals in armed conflict with its government, would have the right to intercept ships owned by other countries, to demand the extradition of wounded, sick or shipwrecked men, and, in fact, would be entitled to demand the observance of all the obligations and to claim all the rights embodied in the four Conventions.[68]

Although the Danish delegate exaggerated the difficulty posed by the term, the question of what constituted a party to an armed conflict was an important one for many delegations involving the drafting of common Article 3.[69] The fear was that the law might be interpreted in a manner that would place insurgents on a footing similar to that of state authorities. Joyce Gutteridge of the United Kingdom voiced reservations similar to those of the Danish delegation concerning the use of the term 'Party to the conflict' instead of 'belligerent': 'The word "belligerent", I need hardly remind the Conference, has a well understood meaning in international law and is used in particular in relation to questions of neutrality. Certain rights are accorded in international law to belligerents, and the wholesale replacement of the word "belligerent" in these Conventions by the expression "Parties to the conflict", the wholesale replacement of one expression in an international treaty by another

[67] *Ibid.* [68] *Final Record*, vol. II-B, Minutes, 29 July 1949, p. 332.

[69] As noted by Ingrid Detter de Lupis, 'Common Article 3 was drafted at a time when the criteria for combatant status were more stringent.' *Law of War*, p. 168, fn. 240.

expression can lead to legal consequences which I am certain are not intended by the framers of these humanitarian Conventions.'[70]

In line with views that had been previously expressed by her delegation, Gutteridge highlighted the doctrine of belligerency as the standard by which to judge the applicability of the Conventions in armed conflicts not of an international character. The UK delegate strongly urged the Conference to give careful consideration to the use of the terms 'Parties to the conflict' and 'belligerents'. In order to address concerns relating to the interpretation of the term 'Party to a conflict', in particular its potential effect on the doctrine of belligerency in international law, the Danish delegation prepared the following resolution: 'The Conference considers that the conditions under which a Party to a conflict can be recognized as a belligerent by Powers not taking part in this conflict, are governed by the general rules of international law on the subject and are in no way modified by the Geneva Conventions.'[71]

In response to the criticisms voiced by delegates on Article 2A, the Swiss representative, Plinio Bolla, remarked that the text represented a balance between the claims of idealism and the rights of realism.[72] Directing his address at those who considered that Article 2A did not go far enough, Bolla stated that 'half a loaf is better than no bread'.[73] To delegations such as that of Burma, who viewed the provision as a danger to state sovereignty, he directed the following comments on the meaning of 'armed conflict not of an international character':

> [O]utbreaks of individual banditism, or even movements of the kind, complicated or aggravated by the existence of a conspiracy, do not really constitute an armed conflict in the proper sense of the term ... An armed conflict, as understood in this provision, implies some form of organization among Parties to the conflict. Such organization will, of course, generally be found

[70] *Final Record*, vol. II-B, Minutes, 29 July 1949, p. 333.

[71] *Final Record*, vol. I, Resolution 10, p. 362. Although the resolution of the Danish delegation was approved by the Conference, it is probable that the absence of the term in the Geneva Conventions was a major contributing factor to the decline of the belligerency doctrine in contemporary international humanitarian law. While clear criteria existed for the recognition of belligerency, it was unclear what would be deemed to qualify as a 'party' to a non-international armed conflict. The ambiguity surrounding what constitutes a 'party' to an armed conflict is one that still affects interpretation of international humanitarian law (see Chapter 4, at section 4.1.1.1). Nevertheless, it is arguable that it has helped to broaden the scope of the Conventions to include the much more prevalent forms of internal armed conflict, such as protracted guerrilla warfare.

[72] *Final Record*, vol. II-B, Minutes, 29 July 1949, p. 336. [73] *Ibid.*, p. 335.

on the governmental side; but there must also be some degree of organization among the insurgents.[74]

Implicit in these remarks is an understanding that the recognition of non-international armed conflict is not subject to the discretion of the state authorities. Referring to the degree of organisation as the distinguishing factor for the recognition of parties to a conflict, the Swiss representative highlighted a feature of non-international armed conflict that is still retained in the contemporary concept.[75]

Another view on what constitutes non-international armed conflict was put forward by Colonel Falcon Briceno of Venezuela. While rejecting the open-ended interpretations expressed by the representatives of Denmark and Burma, Briceno posited an alternative understanding of the term 'armed conflict not of an international character'. He stated that '[t]here is no doubt that this does not apply to the exploits of bandits or to riots of any kind, but to *civil war*, a sociological phenomenon of political history which often in essence is a form of class struggle'.[76]

The debate on the application of the Conventions to situations of non-international armed conflicts concluded with a vote by secret ballot resulting in the adoption of Article 2A, the current common Article 3 text. Of the 47 delegates in attendance, 34 delegates voted in favour, 12 against and 1 abstained.[77] The number of delegates that voted against the provision indicates the reluctance of a significant minority to include non-international armed conflict within the scope of the Geneva Conventions. Despite the opposition expressed in this vote, only two delegations made reservations relating to common Article 3 when signing the Conventions on behalf of their governments. Argentina stated that 'Article 3, common to all four Conventions, shall be the only Article, to the exclusion of all others, which shall be applicable in the case of armed conflicts not of an international character.'[78] However, this reservation was not confirmed at the time of ratification. As a consequence, it is not considered active and carries no legal significance.[79]

[74] *Ibid.* [75] This issue will be returned to in Chapter 4, at section 4.1.1.1.

[76] *Final Record*, vol. II-B, Minutes, 29 July 1949, p. 333. Emphasis added.

[77] *Ibid.*, p. 339.

[78] *Final Record*, vol. I, Reservations made at the time of signature of the Geneva Conventions for the Protection of War Victims of August 12, 1949, Argentina, p. 343.

[79] 'Argentina made a reservation at the time of signature, but did not confirm it at the time of ratification of the Geneva Conventions of 1949. Therefore, the depositary, in this case Switzerland, considers that Argentina made no reservation.' From author's

The second reservation was made by Portugal's Chargé d'Affaires, Goncalo Caldeira Coelho in the following declaration:

> As there is no actual definition of what is meant by a conflict not of an international character, and as, in case this term is intended to refer solely to civil war, it is not clearly laid down at what moment an armed rebellion within a country should be considered as having become a civil war, Portugal reserves the right not to apply the provisions of common Article 3, in so far as they may be contrary to the provisions of Portuguese law, in all territories subject to her sovereignty in any part of the world.[80]

This reservation was later formally withdrawn by Ambassador Ruy Teixeira Guerra at the time of Portugal's ratification of the Geneva Conventions, 14 March 1961. The absence of active reservations strengthens the content of common Article 3. The reservations submitted by the Argentine and Portuguese delegations no longer have any legal significance and may not be interpreted as having any import for the application of common Article 3.

2.1.4 *Comments on the intended scope of common Article 3*

It is clear from the *travaux préparatoires* of the Geneva Conventions that the intended scope of applicability for common Article 3 was far narrower than that which is currently the case. The delegates involved in drafting the provision understood 'armed conflict not of an international character' as having essentially the same meaning as 'civil war'.[81] The existence of 'civil war', a state of armed conflict requiring the application of international humanitarian norms, was understood in terms of the doctrine of belligerency. The conditions required for the recognition of belligerency were reproduced in most of the drafts considered by the Special Committee as alternatives to the original proposal stipulating uniform application for the Conventions to all situations of armed conflict. While the original proposal would have arguably made the application of international humanitarian law more straightforward, lacking a distinction that many still contend is artificial and unnecessary, the idea was too radical for most delegates participating at the Diplomatic Conference.

correspondence with Jacqueline Walters of the Swiss Federal Department of Foreign Affairs, 21 May 2007.

80 *Final Record*, vol. II-A, Reservations made at the time of signature of the Geneva Conventions for the Protection of War Victims of 12 August 1949, Portugal, p. 351.

81 See *Final Record*, vol. II-B, Seventh Report, p. 121.

Although there had been significant opposition to the principle of including a provision relating to non-international armed conflict, the majority of delegations at the Diplomatic Conference favoured extending the Conventions to include such situations. Opinions voiced by the experts of the ICRC had been consistent on the matter. When called upon to speak, ICRC representatives expressed strong support for the application of the Conventions to non-international armed conflict. With unique professional experience of applying international humanitarian law in such situations, the expert opinion of the ICRC delegation had a significant influence in shifting restrictions placed by delegations on the application of the Conventions.

Although the distinction between international and non-international armed conflict has undoubtedly obstructed aspirations towards the formulation of a single body of law applicable in all situations of armed conflict, it has also had the positive consequence of broadening the scope of international humanitarian law. The use of the phrase 'armed conflict not of an international character' in common Article 3 has allowed the scope of the provision to evolve beyond that which was originally intended by its drafters. The non-use of the terms 'civil war' and 'belligerents' has also allowed some latitude for the interpretation of common Article 3's applicability to take into account developments in the conduct of hostilities. These terms represent concepts essential to the application of international humanitarian norms in traditional international law. Their absence from the text of common Article 3 allows for much a less restrictive interpretation of its applicability.

It is important to recognise the concept of non-international armed conflict used by the drafters of the Geneva Conventions to be one essentially akin to contemporaneous international warfare.[82] In the words of Professor Frede Castberg, Head of the Norwegian delegation, it is 'a form of conflict resembling international war, but taking place inside the territory of a State'.[83] According to the Seventh Report of the

[82] This is acknowledged, albeit in loose terms, in the ICRC Commentary on common Article 3:

> Speaking generally, it must be recognized that the conflicts referred to in Article 3 are armed conflicts, with armed forces on either side engaged in hostilities – conflicts, in short, which are in many respects similar to an international war, but take place within the confines of a single country. In many cases, each of the Parties is in possession of a portion of the national territory, and there is often some sort of front.

Pictet (ed.), *Commentary IV*, p. 36.

[83] *Final Record*, vol. II-B, Summary Records, 1st Meeting, p. 11.

Special Committee it is 'an armed conflict resembling an international war in dimensions'.[84]

As the conduct of warfare has evolved, so too has the interpretation of international humanitarian law. The interpretation of what constitutes an armed conflict has changed significantly in the past sixty years. The field of application associated with 'armed conflict not of an international character' has expanded beyond its intended meaning. The conditions required for the recognition of belligerency no longer apply for the application of international humanitarian law. It is important therefore to be aware that references to the intentions of the drafters are likely to imply a threshold requirement that no longer exists in contemporary international law.

2.2 The ICRC Commentary on common Article 3

Soon after the drafting of the Geneva Conventions, the ICRC decided to undertake a commentary on the provisions contained in each Convention.[85] This Commentary, published under the general editorship of Jean S. Pictet, was released in four volumes over a period spanning eight years. The first of these four volumes, on the Geneva Convention for the Amelioration of the Condition of the Wounded and Sick in Armed Forces in the Field (*Commentary I*), was published in 1952.[86] The next volume, on the fourth Geneva Convention on the Protection of Civilian Persons in Time of War (*Commentary IV*), was released first in French in 1956 and then in English in 1958.[87] These were followed by French and English editions on the Convention relating to the Treatment of Prisoners of War (*Commentary III*)[88] and the Convention for the Amelioration of the Condition of Wounded, Sick and Shipwrecked Members of Armed Forces at Sea (*Commentary II*).[89] The latter was the last of the four Commentaries released by the ICRC, published in 1960.

The chronology is of interest as the text on common Article 3 differs in each volume. The section on common Article 3 in the first volume published is the most substantive, spanning 25 pages. In the next volume published (on the fourth Geneva Convention), it is reduced to 20.

[84] *Final Record*, vol. II-B, Seventh Report, p. 121.
[85] Pictet (ed.), *Commentary I*, p. 7. [86] Pictet (ed.), *Commentary I*.
[87] Pictet (ed.), *Commentary IV*. A French edition of this Commentary was published in 1956.
[88] Pictet (ed.), *Commentary III*. [89] Pictet (ed.), *Commentary II*.

In the volume that followed (on the third Geneva Convention), it is again reduced to 18 pages, and then cut to 8 pages for the final volume published, on the second Geneva Convention.[90]

While some of the text on Article 3's field of application is shared by all four Commentaries, some noteworthy developments are visible in the sections dealing with this provision's field of application. In the Commentary on the first Geneva Convention some of the proposals discussed at the Diplomatic Conference are put forward as 'convenient criteria' to help to distinguish situations of non-international armed conflict:

(1) That the Party in revolt against the *de jure* Government possesses an organized military force, an authority responsible for its acts, acting within a determinate territory and having the means of respecting and ensuring respect for the Convention.

(2) That the legal Government is obliged to have recourse to the regular military forces against insurgents organized as military and in possession of a part of the national territory.

(3) (a) That the *de jure* Government has recognized the insurgents as belligerents; or
(b) that it has claimed for itself the rights of a belligerent; or
(c) that it has accorded the insurgents recognition as belligerents for the purposes only of the present Convention; or
(d) that the dispute has been admitted to the agenda of the Security Council or the General Assembly of the United Nations as being a threat to international peace, a breach of the peace, or an act of aggression.

(4) (a) That the insurgents have an organization purporting to have the characteristics of a State.
(b) That the insurgent civil authority exercises *de facto* authority over persons within a determinate territory.
(c) That the armed forces act under the direction of the organized civil authority and are prepared to observe the ordinary laws of war.
(d) That the insurgent civil authority agrees to be bound by the provisions of the Convention.[91]

The above criteria are reproduced in the Commentaries on the fourth and third Geneva Conventions with minor changes.[92] The

[90] The foreword of this volume states that '[f]or more detailed information on general matters, the reader should … refer to Volume I of the Commentary'. Pictet (ed.), *Commentary II*, p. 2.

[91] Pictet (ed.), *Commentary I*, p. 49.

[92] In *Commentary IV*, paragraph 4(b) is amended to refer to a 'determinate portion of the national territory' and paragraph 4(c) is altered to refer to an 'organized

Commentaries on the first and fourth Geneva Conventions state that the criteria 'are useful as a means of distinguishing a genuine armed conflict from a mere act of banditry or an unorganized and short-lived insurrection'.[93] While the content of the criteria indicates a high threshold of applicability, the authors of the Commentaries on the first, fourth and third Conventions were careful not to limit the applicability of common Article 3 to the situations listed therein:

> Does this mean that Article 3 is not applicable in cases where armed strife breaks out in a country, but does not fulfil any of the above conditions (which are not obligatory and are only mentioned as an indication)? We do not subscribe to this view. We think, on the contrary, that the Article should be applied as widely as possible. There can be no reason against this. For, contrary to what may have been thought, the Article in its reduced form does not in any way limit the right of a State to put down rebellion. Nor does it increase in the slightest the authority of the rebel party. It merely demands respect for certain rules, which were already recognized as essential in all civilized countries, and enacted in the municipal law of the States in question, long before the Convention was signed. What Government would dare to claim before the world, in a case of civil disturbances which could justly be described as mere acts of banditry, that, Article 3 not being applicable, it was entitled to leave the wounded uncared for, to inflict torture and mutilations and to take hostages? However useful, therefore, the various conditions stated above may be, they are not indispensable, since no Government can object to respecting, in its dealings with internal enemies, whatever the nature of the conflict between it and them, a few essential rules which it in fact respects daily, under its own laws, even when dealing with common criminals.[94]

While not subscribing to the view that the criteria are obligatory for the application of common Article 3 in 'armed conflicts not of an international character', the Commentaries' content suggests that the kind of situations deemed to qualify are ones that are similar to conventional inter-state warfare. In the Commentary on the first Convention the section dealing with common Article 3's field of application terminates with the paragraph referred to above. However, the Commentary

authority' instead of 'the organized civil authority'. Pictet (ed.), *Commentary IV*, p. 36. In *Commentary III*, the word 'persons' in paragraph in 4(b) is replaced with the word 'population'. Pictet (ed.), *Commentary III*, p. 36. The criteria are omitted from the Commentary on the second Geneva Convention. Pictet (ed.), *Commentary II*, p. 33.

93 Pictet (ed.), *Commentary I*, p. 50; Pictet (ed.), *Commentary IV*, p. 36.

94 Pictet (ed.), *Commentary I*, p. 50. This paragraph is reproduced with minor alterations in the Commentaries on the third and fourth Geneva Conventions. Pictet (ed.), *Commentary IV*, p. 36; Pictet (ed.), *Commentary III*, pp. 36–7.

published subsequently on the fourth Convention includes an additional paragraph. The language it introduces is significant as it outlines in more specific terms an interpretation of 'armed conflict not of an international character': 'Speaking generally, it must be recognized that the conflicts referred to in Article 3 are armed conflicts, with armed forces on either side engaged in hostilities – conflicts, in short, which are in many respects similar to an international war, but take place within the confines of a single country. In many cases, each of the Parties is in possession of a portion of the national territory, and there is often some sort of front.'[95]

This new paragraph was included in the Commentary on the third Convention with some amendments.[96] The terms of this paragraph were also included in the last of the Commentaries published which states that '[i]n general, Article [3] should be recognized as applying to armed conflicts consisting of *hostilities* in which *armed forces* on either side are engaged – in other words, conflicts which are in many respects similar to an international war, but take place within the confines of a single country.'[97] Taken together with the criteria listed in the Commentaries on the first, third and fourth Conventions, the terms of this paragraph support the finding evidenced in the *travaux préparatoires* of the Geneva Conventions, that the term 'armed conflict not of an international character' was generally understood to have the same meaning as that of 'civil war'.[98] As the concept of civil war presupposed a situation similar in kind to that of conventional international warfare, the threshold determining the application of common Article 3 would have been similarly understood. An issue frequently overlooked when interpreting the intended scope of common Article 3, this point will be returned to later when examining how the international criminal tribunals for Rwanda and the former Yugoslavia have used the ICRC criteria.[99]

As noted by the authors of the ICRC Commentaries,[100] the criteria are 'in no way obligatory' for the application of common Article 3. The only

[95] Pictet (ed.), *Commentary IV*, p. 36.

[96] The last sentence was deleted and the words 'armed forces' and 'hostilities' were italicised. Pictet (ed.), *Commentary III*, p. 37.

[97] Pictet (ed.), *Commentary II*, p. 33. Emphasis in original.

[98] In the Commentary on the first Geneva Convention, the term 'civil war' is used twenty-five times in the section dealing with common Article 3. Pictet (ed.), *Commentary I*, pp. 37–61.

[99] See Chapter 4, at section 4.5.2.2.

[100] Jean Pictet is often referred to in secondary sources as the author of the ICRC Commentaries. This is not entirely accurate. The foreword of the Commentary on

requirement is the existence of 'armed conflict not of an international character'. In view of this threshold for the applicability of common Article 3, the section that follows comments on state practice in situations of non-international armed conflict.

2.3 State practice relating to the applicability of common Article 3

Despite the number of non-international armed conflicts that have taken place since the drafting of the Geneva Conventions of 1949, state practice relating to the application of common Article 3 has been relatively scarce.[101] For various reasons, states are generally not inclined to acknowledge the applicability of this provision within their own territory. While the final clause of common Article 3 states that its application 'shall not affect the legal status of the Parties to the conflict',[102] state authorities engaged with non-international armed conflict have a tendency not to recognise its applicability. As noted by the UK Ministry of Defence, 'although Common Article 3 specifically provides that its application does not affect the legal status of the parties to a conflict, *states have been, and always will be, reluctant to admit that a state of armed conflict exists*'.[103]

The final clause of Article 3 was included to verify that it serves a strictly humanitarian purpose and as such possesses no threat to the security of a state by compromising any of the legal means at its

the Geneva Convention for the Amelioration of the Condition of the Wounded and Sick in Armed Forces in the Field states that the Commentary was 'written mainly by Mr. Jean S. Pictet, who called on M. Fédéric Siordet for Articles 1 to 3 and 8 to 10, M. Claude Pilloud for Articles 11 and 49 to 52, M. Jean-Pierre Schoenholzer for Articles 12 to 18, M. René-Jean Wilhelm for Articles 6, 7 and 46, and M. Oscar M. Uhler for Articles 45, 47, 48 and 52 to 64'. Pictet (ed.), *Commentary I*, p. 8. Fédéric Siordet is also referred to in the other Commentaries as a contributor to sections dealing with Articles 1 to 3. Pictet (ed.), *Commentary II*, p. 2; Pictet (ed.), *Commentary III*, p. 2; Pictet (ed.), *Commentary IV*, p. 2.

101 For a survey of state practice relating to the application of common Article 3, see Moir, *Internal Armed Conflict*, pp. 67–88. See also Forsythe, 'Legal Management', 272, at 275–7; Cho, 'International Humanitarian Law', pp. 32–41.

102 According to the ICRC Commentary on the first Geneva Convention, this clause 'makes it absolutely clear that the object of the Convention is a purely humanitarian one, that it is in no way concerned with the internal affairs of States, and that it merely ensures respect for the few essential rules of humanity which all civilized nations consider as valid everywhere and under all circumstances and as being above and outside war itself'. Pictet (ed.), *Commentary I*, p. 60.

103 UK Ministry of Defence, *Manual*, p. 384. Emphasis added.

disposal to suppress insurgency. It is worth noting in this regard that there is no provision in the body of international humanitarian law that would prevent a government from treating rebels or insurgents in a non-international armed conflict as ordinary criminals. The application of common Article 3 in particular does not in any way prevent the criminalisation of acts committed by those who take up arms against the state. The use of emergency powers by the state to deal with a situation of insurgency is in no way precluded by the provision provided such measures do not conflict with the standards contained therein. A plain reading of the final clause of common Article 3 makes it clear that the application of this provision has no effect on the legal status of non-state actors and as such does not in any way prevent a *de jure* government from treating them as criminals for their participation in a non-international armed conflict.

Despite the presence of the provision stating that the legal status of parties to the conflict will not be affected, and the fundamental nature of the humanitarian standards stipulated, the main problem with the implementation of common Article 3 is in the recognition of situations as constituting armed conflict. In such scenarios, governments often find it less expedient to recognise it formally than to treat the conflict as a mere internal disturbance, aggressively suppressing it. According to Eldon van C. Greenberg, such a response is understandable if the political sensibilities of state authorities are taken into account: 'In a revolutionary war ... status is the prize for which fighting is waged. Thus, in spite of the plea contained in Article 3 of the Geneva Conventions to put aside (at least to some extent) questions of status, this politically is impossible'.[104] In terms of recognising the existence of armed conflict, the political significance of common Article 3 has also been highlighted by Professor Andrew Clapham:

> The designation of a situation as 'armed conflict not of an international character' so as to trigger the application of Common Article 3 to the Geneva Conventions of 1949 is obviously an act of considerable political importance for all sides to the conflict. The insurgents will often welcome the designation of their attacks as constituting armed conflict as this confers a curious sort of international recognition on them; the applicability of Common Article 3 reinforces the special role of the International Committee of the Red Cross (ICRC). On the other hand the government may be less willing to acknowledge

[104] Greenberg, 'Law and the Conduct of the Algerian Revolution' (1970) 11 *Harvard International Law Journal* 37, at 70–1, as cited in Moir, *Internal Armed Conflict*, p. 66.

the situation as one of armed conflict, preferring instead to portray it as a fight against criminals and terrorists.[105]

For Colonel G.I.A.D. Draper, the lack of juridical precision in the formulation of common Article 3 has caused many of the problems surrounding its implementation. He stated that the drafters of this provision left it 'open to much ambiguity of interpretation. As is so often the case with humanitarian law instruments, this is the outcome of the desire for maximum width for the play of the humanitarian norms, overriding the desire for that element of certainty which legal norms demand if they are to be effective.'[106] The ambiguity in the scope of common Article 3 is cited by many commentators as allowing states the opportunity to evade the responsibility to adhere to its provisions. States are often reluctant to recognise the applicability of the common Article due to the perception that it increases the authority of the insurgents. The act of formally recognising the existence of an armed conflict is, from the state's point of view, disadvantageous for a number of reasons. First, it highlights the failure of the state in preventing such a situation; second, it is possible for it to contribute to the *perceived* recognition of insurgents as legitimate combatants; and, third, acknowledging the existence of an armed conflict automatically brings into force the most basic provisions of international humanitarian law, limiting the state's use of repressive measures. These reasons serve as examples explaining states' reluctance to acknowledge the existence of armed conflict. As noted by Lindsay Moir:

> [g]iven the political factors which are bound to influence these circumstances, and common Article 3's silence as regards the party who is to determine the existence or otherwise of an armed conflict (and indeed the method by which this determination is to be made), decisions on the issue will inevitably be made by the State itself. Naturally reluctant to bind themselves to rules which could be perceived as favouring political opponents, States can therefore hide behind the lack of a definition to prevent the application of humanitarian law by denying the very existence of armed conflict.[107]

As there is no formula built into common Article 3 determining the conditions of its application, the act of recognising the existence of armed conflict is in practice left to the discretion of the central government authorities of the state hosting the conflict.[108] As pointed out by

105 Clapham, *Human Rights*, pp. 112–13.
106 Draper, 'Humanitarian Law', at 264.
107 Moir, *Internal Armed Conflict*, p. 34.
108 See *Ibid.*, p. 45. See Menon, 'Recognition of Belligerency', in Menon, *Law of Recognition*, pp. 109–37.

Moir, this is 'clearly unsatisfactory from a humanitarian standpoint'.[109] The lack of a formula for distinguishing 'armed conflict not of an international character' has been cited by some scholars as a major obstacle to the implementation of international humanitarian law.[110] According to Moir, '[t]he failure of the drafters to define the term "armed conflict not of an international character" allowed States reluctant to hinder their ability to deal with insurrection by accepting any international humanitarian obligations simply to deny the existence of armed conflict, and thus the applicability of international regulation'.[111]

Another feature of common Article 3 making its application problematic is the wording of some provisions. The ICRC Commentary on Additional Protocol II states that the concise wording of common Article 3

> lays down the principles without developing them, which has sometimes given rise to restrictive interpretations. This particularly applies to the scope of judicial guarantees (paragraph 1(1)(d)) which does not go into details. The precarious position in which insurgent combatants find themselves requires that such guarantees should be clarified and reinforced for their benefit, particularly with regard to matters of judicial procedure. In fact, an insurgent combatant does not enjoy immunity when charged with having taken up arms, as do members of the armed forces in a conflict between States; on the contrary, he may be punished for having violated the national law.[112]

Despite the vague nature of its content, common Article 3 arguably represents one of the most important developments in the history of international humanitarian law. Jean Pictet describes the significance of common Article 3 as 'marking a decisive step in the evolution of modern law and tending to limit the sovereignty of the state for the benefit of the individual'.[113] He also notes, however, that 'it must be acknowledged that some [states] evade their responsibilities simply by denying the existence of an armed conflict'.[114] Higgins comments that, despite its shortcomings, common Article 3 represents 'a step in the right direction – its application is not based on reciprocity by the other party, nor does it depend upon the fulfilment of a technical definition of civil war'.[115] Indeed, the achievement of common Article 3 as a

[109] Moir, *Internal Armed Conflict*, p. 34.

[110] See Meron, 'Humanitarian Decision', at 818; Moir, *Internal Armed Conflict*, p. 34; Pictet, *Development and Principles*, p. 47.

[111] Moir, *Internal Armed Conflict*, p. 88.

[112] Pilloud, *Commentary*, p. 1325.

[113] Pictet, *Development and Principles*, p. 47.

[114] *Ibid.*

[115] Higgins, 'Civil Conflict', in Luard (ed.), *International Regulation*, p. 183.

universal standard applicable to situations of non-international armed conflict ought not to go unrecognised. As noted by Suter, at the very least 'it was useful in enabling governments to become accustomed to the principle of non-international armed conflicts being regulated by international law'.[116]

2.4 Concluding observations

The formulation of common Article 3, despite its failings, has come to be recognised as the first major achievement in the codification of a universally acceptable set of standards for situations of non-international armed conflict. As customary international law, the provision embodies a set of minimum standards of humane treatment to be adhered to in all circumstances. The progress achieved in this development of international humanitarian law is extremely significant. As the first substantive provision of international law specific to situations of non-international armed conflict, it represents a major advancement into an area that had previously been taken as the remit of state sovereignty. Described by David A. Elder as an 'initial but very important first step', the codification of common Article 3 represents a development of tremendous value for the victims of non-international armed conflict.[117] As noted by Heather A. Wilson:

> Article 3 of the Geneva Conventions was a milestone in the development of the law of war. Although the Article does not grant any legal status to the rebels, as evidenced by the final paragraph, its adoption affirmed that internal wars are not entirely beyond the scope of international law. Each of the States party to the Conventions has the right to demand that its provisions be respected by a government engaged in a civil war. To this degree at least, humanitarian protection in non-international armed conflicts was effectively internationalized.[118]

While the achievements of common Article 3 are laudable, the provision also has serious shortcomings. The two most significant were summed up by the UN Secretary-General in an analytical report to the UN Commission on Human Rights (UNCHR):

> First, it provides only a minimum of protection; for example, it is silent on issues relating to freedom of movement, does not explicitly prohibit rape, and does not explicitly address matters relating to the methods and means

[116] Suter, *Guerrilla Warfare*, p. 16. [117] Elder, 'Historical Background', at 68.
[118] Wilson, *International Law*, p. 44.

of warfare. Second, while common article 3 does not define 'armed conflicts not of an international character', in practice this wording has left room for Governments to contest its applicability to situations of internal violence inside their countries.[119]

It is clear from the *travaux préparatoires* of the Geneva Conventions that the threshold of 'armed conflict not of an international character' was that of civil war. If a definition of this term had been included in the Geneva Conventions, there is evidence to suggest that it would have been based on the doctrine of belligerency. Given the conditions attached to the recognition of belligerency, it is fortunate that the term was not included in the text of common Article 3. To do so would have created serious problems in the applicability of this provision. The use of belligerency would have set the threshold of hostilities required for the characterisation of armed conflict to that of full-scale civil war. All situations not qualifying as such would consequently have been excluded from the remit of common Article 3.

It is fortunate that the applicability of common Article 3 is no longer interpreted in the terms discussed at the Diplomatic Conference of 1949. If 'armed conflict not of an international character' was still understood as indicating a field of application similar to civil war, the majority of contemporary non-international armed conflicts would be excluded from the remit of international humanitarian law. The non-inclusion of a definition in common Article 3 and the absence of criteria governing the applicability of this provision in the Geneva Conventions has allowed the concept of non-international armed conflict to develop considerably since 1949. According to Heike Spieker:

> [T]he positive effect of a lack of agreed distinctive criteria is the flexibility provided by such lacuna. Doors might be opened to apply international humanitarian law in situations which traditionally would not necessarily qualify as non-international armed conflicts. In theory, weaknesses in protecting civilian population and discretion in qualifying armed hostilities are balanced by an increased flexibility and an enhancement of the protection of the civilian population in non-international armed conflicts.[120]

While it was prudent not to define the term at the Diplomatic Conference, in order to avoid narrowing the applicability of the Conventions, the ambiguity in common Article 3's field of application

[119] Minimum Humanitarian Standards: Analytical Report of the Secretary-General Submitted pursuant to Commission on Human Rights Resolution 1997/21, UN Doc. E/CN.4/1998/87, para. 74 (1998).

[120] Spieker, 'Twenty-fifth Anniversary', at 141.

has allowed some states an opportunity to deny the applicability of international humanitarian law by not recognising the existence of an armed conflict. As there is no internationally agreed mechanism for determining the applicability of common Article 3, its implementation has in many cases been dependent upon the will of parties to acknowledge the applicability of international humanitarian law. This is perhaps the most problematic aspect of the law governing situations of non-international armed conflict.[121]

The interpretation of the threshold contained in common Article 3 will be returned to in Chapter 4. The chapter that follows examines the thresholds of application contained in the Additional Protocols of 1977. In doing so, the significance of these developments and their impact on the concept of non-international armed conflict in international humanitarian law will also be explored.

121 According to the UK Ministry of Defence, 'states have been, and always will be, reluctant to admit that a state of armed conflict exists'. *Manual*, p. 384.

3 Changes in the scope of non-international armed conflict resulting from the Additional Protocols of 1977

In 1977, driven by developments in armed conflict subsequent to the Second World War, there was a major revision and updating of the Geneva Conventions.[1] Two protocols to the Conventions, one dealing with international armed conflict, the other dealing with non-international armed conflict, were adopted at a diplomatic conference convened by the Swiss Federal Council. The existence of the two protocols, and the distinctions between them, highlight the importance of the issue of thresholds of armed conflict with respect to the implementation of international humanitarian law. In a number of respects, the two Additional Protocols refine and complicate issues relating to the determination of the existence of armed conflict.

This chapter, in two parts, examines each of the two Protocols.[2] The first part studies Additional Protocol I, which is devoted to international

[1] Protocol Additional to the Geneva Conventions of 12 August 1949, and Relating to the Protection of Victims of International Armed Conflicts (Additional Protocol I), 1125 UNTS 3, 1977; Protocol Additional to the Geneva Conventions of 12 August 1949 and Relating to the Protection of Victims of Non-International Armed Conflicts (Additional Protocol II), 1125 UNTS 609, 1977.

[2] Unlike the Geneva Conventions of 1949, the Additional Protocols of 1977 have yet to be ratified by all member states of the UN. To date 168 states have ratified Additional Protocol I while 164 have ratified Additional Protocol II. The non-ratification of Additional Protocol I and II by states such as India, Pakistan, Indonesia and the United States does not impact significantly on how the internal armed conflict is conceptualised contemporaneously in international humanitarian law. David J. Scheffer, the former United States Ambassador at Large for War Crimes Issues, stated in an address to I Corps Soldiers and Commanders on 4 May 2000 that 'we continue to recognize that many of the substantive provisions of both Protocol I and Protocol II, which covers internal armed conflicts, reflect the development of customary international norms'. In the same speech he stated that '[t]hirteen years ago, President Reagan asked the Senate for its advice and consent to Additional Protocol II to the 1949 Geneva Convention, which governs internal armed conflicts.

armed conflict, demonstrating the way in which the concept of non-international armed conflict was narrowed to exclude wars of national liberation. The second part scrutinises Additional Protocol II, which addresses non-international armed conflict, paying specific attention to provisions governing its application. While the two new categories of armed conflict created by the Additional Protocols are considered not advantageous to the implementation of international humanitarian law, it is contended that the distinctions introduced in these instruments do not represent codifications of customary international law. It is also held that they do not affect the threshold of application associated with common Article 3.

3.1 Additional Protocol I

The significance of Additional Protocol I to the present discussion concerns its characterisation of wars of national liberation as situations of international armed conflict. The title of the instrument states that it relates to 'the Protection of Victims of International Armed Conflicts'.[3] While the scope of international armed conflict had previously been defined by Article 2 common to the four Geneva Conventions of 1949, Additional Protocol I broadened the concept of international armed conflict to include other situations. Article 1 outlines the Protocol's general principles and scope of application:

> 1. The High Contracting Parties undertake to respect and to ensure respect for this Protocol in all circumstances.
> 2. In cases not covered by this Protocol or by other international agreements, civilians and combatants remain under the protection and authority of the principles of international law derived from established custom, from the principles of humanity and from dictates of public conscience.
> 3. This Protocol, which supplements the Geneva Conventions of 12 August 1949 for the protection of war victims, shall apply in the situations referred to in Article 2 common to those Conventions.
> 4. The situations referred to in the preceding paragraph include armed conflicts which peoples are fighting against colonial domination and alien occupation and against racist regimes in the exercise of their right of self-determination, as enshrined in the Charter of the United Nations and the Declaration on Principles of International

President Clinton renewed that request in January 1999.' (Transcript of speech on file with author.)

[3] Additional Protocol I; Additional Protocol II.

> Law concerning Friendly Relations and Co-operation among States in accordance with the Charter of the United Nations.[4]

The last paragraph of this Article expanded the concept of international armed conflict provided by common Article 2 to include situations of conflict arising from armed campaigns for national liberation. Prior to the formulation of this instrument, the status of such situations under international humanitarian law was a subject of considerable debate.[5] While the international character of such conflicts had been supported by resolutions adopted by the UN General Assembly,[6] there existed no consensus on their status under international humanitarian law.[7] In an article published shortly before the Diplomatic Conference on the Reaffirmation and Development of International Humanitarian Law Applicable in Armed Conflicts (1974–1977),[8] Richard R. Baxter commented that '[t]he law of war as presently conceived and codified makes no distinction between one belligerent and the other according to the legality of the resort to force by each. The *jus in bello* incorporated in the Geneva Conventions of 1949, the Hague Regulations, the Geneva Protocol of 1925, and the Hague Cultural Property Convention of 1954 is based upon the principle that the law relating to the conduct of warfare and the protection of war victims will be neutral and that there will be an equality of treatment for the participants in a conflict.'[9] The *jus in bello* and equality of treatment referred to by Baxter were viewed by some states as negating the possibility of classifying wars of national liberation, which would be characterised as such on account of their cause, as international armed conflicts.[10] The ICRC Commentary on the

[4] Additional Protocol I, Article 1(4).

[5] See *ICRC Conference of Government Experts on the Reaffirmation and Development of Humanitarian Law Applicable in Armed Conflicts, Geneva, 24 May–12 June 1971: Report on the Work of the Conference*, paras. 312–56.

[6] E.g. UNGA Res. 3103 (XXVII), Basic Principles of the Legal Status of the Combatants Struggling Against Colonial and Alien Domination and Racist Regimes, 12 December 1973.

[7] For literature on the status of national liberation movements prior to the adoption of Article 1 of Additional Protocol I in 1974, see Abi-Saab, 'Wars of National Liberation', 93; Baxter, 'Geneva Conventions', 193; Yorham, 'Terrorism and Wars', 78; Ginsburgs, '"Wars of National Liberation"', 911; Paust, 'Guerrilla Conflict', 39.

[8] See *Official Records of the Diplomatic Conference on the Reaffirmation and Development of International Humanitarian Law Applicable in Armed Conflicts, Geneva (1974–1977)*; vols. 1–14; Berne: Federal Political Department, 1978. Hereafter *Official Records.*

[9] Baxter, 'Geneva Conventions', at 199.

[10] For examples, see the statements made by representatives of Canada (*Official Records*, vol. V, CDDH/SR.18, p. 183); Switzerland (*Official Records*, vol. V, CDDH/SR.13, p. 138);

Additional Protocols suggests that wars of liberation were considered as non-international in character by the majority of experts involved in discussions leading up the drafting of Additional Protocol I at the Diplomatic Conference on the Reaffirmation and Development of International Humanitarian Law Applicable in Armed Conflict. The Commentary states that during the 'various meetings of experts devoted specifically to the reaffirmation and development of international humanitarian law applicable in armed conflicts, whether these were consultations in groups with restricted participation or the Conferences of Government Experts or Red Cross experts, the majority of experts considered that wars of national liberation were conflicts not of an international character. Indeed, although they all recognized the need for improving the protection provided by humanitarian law to victims of the armed conflicts for self-determination – and those of other conflicts qualified as not having an international character – only a minority advocated the extension of the mandatory legal application of the whole of the Conventions and of Protocol I to such conflicts.'[11] The UK Ministry of Defence *Manual of the Law of Armed Conflict* reflects a similar view on the situation prior to the adoption of Article 1(4): 'Conflicts of this nature within the territory of a state had hitherto been regarded as internal. Under the Protocol, such conflicts are treated as if they were international armed conflicts.'[12]

As there was no consensus on the international status of wars of resistance against colonial powers, common Article 3 to the 1949 Geneva Conventions would generally have been considered as the main applicable standard of international humanitarian law in such situations.[13] Given the limited protection provided by this provision, and

the UK (*Official Records*, vol. V, CDDH/SR.13, p. 134; *Official Records*, vol. VIII, CDDH/I/SR.2, pp. 13–14); Iran (*Official Records*, vol. V, CDDH/SR.18, p. 189); the Netherlands (*Official Records*, vol. VIII, CDDH/I/SR.4, p. 31); France (*Official Records*, vol. VIII, CDDH/I/SR.2, p. 14); and the US (*Official Records*, vol. V, CDDH/SR.11, pp. 109–10).

11 Pilloud *et al.*, *Commentary*, p. 47, para. 89. The report of an ICRC Conference of Government Experts which took place in 1971 shows an exception: 'Most of the experts of Committee II who spoke on the subject considered that wars of national liberation were international armed conflicts.' *ICRC Conference, 24 May–12 June 1971*, para. 312.

12 UK Ministry of Defence, *Manual*, p. 29.

13 According to Professor Masayuki Takemoto, '[e]ven if the field of application of paragraph 4 is very limited as maintained by several scholars, it is still true that paragraph 4 has expanded the application of the Protocol to armed conflicts which the Geneva Conventions intended to govern only by Article 3 common to the all

the number of wars of national liberation raging across the globe, this was deemed an unsatisfactory situation by many states sympathetically inclined towards such resistance movements. Considering the intensity of many of these conflicts, the need to develop international humanitarian law was clear to all concerned with its implementation. The Diplomatic Conference on the Reaffirmation and Development of International Humanitarian Law Applicable in Armed Conflicts served as a platform to address this deficiency in the law of armed conflict. While there was general agreement that the law needed to be strengthened to ensure a greater level of protection to the victims of wars of national liberation, the approach taken by the Diplomatic Conference departed sharply from conventional interpretations of international humanitarian law to create a new category of armed conflict in Article 1(4) of Additional Protocol I.

3.1.1 *The drafting history of Article 1(4)*

In interpreting Article 1(4) of Additional Protocol I it is important to take into consideration the drafting history of the provision. The Diplomatic Conference responsible for drafting the Additional Protocols of 1977 debated at length the issue of extending the applicability of the Geneva Conventions to wars of national liberation. While interpretation of Article 1(4) is not limited to that assumed by its drafters, the *Official Records* indicate how delegates at the Diplomatic Conference understood the terms contained in the provision. The *travaux préparatoires* of the Additional Protocols illuminate the rationale for expanding the scope of international armed conflict to include wars of national liberation. In doing so they also shed light on the consequent narrowing of the concept of non-international armed conflict in international humanitarian law.

3.1.1.1 The status of national liberation movements at the Diplomatic Conference on the Reaffirmation and Development of International Humanitarian Law Applicable in Armed Conflicts (1974–1977)

Prior to the adoption of rules of procedure and the commencement of work on the substance of the draft Protocols, the attention of delegates at the Diplomatic Conference focused on the question of allowing national

four Conventions'. 'The Additional Protocols and the Law of Treaties', in Swinarski (ed.), *Études*, p. 257.

liberation movements to participate in proceedings. Debate on the issue at the first session of the Diplomatic Conference (20 February–29 March 1974) centred in particular on whether to allow the participation of two national liberation movements, the Republic of Guinea-Bissau and the Provisional Revolutionary Government of the Republic of South Vietnam. While participation of the former was approved in a resolution adopted on 28 February 1974,[14] participation of the latter was rejected the same day by a margin of one vote.[15] The following day, at the seventh plenary meeting of the Diplomatic Conference, the participation of national liberation movements recognised by intergovernmental organisations was approved in a resolution adopted by consensus.[16] This resolution secured a strong position for representatives of national liberation movements at the Conference. In approving such participation, the text of the resolution states that the Diplomatic Conference,

> 1. *Decides* to invite the national liberation movements, which are recognized by the regional intergovernmental organizations concerned, to participate fully in the deliberations of the Conference and its Main Committees;
> 2. *Decides further* that, notwithstanding anything contained in the rules of procedure, the statements made or the proposals and amendments submitted by delegations of such national liberation movements shall be circulated by the Conference Secretariat as Conference documents to all the participants in the Conference, it being understood that only delegations representing States will be entitled to vote.[17]

In addition to the Republic of Guinea-Bissau, other national liberation movements permitted to participate in the Conference included the African National Congress, the Angola National Liberation Front, the Mozambique Liberation Front, the Palestine Liberation Organisation, the Panafricanist Congress, the People's Movement for the Liberation of Angola, the Seychelles People's United Party, the South West Africa People's Organisation, the Zimbabwe African National Union and the Zimbabwe African People's Organisation.[18]

[14] For the text of Res. 2(1) see *Official Records*, vol. I, CDDH/55, p. 4.

[15] Voted in favour: 37, 38 against and 33 abstained. See *Official Records*, vol. V, CDDH/SR.6, p. 53.

[16] *Official Records*, vol. V, CDDH/SR.7, p. 65.

[17] *Official Records*, vol. I, CDDH/55, p. 5.

[18] *Official Records*, vol. II, CDDH/51/Rev.1, p. 671.

While these movements lacked voting rights, resolution 3(1) situated them in a strong position to influence the proceedings of the Conference. Prior to the adoption of this resolution, the proposal to allow the participation of national liberation movements had been objected to by several delegates. The representatives of states such as the United Kingdom,[19] the United States,[20] Israel,[21] South Africa and Portugal[22] had raised concerns about the appropriateness of allowing the participation of such movements in a diplomatic conference.[23] An example of the position commonly adopted by such states is provided in the statement of the Portuguese Ambassador, Fernando de Alcambar Pereira, who argued that:

> national liberation movements had no *locus standi* and therefore could not take part in a conference to deal with the codification of international humanitarian law. The very character of the Conference would be changed if it discussed and approved the admission of national liberation movements. The Conference would lose its diplomatic character and become political, and the possibility of its achieving its humanitarian aims would be compromised. The Portuguese delegation was not a party to the consensus which had been reached by the regional groups on draft resolution CDDH/22 and Corr.1 and could not approve of invitations being extended to national liberation movements.[24]

Despite the strength of objections to the participation of national liberation movements, delegations favouring the initiative formed a clear majority at the Diplomatic Conference. Representatives of the African group,[25] the Latin-American group,[26] and Asian states such as India[27] and China,[28] were vocal in their support for the position of national liberation movements. While the strength of this support helped to ensure that the resolution on the participation of national liberation movements was adopted by consensus, it is clear that the issue caused deep division among delegations. The depth of disagreement on the participation of national liberation movements was reflected in the time spent debating the issue prior to adopting rules of procedure. Of the 22 plenary meetings of the first session of the Diplomatic conference,

[19] *Official Records*, vol. V, CDDH/SR.7, p. 67. [20] *Ibid.*, p. 69.
[21] *Official Records*, vol. V, CDDH/SR.6, p. 57.
[22] *Official Records*, vol. V, CDDH/SR.7, p. 68.
[23] *Official Records*, vol. V, CDDH/SR.6, p. 56. [24] *Ibid.*, p. 61.
[25] *Official Records*, vol. V, CDDH/SR.1, pp. 12–14.
[26] *Official Records*, vol. V, CDDH/SR.3, p. 28.
[27] *Official Records*, vol. VIII, CDDH/I/SR.6, p. 47.
[28] *Official Records*, vol. V, CDDH/SR.6, p. 60.

6 were specifically concerned with the question of invitations to the representatives of national liberation movements.

The involvement of national liberation movements in deliberations on the drafting of the Additional Protocols represented a significant departure from the practice of previous diplomatic conferences. As an implicit recognition of their role in the implementation of international humanitarian law, it showed a considerable shift in state practice. The high level of support enjoyed by national liberation movements at the Diplomatic Conference placed the representatives of these organisations in a strong position to lobby for the internationalisation of wars of national liberation.

3.1.1.2 Arguments for the internationalisation of wars of national liberation

The characterisation of wars of national liberation as international armed conflicts was to a large extent based on resolutions of the UN General Assembly relating to the right of self-determination.[29] The move to recognise wars of national liberation as international armed conflicts in Article 1(4) of Additional Protocol I was an issue that dominated much of the discussion both in the Plenary and in Committee I of the Diplomatic Conference during its first session. This initiative to secure the international characterisation of wars of national liberation at the Diplomatic Conference was driven by the delegations of 'Third World' states. According to Ould Dada, the President of the Islamic Republic of Mauritania:

> the countries of the Third World were asking very little: only that the Conference should not exclude freedom fighters from protection. Such fighters would never renounce their rights. Representatives at the Conference would be preparing rules to enable the ICRC and the various relief agencies to secure respect for human rights. If, for one reason or another, the Conference did not grant freedom fighters the same protection as the oppressors, it would be making a serious mistake, for it would be contravening the principles set out in the Charter of the United Nations, the United Nations Declaration of Human Rights, the Declaration on the Granting of Independence to Colonial Countries and Peoples, (United Nations General Assembly Resolution 1514

[29] See UNGA Res. 1514, 2625, 3103, 3042 and 3076. For the use of such Resolutions at the Diplomatic Conference, see *Official Records*, vol. V, CDDH/SR.1, pp. 13–14; *Official Records*, vol. V, CDDH/SR.5, p. 46; *Official Records*, vol. V, CDDH/SR.11, p. 105; *Official Records*, vol. VIII, CDDH/I/SR.2, p. 8.

(XV)), and in the Geneva Conventions of 1949 which the Conference was designed to supplement.[30]

President Dada's statement, made at the opening of the Diplomatic Conference on 20 February 1974, outlines some of the sources employed for expanding the scope of international armed conflict. While none of these sources refer to wars of national liberation as international armed conflicts, it was nevertheless argued that they could be interpreted to support such a characterisation. According to Victor Cristescu of the Romanian delegation:

> national liberation movements could not be considered as protagonists in internal conflicts because the colonial and Trusteeship territories, according to the United Nations Declaration on the Granting of Independence to Colonial Countries and Peoples (General Assembly resolution 1514 (XV)) and the Declaration on Principles of International Law concerning Friendly Relations and Co-operation among States in accordance with the Charter of the United Nations (General Assembly resolution 2625 (XXV)), had retained a status distinct from that of the administrative Power. International law [has] to be adapted to the realities of the international situation.[31]

The argument was put forward that wars of national liberation had already received recognition of their status as being not of a non-international character. Such conflicts must therefore be characterised as international. Vuko Gozze-Gucetic, Head of the Yugoslavian delegation, expressed a similar view on the characterisation of wars of national liberation:

> General Assembly resolutions 3042 (XXVII), 3076 (XXVIII) and 3103 (XXVIII) formed an adequate basis for the Conference's work. They emphasized certain basic problems and pointed the way towards certain solutions [...]
>
> The body of law to be drawn up should prohibit wars of aggression and facilitate all forms of armed and political struggle against aggression [...]
>
> The question of combatants fighting to free their peoples from the colonial yoke deserved close consideration, since the existing Conventions were not adapted to that particular form of armed struggle. The Fourth Conference of Heads of State or Government of Non-Aligned Countries had recognized the need to encourage such forms of struggle and to protect the victims thereof, and the necessary provisions must be embodied in the new international humanitarian law. The best way of doing so would be to state that such struggles were international conflicts, as had already been recognized in many United Nations documents.[32]

[30] *Official Records*, vol. V, CDDH/SR.1, pp. 13–14.
[31] *Official Records*, vol. V, CDDH/SR.5, p. 46.
[32] *Official Records*, vol. V, CDDH/SR.11, p. 105.

The comments of the Yugoslav delegate on the necessity of creating new international humanitarian law to cover wars of national liberation reflect a position commonly adopted by the delegates of African and East European (Soviet Bloc) countries at the Diplomatic Conference. The argument that the Geneva Conventions of 1949 were not adapted to such conflicts was voiced by many delegates supporting the inclusion of wars of national liberation within the scope of Article 1 of Additional Protocol I.

A more simplistic approach was adopted by other delegations through the use of a distinction between just and unjust wars. Addressing the Plenary of the Conference, the Chinese Head of Delegation, Chi-Lung Pi, stated the following:

> Wars were divided into two kinds, just and unjust. Imperialism was at the root of all wars of aggression. While imperialism persisted in the world, there would always be the danger of war. The two world wars launched by imperialism had inflicted tremendous losses of life and property on the peoples of the world. The first step in protecting victims of international armed conflicts was therefore to condemn imperialist policy of aggression and to mobilize the people of the world in a resolute struggle against the policies pursued by the imperialist countries. Moreover, a distinction between just and unjust wars, should be made in the new Protocols.[33]

Perhaps the most erudite proponent for the internationalisation of wars of national liberation at the Diplomatic Conference was Professor Georges Abi-Saab of the Egyptian delegation. Speaking before Committee I, the organ of the Diplomatic Conference responsible for the consideration of Article 1 of draft Protocol I among other provisions, Abi-Saab stated that

> Wars of national liberation had formed a very important category of armed struggle in the post-1945 period and a number of them were still continuing. Contemporary international law recognized such wars as international armed conflicts. United Nations General Assembly resolution 3103 (XXVIII) was the latest in a stream of resolutions of important international bodies proclaiming that principle. The General Assembly had, indeed, gone further by recommending sanctions against colonial, alien and racist régimes and the provision of assistance to specific liberation movements, and the Security Council in one case had ordered mandatory sanctions. It would be difficult to explain all such international action if wars of national liberation were to be considered merely as armed conflicts of a non-international character. Existing practice provided abundant proof of the international nature of such conflicts.[34]

[33] *Official Records*, vol. V, CDDH/SR.12, p. 120.
[34] *Official Records*, vol. VIII, CDDH/I/SR.2, p. 8.

While it is possible, depending on the context of their adoption, to interpret some resolutions of the UN General Assembly as indicative of state practice, it would be fallacious to assume their status as a codification of international law.[35] Reliance on such resolutions nevertheless formed the core of many arguments without consideration of other aspects that would indicate the development of customary international law.[36] Referring to the most recent resolution of the UN General Assembly relating to the right to self-determination, Professor Bernhard Graefrath of the German Democratic Republic spoke in support of the inclusion of wars of national liberation in Article 1 of Additional Protocol I:

> Despite numerous appeals by the United Nations, the provisions of international humanitarian law were not yet being applied to peoples fighting for their national liberation. That was why the General Assembly, in operative paragraph 3 of resolution 3103 (XXVIII), had declared that 'armed conflicts involving the struggle of peoples against colonial and alien domination and racist regimes are to be regarded as international armed conflicts in the sense of the 1949 Geneva Conventions'. That resolution was extremely important because it confirmed that the colonial Power had no rights of sovereignty over colonial territories and peoples, that assistance by foreign States to the liberation struggle of colonial peoples did not constitute interference in the domestic affairs of the colonial Power; and that article 2, not article 3 of the Geneva Conventions, was applicable to armed conflicts of that kind.[37]

In addition to the statements made by the representatives of the German Democratic Republic, Egypt, Yugoslavia, Romania and Mauritania, numerous other delegates took the floor at the Diplomatic Conference to voice support for the internationalisation of wars of national liberation. These included representatives of Burundi, China, Poland, Ukraine, USSR, Uganda, Czechoslovakia, German Democratic Republic, Madagascar, Venezuela, Uganda, Albania, Algeria, Byelorussian SSR, Sri Lanka, Zaire, Mongolia, Senegal, India and Yugoslavia. The bulk of deliberations on the amendment of Article 1 of Additional Protocol I took place in Committee I of the Diplomatic Conference. The Report of Committee I confirms that '[t]he great majority of delegations were in favour of article 1 mentioning that the international armed conflicts

[35] See ICJ, *North Sea Continental Shelf* cases, Judgment, 20 Feburary 1969, *ICJ Reports 1969*, paras. 70–4.

[36] This point will be returned to later in exploring the customary status of Article 1(4), at section 3.1.2.

[37] *Official Records*, vol. VIII, CDDH/I/SR.2, p. 12.

referred to in Article 2 common to the four Geneva Conventions of 1949 included those armed conflicts in which peoples, in exercise of their right to self-determination, fight colonial domination and alien occupation against racist regimes. Other delegations did not share that view.'[38]

The 'great majority' referred to in the Report of Committee I alludes to the seventy delegations who voted in favour of an amendment to Article 1 of draft Protocol I allowing the inclusion of wars of national liberation within the scope of the instrument.[39] This represents over two-thirds of states present at the Diplomatic Conference. Nevertheless, in reflecting on the merit of the initiative to expand the scope of international armed conflict and thus limit the scope of non-international armed conflict, it is important to access the position of those opposed to this development of international humanitarian law. The section that follows probes their arguments.

3.1.1.3 Arguments against the internationalisation of wars of national liberation

While international status for wars of national liberation was strongly supported by delegations from the 'Third World' along with those of socialist states, the representatives of most Western states held a different position.[40] Speaking on behalf of the Canadian government, Minister David Miller stated that his delegation was

> deeply concerned about the suggestion that the Protocol should contain provisions that could result in the standard of humanitarian protection becoming dependent upon the declared purpose of an armed conflict. A case in point

[38] *Official Records*, vol. X, CDDH/48/Rev.1, p. 6.

[39] For the text of the amendment, see *Official Records*, vol. III, CDDH/I/71, pp. 8–9; the following states voted in favour: Albania, Algeria, Arab Republic of Egypt, Argentina, Bangladesh, Bulgaria, Burundi, Byelorussian Soviet Socialist Republic, Cuba, Chad, Czechoslovakia, China, Cyprus, Democratic People's Republic of Korea, Democratic Yemen, El Salvador, Finland, Gabon, German Democratic Republic, Ghana, Guinea-Bissau, Honduras, Hungary, India, Indonesia, Iran, Iraq, Ivory Coast, Jordan, Khmer Republic, Kuwait, Lebanon, Liberia, Libyan Arab Republic, Madagascar, Mali, Morocco, Mauritania, Mexico, Mongolia, Nigeria, Norway, Pakistan, Panama, Peru, Poland, Qatar, Republic of Vietnam, Romania, Saudi Arabia, Senegal, Sri Lanka, the Sudan, Sultanate of Oman, Syrian Arab Republic, Thailand, Togo, Trinidad and Tobago, Tunisia, Uganda, Ukrainian Soviet Socialist Republic, Union of Soviet Socialist Republics, United Arab Emirates, United Republic of Cameroon, United Republic of Tanzania, Venezuela, Yemen, Yugoslavia, Zaire, Zambia.

[40] See generally Lysaght, 'The Attitude of Western Countries', in Cassese (ed.), *New Humanitarian Law*, pp. 349–56.

was the proposed new paragraph 3 appearing in a foot-note to article 42, which would accord extraordinary protection to persons captured in conflicts relating to self-determination. Yet no single principle was more necessary to humanitarian law than that of non-discrimination, and the Conference should reflect carefully before incorporating a concept totally alien to both the spirit and letter of humanitarian law.[41]

The provision referred to by the Canadian delegate concerned prisoner-of-war status. While Article 42 of the ICRC draft Protocol had developed the concept of prisoner of war to include members of organised resistance movements,[42] there was no reference in the main text of the provision to members of liberation movements. A footnote was however included in the ICRC draft of Protocol I containing the proposal that, subject to approval by the Diplomatic Conference, the following would be incorporated as the final clause in Article 42 dealing with prisoner-of-war status: 'In the case of armed struggle where peoples exercise their right to self-determination as guaranteed by the United Nations Charter and the "Declaration on Principles of International Law concerning Friendly Relations and Co-operation among States in accordance with the Charter of the United Nations", members of organized liberation movements who comply with the aforementioned conditions shall be treated as prisoners of war for as long as they are detained.'[43]

This clause was put forward by the ICRC as a means of compromising with delegations of the 'Third World' on the internationalisation of wars of national liberation. This provision however was considered insufficient in terms of the recognition it conferred upon national liberation movements. A more explicit acknowledgement of status was needed. As previously indicated, it was thus proposed that Article 1 of draft Protocol I be amended so that the concept of international armed conflict would include 'armed conflicts in which peoples are

[41] *Official Records*, vol. V, CDDH/SR.18, p. 183.

[42] The ICRC draft Protocol broadened the concept of prisoner of war beyond that contained in the Geneva Conventions to include members of organised resistance movements provided:

> (a) that they are under a command responsible to a Party to the conflict for its subordinates; (b) that they distinguish themselves from the civilian population in military operations; (c) that they conduct their military operations in accordance with the Conventions and present Protocol.

Official Records, vol. I, part 3: ICRC, 'Draft Additional Protocols to the Geneva Conventions of 1949', 1973, p. 14.

[43] *Ibid.*

fighting against colonial domination and alien occupation and against racist régimes in exercise of their right to self-determination'.[44] This amendment drew criticism from a number of different angles.

A concern expressed by several delegations opposed to the amendment was that it would undermine the implementation of international humanitarian law through introducing a notion of 'just war'. Ambassador Rudolf Bindschedler of the Swiss delegation argued that '[t]he idea of "just" or "unjust" wars had no place in the work of the Conference. The Conference must endeavour to limit violence in armed conflict, regardless of the motives which had provoked such conflict.'[45] A problem related to this issue of 'just' war, was that of the discriminatory application of international humanitarian law. For some delegates, the idea of making the application of international humanitarian law dependent upon the question of political motivation negated the principle of non-discrimination underlying the Geneva Conventions. The United Kingdom delegation was particularly vocal in expressing its concern on the issue. Colin Crowe, the British Head of delegation, made the following statement before the Plenary of the Diplomatic Conference on the question of internationalising wars of national liberation:

> Some speakers had suggested that political motivation for the resort to armed conflict should be made a relevant criterion in the draft Protocols. The same idea appeared to be the basis of the proposed paragraph 3 of article 42 of draft Protocol I, as set out in the foot-note on page 14 of that document. Some delegations had even divided wars into just and unjust wars. Those were extremely dangerous approaches and totally alien to all the principles of international humanitarian law. They struck at the very heart of the Geneva Conventions and the philosophy of equality of rights and non-discrimination which inspired them. Humanitarian protection for the individual could not depend on the subjective and political views of the party to the conflict in whose power an individual victim of war happened to find himself. A Detaining Power was not entitled to deny prisoners of war conventional humanitarian protection, merely because it considered they were fighting for [an] unjust cause. Likewise, parties to a conflict were not entitled to claim that protection for their personnel solely on the grounds that the cause for which they were fighting was just. Humanitarian law was concerned not with who was right or wrong, but with the unfortunate victim of events, the human being who was caught in the jaws of fate.[46]

[44] *Official Records*, vol. X, CDDH/48/Rev.1, p. 7.
[45] *Official Records*, vol. V, CDDH/SR.13, p. 138. [46] *Ibid.*, p. 134.

Elaborating on the position of the United Kingdom in Committee I of the Diplomatic Conference, Colonel G.I.A.D. Draper stated that:

> The various arguments had presented no convincing case for considering an internal struggle as an international one. Moreover, it was a basic principle of the Geneva Conventions, The Hague Regulations and other instruments that legal and humanitarian protection should never vary according to the motives of those engaged in a particular armed struggle. Deviation from that principle would mean damaging the structure of The Hague and Geneva Conventions and would involve the need to reconstruct the whole of humanitarian law. Moreover, to discriminate between the motives of those engaged in the struggle, would violate essential principles of human rights.[47]

The potential for the politicisation of international humanitarian law through the internationalisation of wars of national liberation was a serious point of concern for several delegates not favouring the proposal to amend Article 1 of draft Protocol I. The introduction of a political or ideological basis for the application of this body of law was viewed as effectively undermining principles of equality and non-discrimination fundamental to the implementation of the Geneva Conventions. Ambassador Houchang Amir-Mokri of Iran stated that his government

> Considered that political and ideological considerations should not be introduced into discussions on humanitarian law. It was accordingly not in favour of establishing a distinction between 'just' and 'unjust' wars, which would necessarily be an arbitrary one. [The Iranian delegation's] position on that point was in fact very close to those of the delegations of Switzerland and the United Kingdom.[48]

Speaking on behalf of the Dutch delegation, Professor Fritz Kalshoven also raised the problem of an arbitrary distinction being introduced into international humanitarian law by including wars of national liberation within the scope of international armed conflict. He stated that those proposing the amendment to Article 1 of Additional Protocol I were 'introducing the idea that a distinction must be drawn between the parties according to the legitimacy or illegitimacy of their cause. Although it was true that humanitarian law was not immutably fixed, certain basic values must be respected, including the idea of equality as between the parties.'[49]

[47] *Official Records*, vol. VIII, CDDH/I/SR.2, pp. 13–14.
[48] *Official Records*, vol. V, CDDH/SR.18, p. 189.
[49] *Official Records*, vol. VIII, CDDH/I/SR.4, p. 31.

In addition to criticisms concerning the arbitrary nature of terms contained in the proposed amendment to Article 1 of draft Protocol I, and their consequences for the politicisation of international humanitarian law, the proposal was faulted on account of its vagueness. Colonel G.I.A.D. Draper stated

> It was true that self-determination was mentioned in the Charter of the United Nations, but as a principle, not as a right. Nowhere in the Charter did the right to engage in armed struggle appear. No resolution of the United Nations could amend the Charter, which would remain inviolate until amended in the proper manner. Terms like 'struggle for the self-determination of peoples' were all too vague. What was a 'people'? Such terms were elastic, as Biafra and Bangladesh had shown. They could not be used as a basis for law making.
>
> It would not advance the cause of international humanitarian law to insert the proposed amendments to Protocol I, for endless political debate would ensue.[50]

Similarly, Charles Lysaght of the Irish delegation commented that '[t]he expression "armed struggles waged by peoples in the exercise of their right to self-determination" was too vague to be useful in a legal instrument. Any separatist movement, any band of armed criminals in a colonial territory might claim to be engaged in an armed struggle in furtherance of their people's right to self-determination.'[51]

A further criticism of the proposal to internationalise wars of national liberation was made by Christian Girard, Head of the French delegation. Speaking before Committee I of the Diplomatic Conference, Girard pointed to the flawed approach adopted by those who had interpreted international humanitarian law on the basis of UN resolutions in order to support the amendment to Article 1 of draft Protocol I:

> Two completely different concepts were emerging from the discussion. The first was the concept upon which the Egyptian representative had based his statement and the second was the concept to which his Government subscribed, namely, that the United Nations and the ICRC pursued their activities on entirely different levels. The United Nations was the political body whose role was to find political solutions to specific problems of the moment, whereas humanitarian law must provide protection for all war victims at all

[50] *Official Records*, vol. VIII, CDDH/I/SR.2, pp. 13–14.

[51] *Official Records*, vol. VIII, CDDH/I/SR.4, p. 26. Lysaght added that '[t]he amendment was objectionable in that it would apply where a people were content to seek independence by constitutional, non-violent, means and where a minority, with no popular mandate, resorted to violence in the same cause'. *Ibid.*

times and must not be subordinated to subjective considerations of any sort. Consideration of elements such as motivation, justice and legitimacy, which it was quite normal to discuss in the United Nations, would be fatal in an assembly held under the auspices of the ICRC. Humanitarian law must remain free of any notion of political motivation or subjective judgment, and his government was not prepared, under any circumstances, to sacrifice that basic principle.[52]

An issue underlying all criticisms of the proposed amendment to internationalise wars of national liberation was its potential effect on the implementation of international humanitarian law. It was contended that if adopted, the proposal would not serve the interests of the victims of such armed conflicts. On the contrary, it would discourage states from recognising the existence of such conflicts and thus also the applicability of international humanitarian law. Highlighting the general lack of compliance in recent years, George Aldrich, the deputy legal adviser of the United States Department of State, argued that the introduction of a distinction into international humanitarian law based on the cause for which a particular group was fighting would not help to improve the implementation of this body of law:

The argument that the end justified the means [...] was the antithesis of international humanitarian law and in particular, of the Geneva Conventions, the philosophy of which was concern not for who was right and who was wrong, but for the protection of all victims of armed conflict, irrespective of the cause they supported. His government firmly held the view that the Conference should reaffirm the philosophy of the Geneva Conventions and reject any efforts to introduce into the law discriminatory levels of protection based on subjective criteria such as the justness of the cause for which a particular group was fighting. Agreed humanitarian standards must be applied equally to the victims of war whichever cause they supported.

The introduction into international humanitarian law of 'just war' concepts would inevitably result in a lowering of the standards of protection accorded to war victims. Rare was the man who thought his enemy right and even rarer the State which, when combating rebellion, could afford to apply international standards to captured rebels if by so doing it implicitly acknowledged the justness of the rebels' cause of their right to self-determination. If the Conference was to succeed in the development of the Protocols it must make a law to protect all war victims, friend and foe alike.[53]

In addition to the statements referred to by representatives of the United States, France, Ireland, Iran, United Kingdom, Switzerland and

[52] *Official Records*, vol. VIII, CDDH/I/SR.2, p. 14.
[53] *Official Records*, vol. V, CDDH/SR.11, pp. 109–10.

Canada, delegates from New Zealand, Israel, Tunisia, Belgium, the Holy See and the Federal Republic of Germany also took the floor at the Diplomatic Conference to voice their concerns about the internationalisation of wars of national liberation. The arguments raised by these states clearly contradicted those contending that wars of national liberation were already being recognised by the international community as constituting international armed conflicts. As a means of clarifying the issue, and its import on the scope of non-international armed conflict in international humanitarian law, the customary status of Article 1(4) will be returned to later in this chapter. Before doing so, the conditions surrounding the adoption of Article 1 at the Diplomatic Conference will first be examined.

3.1.1.4 The adoption of Article 1 and the internationalisation of wars of national liberation

The final version of Article 1 of Additional Protocol I was adopted by Committee I of the Diplomatic Conference. It was approved with 70 delegations voting in favour,[54] 21 against[55] and 13 abstentions.[56] Many of the delegations that voted against or abstained took the opportunity after the vote to voice their dissatisfaction about the provision and the context of its adoption. Speaking on behalf of the Swiss delegation, François Pictet stated that

[54] *Official Records*, vol. V, CDDH/SR.11, p. 102. The following states voted in favour: Albania, Algeria, Arab Republic of Egypt, Argentina, Bangladesh, Bulgaria, Burundi, Byelorussian Soviet Socialist Republic, Cuba, Chad, Czechoslovakia, China, Cyprus, Democratic People's Republic of Korea, Democratic Yemen, El Salvador, Finland, Gabon, German Democratic Republic, Ghana, Guinea-Bissau, Honduras, Hungary, India, Indonesia, Iran, Iraq, Ivory Coast, Jordan, Khmer Republic, Kuwait, Lebanon, Liberia, Libyan Arab Republic, Madagascar, Mali, Morocco, Mauritania, Mexico, Mongolia, Nigeria, Norway, Pakistan, Panama, Peru, Poland, Qatar, Republic of Vietnam, Romania, Saudi Arabia, Senegal, Sri Lanka, the Sudan, Sultanate of Oman, Syrian Arab Republic, Thailand, Togo, Trinidad and Tobago, Tunisia, Uganda, Ukrainian Soviet Socialist Republic, Union of Soviet Socialist Republics, United Arab Emirates, United Republic of Cameroon, United Republic of Tanzania, Venezuela, Yemen, Yugoslavia, Zaire, Zambia.

[55] *Official Records*, vol. V, CDDH/SR.11, p. 102. The following states voted against: Belgium, Canada, Denmark, Federal Republic of Germany, France, Israel, Italy, Japan, Liechtenstein, Luxembourg, Monaco, Netherlands, New Zealand, Portugal, Republic of Korea, South Africa, Spain, Switzerland, United Kingdom, United States, Uruguay.

[56] *Ibid.* The following states abstained: Australia, Austria, Burma, Brazil, Colombia, Chile, Greece, Guatemala, Holy See, Ireland, Philippines, Sweden, Turkey.

He regretted the amendment in document CDDH/I/71 had been put to the vote, since key provisions should be adopted by consensus, even at the expense of the long and arduous search. All possibilities of reaching a generally acceptable text had not been completely explored. [...]

His delegation had doubts concerning the opportuneness of introducing concepts of a political nature into matters of humanitarian law. The Geneva Conventions had always been above all considerations of that type in order the better to protect the victims of all conflicts whatever their origins. He hoped that the question would be studied more deeply.[57]

Other delegations that expressed concern about the premature closure of discussion on the issue during the first session of the Diplomatic Conference included the delegations of Australia, Belgium, and the Holy See.

The deep division that existed between delegations at the Diplomatic Conference was exacerbated further by the action of calling a vote on the amendment to Article 1. The representative of the Holy See, Mgr. Muoni, highlighted inappropriateness of treating such an important provision of the Protocol in this way:

His delegation had kept silent during the discussion which had preceded the vote on amendment CDDH/I/71, but would not conceal its anxiety as to what the consequence of that vote might be for the future of the Conference. Other international organisations were responsible for taking decisions of a fundamentally political nature and for the Conference to take such decisions could only increase the existing confusion concerning the competence of the different organisations. The vote had split the Conference into two groups. The value of any rules that might be adopted would be diminished if there were a certain number of States which thought it against their interests to apply them, as had been the case in the past, when a number of countries had refused to accept a draft proposed by the ICRC. In the case of rules of international humanitarian law, it was desirable to seek a consensus.[58]

Despite the clear majority that supported the amendment of Article 1, the strength of this provision was seriously weakened by the vote. Its adoption by consensus would have supported the view expressed by proponents of the initiative that customary international law had evolved to recognise wars of national liberation as international armed conflicts. However, given the strength of statements made by the representatives of states opposed to the amendment, the circumstances of Article 1(4)'s adoption make it difficult to conclude that this was

[57] *Official Records*, vol. VIII, CDDH/I/SR.14, p. 107. [58] *Ibid.*, p. 108.

an exercise in codifying existing international humanitarian law with respect to the threshold for international armed conflict.

Considering that Article 1 forms the cornerstone of the instrument it is regrettable that consensus was not achieved in its formulation. The outcome of the vote on the amendment to Article 1 clearly weakened the status of the provision as a whole. In view of the fact that Article 1 stipulated the field of application for the Protocol, it was inevitable that such action would also have the potential to weaken the instrument as a whole. The section that follows will now explore the status of this provision as a codification of customary international law.

3.1.2 The customary status of wars of national liberation

Some delegates at the Diplomatic Conference argued that the international character of wars of national liberation had acquired the status of a customary norm. Relying heavily on General Assembly resolutions as the basis for this contention, it was argued that state practice had shifted since the drafting of the Geneva Conventions to incorporate wars of national liberation into the concept of international armed conflict. Ambassador M.N. Rattansey, Head of the United Republic of Tanzania delegation, stated that:

> It was now generally accepted by jurists that the international law governing armed conflicts of the kind with which they were concerned was customary law, not statute law. United Nations General Assembly resolution 3103 (XXVIII) dealt with the legal status of the combatants struggling against colonial and alien domination and racist regimes. The armed conflicts resulting from such struggles were no longer regarded as internal conflicts but as international conflicts and as legitimate in the eyes of the United Nations.[59]

The third paragraph of the General Assembly resolution referred to by Rattansey states the position that the delegates of socialist and 'Third World' states wished to have incorporated into Additional Protocol I: 'The armed conflicts involving the struggle of peoples against colonial and alien domination and racist régimes are to be regarded as international armed conflicts in the sense of the 1949 Geneva Conventions, and the legal status envisaged to apply to the combatants in the 1949 Geneva Conventions and other international instruments is to apply to the persons engaged in armed struggle against colonial and alien domination and racist régimes.'[60]

[59] *Official Records*, vol. V, CDDH/SR.6, pp. 62–3.
[60] UNGA Res. 3103, para. 3.

While acknowledging the strong support such initiatives received within the General Assembly, it is important to recognise that this resolution was not adopted by consensus. Resolution 3103 had been adopted with 83 states voting in favour, 13 against, and 19 abstaining. The fact that this resolution lacked the support of over 25 per cent of the General Assembly indicates a level of acceptance that is arguably short of that required to evidence a trend in state practice.[61] According to the International Court of Justice the formation of a new rule of customary international law requires the existence of state practice that is 'both extensive and virtually uniform in the sense of the provision invoked; – and should moreover have occurred in such a way as to show a general recognition that a rule of law or legal obligation is involved'.[62] This was clearly lacking in the case of Article 1(4). It is furthermore worth considering that the practice required should also include 'states whose interests are specially affected'.[63] As states engaged in the suppression of national liberation movements would oppose recognition of such situations as international armed conflicts, it is difficult to conclude that this requirement is fulfilled.[64] According to Dietrich Schindler:

> A rule of customary law may well have come into existence with regard to the application of the Geneva Conventions to the principle of self-determination, but not with regard to the application of the Geneva Conventions to wars of national liberation. The requirements for a new rule of customary law in this respect are hardly fulfilled, as the States particularly affected by such a rule as well as other important States have consistently taken up a stand against it.[65]

As the wording of Article 1(4) ensures its non-application by 'states whose interests are specially affected',[66] i.e. states interested in suppressing national liberation movements, the characterisation of the provision as customary international law is questionable. It is worth noting that delegates at the Diplomatic Conference had not been tasked with the codification of customary international law but with 'reaffirmation and development' of international humanitarian law. The fact that Article 1(4) was adopted by the Conference does not in itself provide grounds for asserting the customary status of the provision. Considering the manner in which Article 1(4) was adopted, and that its inclusion in Additional Protocol I was opposed by specially affected states, it is difficult to conclude that this provision secured

[61] See ICJ, *Continental Shelf* cases, para. 74. [62] *Ibid.*
[63] *Ibid.* [64] See Schindler, 'Different Types of Armed Conflicts', at 136.
[65] *Ibid.* [66] *Continental Shelf* cases, para. 74.

the international character of wars of national liberation as a norm of customary international law.

The move to codify wars of national liberation as international armed conflicts at the Diplomatic Conference was not on account of their status as such under customary international law. The motivation behind the initiative was intrinsically political.[67] The fact that Article 1(4) has yet to be positively applied for the implementation of international humanitarian law is noteworthy.[68] As the section that follows will show, the scope of the provision is so narrow that virtually all situations of armed conflict that have occurred since are excluded.

3.1.3 *The applicability of Article 1(4)*

The question of the applicability of Additional Protocol I to wars of national liberation is determined by the categories of situations listed in Article 1(4): 'colonial domination', 'alien occupation', and 'racist regimes'. In order for a situation to be characterised as an international armed conflict under the Protocol it must fit into one of these three categories. While the scope of each category is clearly of importance in determining the issue of applicability, the meaning of the terms in Article 1(4) were left undefined by the provision's drafters. As noted by Leslie C. Green, 'neither the Protocol nor the Declaration on Friendly Relations makes any provision for determining what movement is seeking self-determination and thus qualifies as a national liberation movement. Nor does either instrument offer any assistance in determining whether a country is self-governing or what constitutes a people.'[69]

In the absence of definitions that would help demarcate the scope of Article 1(4), the Commentary of the International Committee of the Red Cross interprets the three categories of armed conflict as follows:

> The expression 'colonial domination' certainly covers the most frequently occurring case in recent years, where a people has had to take up arms to free itself from the domination of another people; it is not necessary to explain this in greater detail here. The expression 'alien occupation' in the sense of this

[67] Suter, *Guerrilla Warfare*, p. 146

[68] The Additional Protocol currently has 163 state parties. The following states have yet to ratify: Andorra, Afghanistan, Azerbaijan, Bhutan, Eritrea, Fiji, Haiti, India, Indonesia, Iran, Iraq, Israel, Kiribati, Malaysia, Marshall Islands, Morocco, Myanmar, Nepal, Pakistan, Papua New Guinea, Philippines, Singapore, Somalia, Sri Lanka, Sudan, Thailand, Turkey, Tuvalu and the United States.

[69] Green, *Law of Armed Conflict*, pp. 63–4.

paragraph – as distinct from belligerent occupation in the traditional sense of all or part of the territory of one State being occupied by another State – covers cases of partial or total occupation of a territory which has not yet been fully formed as a State finally, the expression 'racist régimes' covers cases of régimes founded on racist criteria. The first two situations imply the existence of distinct peoples. The third implies, if not the existence of two completely distinct peoples, at least a rift within a people which ensures hegemony of one section in accordance with racist ideas. It should be added that a specific situation may correspond simultaneously with two of the situations listed, or even with all three.[70]

The approach taken by the ICRC Commentary in its interpretation of Article 1(4) is to limit the meaning of the terms contained in this provision to the situations considered by the Diplomatic Conference. According to George Aldrich, 'Paragraph 4 of Article 1 was designed by its sponsors with certain conflicts in mind, specifically those in Palestine and southern Africa, and was drafted in terms fashioned to exclude its application to civil wars within existing states. That is why it uses emotionally loaded terms like "colonial domination," "alien occupation" and "racist regimes"; indeed, the use of these terms goes far to ensure that the provision will never be applied.'[71]

Some scholars have approached the interpretation of this provision in a more expansive manner. According to Green, '[s]o long as an internal conflict is directed towards self-government, the Protocol provides for its recognition as an international conflict governed by the Conventions and the Protocol, as well as the ordinary law regarding international armed conflicts'.[72] The ICRC Commentary interprets Article 1(4) more restrictively: it states that the three cases recorded therein (colonial domination, alien occupation and racist regimes), constitute an 'exhaustive' list of situations deemed to be international.[73]

The application of the humanitarian norms contained in the Protocol to other categories of armed conflict would no doubt benefit the victims of such situations. However, given the reluctance of states to be self-identified according to the terms of Article 1(4), it appears unlikely

[70] ICRC, *Commentary on the Additional Protocols*, p. 54, para. 112.

[71] Aldrich, 'Prospects for United States Ratification', 6–7.

[72] Green, 'Strengthening Legal Protection', at 503.

[73] ICRC, *Commentary on the Additional Protocols*, p. 54. The Commentary's narrow interpretation of the three categories contained Article 1(4) is supported by the decision of the Netherlands District Court of Utrecht in the *Folkerts* decision. See *Folkerts*, Netherlands District Court of Utrecht, 20 December 1997. Reprinted in Sassoli and Bouvier (eds.), *How Does Law Protect?*, vol. I, p. 2451.

that the provision will ever be utilised as a mechanism for extending the applicability of international humanitarian law to wars of national liberation.[74]

Given the fact that Article 1(4) has never positively enabled the application of the Protocol, and that the interpretation of this provision is to be narrowly construed, its effect on the threshold of non-international armed conflict in international humanitarian law is negligible. As noted by Heather Wilson, 'the scope of Article 1(4) is actually very limited. If it opens up a Pandora's box at all, it is an unexpectedly small one.'[75]

Article 1(4) was a product of the international environment of Cold War and de-colonisation which framed the context of the Diplomatic Conference. As such, it represents an anomaly in the development of international humanitarian law, importing considerations of *jus ad bellum* into the domain of *jus in bello*.[76] While Article 1(4) clearly boosted the status of national liberation movements at the Diplomatic Conference, the import of this development should not be overstated. It did not have sufficient support at the Diplomatic Conference for it to be recognised as a codification of customary international law and subsequent practice does not suggest any change in this status.

Despite the restrictions implicit in Article 1(4), its inclusion in the Additional Protocol represented a major victory for the 'Third World' countries participating in the first session of the Diplomatic Conference. A side effect of this victory, however, was a lessening of interest in the formulation of Additional Protocol II during subsequent sessions. The view expressed by the Nigerian delegate, M. Abdul-Malik, was one commonly adopted by delegates of 'Third World' states:

> His delegation ... wondered whether draft Protocol II was necessary, since draft Protocol I, article 1 covered the three possible situations, namely those

[74] According to Greenwood:

> [T]he provisions on wars of national liberation are less than ideal and the language in which Article 1(4) is cast is particularly inappropriate. Nevertheless, if one examines the practical aspects of these provisions, they turn out to be very limited. The provisions on wars of national liberation were very much a product of the decolonisation era that came to an end not long after the adoption of the Additional Protocols. They are an example of how international agreements on international humanitarian law always focus upon the last conflict rather than the next one ... for the conditions of Article 1(4) are drawn so narrowly that very few conflicts are likely to fall within them.

'Critique of the Additional Protocols', in Durham and McCormack (eds.), *Changing Face of Conflict*, 16. See also Aldrich, 'Prospects', at 6–7.

[75] Wilson, *International Law*, p. 168. [76] See Gardam, 'Protocol I', at 120.

in which peoples were fighting against colonial domination, alien domination, or racist regimes.[77]

As the situations of colonial states were now deemed to be international, little impetus was left for the expansion of international humanitarian law governing the conduct of hostilities in non-international armed conflict. Indeed, many of the developing countries that participated in the Diplomatic Conferences were in favour of restricting the scope of Additional Protocol II so that their situation would remain under the ambit of Additional Protocol I.[78] The section that follows examines Additional Protocol II, focusing in particular on the scope of the instrument relating to situations of non-international armed conflict.

3.2 Additional Protocol II

Until the adoption of Additional Protocol II by the Diplomatic Conference on the Reaffirmation and Development of International Humanitarian Law,[79] common Article 3 encapsulated the main body of international humanitarian law governing situations of non-international armed conflict, hence its description as a '[c]onvention in miniature'.[80] At the Diplomatic Conference, Daniele Louise Bujard of the International Committee of the Red Cross remarked upon the need to develop further the law governing situations of non-international armed conflict: 'When put to the test ... the rules of protection in Article 3 common to the four Geneva Conventions of 1949 had been shown to require elaboration and completion. Government and Red Cross experts consulted by the ICRC since 1971 had confirmed the urgent need to strengthen the protection of victims of non-international armed conflicts by developing international humanitarian law applicable in such situations.'[81]

[77] *Official Records*, vol. VIII, CDDH/I/SR.24, p. 232.

[78] For examples of these positions, see the statements made by representatives of India (*Official Records*, vol. VIII, CDDH/I/SR.23, p. 224; *Official Records*, vol. V, CDDH/SR.29, p. 345), Nigeria (*Official Records*, vol. VIII, CDDH/I/SR.24, p. 232) and the Philippines (*Official Records*, vol. V, CDDH/SR.29, pp. 350–1). See also Elder, 'Historical Background', at 69; and Lysaght, 'Attitude of Western Countries', p. 382.

[79] Diplomatic Conference on the Reaffirmation and Development of International Humanitarian Law Applicable in Armed Conflicts, Geneva (1974–1977); vols. 1–14; Berne: Federal Political Department, 1978.

[80] Pictet (ed.), *Commentary I*, p. 48.

[81] *Official Records*, vol. VIII, CDDH/I/SR.22, p. 201.

For Adam Roberts and Richard Guelff, the need for a new instrument applicable to non-international armed conflict had been evidenced by the way in which 'experience demonstrated the inadequacy of the common article. While its provisions do extend certain fundamental humanitarian protections to non-combatants, they do not provide any definitive codification of the laws of war for non-international armed conflicts. Moreover, the provisions are so general and incomplete that they cannot be regarded as an adequate guide for the conduct of belligerents in such conflicts.'[82]

Having recognised that the rules contained in common Article 3 'needed to be confirmed and clarified',[83] the initiative was taken to expand on the protection provided by the Geneva Conventions to situations of non-international armed conflict.[84] According to Christopher Greenwood, Additional Protocol II 'goes a long way to putting flesh on the bare bones of common Article 3 of the 1949 Geneva Conventions. In particular, Additional Protocol II contains the first attempt to regulate by treaty the methods and means of warfare in internal conflicts.'[85] Georges Abi-Saab comments that the Protocol provides a 'much greater, and greatly needed, elaboration of the elliptic declarations of principle of common article 3, and through introducing new fundamental rules concerning the protection of civilians against the effects of hostilities, as well as the protection of medical personnel and transports'.[86]

While the expansion of international humanitarian law applicable to situations of non-international armed conflict was broadly welcomed, the field of application associated with the Protocol was criticised by many scholars for narrowing unnecessarily the scope of protection provided by the instrument.[87] This part of the study

[82] Roberts and Guelff, *Documents*, p. 482.

[83] ICRC, *Commentary on the Additional Protocols*, p. 1326, para. 4365.

[84] Article 1(1) states that the Protocol 'develops and supplements Article 3 common to the Geneva Conventions of 12 August 1949 without modifying its existing conditions of application'. The first paragraph of the Preamble emphasises the importance of common Article 3, stating 'that the humanitarian principles enshrined in Article 3 common to the Geneva Conventions of 12 August 1949 constitute the foundation of respect for the human person in cases of armed conflict not of an international character'.

[85] Greenwood, 'Critique of the Additional Protocols', p. 14.

[86] Abi-Saab, 'Non-international Armed Conflict', in UNESCO, *International Dimensions*, p. 236.

[87] Cullen, 'Key Developments', at 94–7; Greenwood, 'Critique of the Additional Protocols', p. 19; Eide, 'New Humanitarian Law', in Cassese (ed.), *New Humanitarian Law*, p. 308.

focuses on the threshold for the application of Additional Protocol II to situations of non-international armed conflict. Here an attempt will be made to outline the origins of this threshold and to evaluate its impact on the concept of non-international armed conflict in international humanitarian law.

3.2.1 The drafting history of Additional Protocol II

The original draft of Protocol II considered by the Diplomatic Conference consisted of four preambular paragraphs and forty-seven articles.[88] In order to secure the support needed for its adoption, the number of articles in the Protocol was reduced considerably and its threshold of application was raised above that originally supported by the ICRC. This section examines the different views expressed by delegates in deliberations on the drafting of Additional Protocol II. In doing so, particular attention will be paid to the field of application for the instrument set out in Article 1(1).

3.2.1.1 Calls for a single protocol applicable to all situations of armed conflict

Some delegates at the Diplomatic Conference favoured an approach that would adopt one protocol applicable to all situations of armed conflict. It was contended that such an approach would be preferable to one maintaining a distinction between international and non-international armed conflict as it would bypass problems surrounding classification of situations. Edvard Hambro, the Head of the Norwegian delegation, stated early in discussions that his government,

> [B]elieved that all war victims must be protected, whatever the political or legal classification of the conflict. For that reason, the Norwegian experts had proposed, at the meetings of experts organized by the ICRC, that there should be only one additional protocol applicable to all armed conflicts. [The Norwegian] delegation reserved the right to revert to that question later.[89]

The representative of the Swedish delegation also spoke out in support of having one Protocol applicable to all situations of armed conflict:

> All armed conflicts, whatever their magnitude, should be subject to the same humanitarian rules. Since the existing conventions were limited to

[88] Draft Protocol Additional to the Geneva Conventions of 12 August 1949, and Relating to the Protection of Victims of Non-international Armed Conflicts; *Official Records*, vol. I, part three, pp. 33–46.

[89] *Official Records*, vol. V, CDDH/SR.10, p. 91.

international armed conflicts, non-international conflicts were sometimes claimed to be international so that the humanitarian law in force might apply. One set of legal rules for all conflicts would obviate allegations of foreign intervention. That approach had not been accepted by the majority of countries. The most appropriate solution would be to define rules relating to non-international armed conflicts which would closely resemble the rules applicable in international conflicts. It was absolutely vital for combatants in the field to be protected by clear and uncomplicated rules.[90]

The need for one uniform body of international law applicable in all situations of armed conflict was furthermore stressed by the representative of the Syrian Arab Republic. Speaking before the Plenary of the Diplomatic Conference, Abdul-Latif Abdine stated that, '[i]t was unfortunate that there were two draft Protocols, providing for two kinds of treatment. But surely humanitarian law was concerned with man; why then should there be two sets of rules? There was no excuse for such a differentiation.'[91]

The idea of having one body of international humanitarian law applicable to all situations of armed conflict had been discussed at the Diplomatic Conference which drafted the Geneva Conventions of 1949. As illustrated in Chapter 2, support for the realisation of this approach had been lacking due to concerns about its impact on state sovereignty. While similar concerns were raised at the Diplomatic Conference responsible for drafting the Additional Protocols, the situation differed from that of twenty-five years earlier. The starting point for discussions on the scope of the Geneva Conventions in 1949 concerned the universal application of these instruments to all situations of armed conflict. In contrast, the starting point for discussions at the Diplomatic Conference in 1974 was provided by two draft additional protocols: one 'relating to the protection of victims of international armed conflicts' and one 'relating to the protection of victims of non-international armed conflicts'. Given that the Conference had been organised on the basis of adopting two protocols, clearly reinforcing a distinction between international and non-international armed conflict, the prospects for the success of proposals allowing a more unified approach were extremely limited. In addition to the format of the Conference, oriented towards the adoption of two instruments instead of one, the majority of delegations did not support the idea of international humanitarian law relating to situations of non-international armed conflict being equivalent

[90] *Official Records*, vol. V, CDDH/SR.14, p. 142.
[91] *Official Records*, vol. V, CDDH/SR.18, p. 193.

to that of international armed conflict. Some delegates went so far as to question the need for an additional protocol relating to situations of non-international armed conflict. Protective of state sovereignty and fearful of external intervention in the internal affairs of their government, efforts were made to limit the scope of the protocol. The arguments expressed by delegations assuming this position will be considered later in the chapter. Before doing this, the original threshold of application proposed by the ICRC in draft Protocol II will be examined.

3.2.1.2 The ICRC proposal on the field of application for Additional Protocol II

The idea of formulating two protocols instead of a single instrument relating to the protection of all situations of armed conflict was one that was strongly supported by representatives of the ICRC at the Diplomatic Conference. Expressing the position of the ICRC on the need to distinguish between situations of international armed conflict and situations of non-international armed conflict, Mrs Daniele Louise Bujard stated that: 'In order to take into account the fundamentally different political aspects which existed between international and non-international armed conflicts, the ICRC had respected the distinction, well established in public international law, between those armed conflicts, in conformity with the wish expressed by the vast majority of experts consulted.'[92]

Explaining the background of Article 1, the provision relating to the draft Protocol's material field of application, Bujard stated that prior to the Diplomatic Conference:

> The Conference of Government Experts on the Reaffirmation and Development of Humanitarian Law applicable in Armed Conflicts had drawn up six alternative texts: the first was based on the idea that a single Protocol should apply without distinction to all armed conflicts; the other five alternative texts, applicable only to non-international armed conflicts, ranged from the broadest possible definition, covering all situations of non-international armed conflict, including those which were limited, to the narrowest definition, covering only non-international armed conflicts with all the characteristics of a war. The Government Experts had concluded that a choice would have to be made between a Protocol with a narrow field of application and broad rules and one with a broad field of application and only a few basic humanitarian rules. Those views had also been expressed by a number of delegations at the first session of the Conference.

[92] *Official Records*, vol. VIII, CDDH/I/SR.22, p. 202.

The ICRC had had the difficult task of determining the field of application of draft Protocol II; it had chosen a broad field to cover all non-international armed conflicts and for that purpose had endeavoured to specify the characteristics of a non-international armed conflict by means of objective criteria so that the Protocol could be applied when those criteria were met and not be made subject to other considerations.[93]

The approach adopted by the ICRC was pragmatic, seeking to achieve 'a delicate balance between the needs of humanity and the security requirements of the State intending to take the requisite steps to maintain and re-establish order on its territory'.[94] While possessing a higher threshold of application than that of common Article 3, the characteristics of non-international armed conflict contained in draft Protocol II were still considered broad by the ICRC. The text of draft Article 1 stated the Protocol's material field of application as follows:

1. The present Protocol shall apply to all armed conflicts not covered by Article 2 common to the Geneva Conventions of August 12, 1949, taking place between armed forces or other organized armed groups under responsible command.
2. The present Protocol shall not apply to situations of internal disturbances and tensions, *inter alia* riots, isolated and sporadic acts of violence and other acts of a similar nature.
3. The foregoing provisions do not modify the conditions governing the application of Article 3 common to the Geneva Conventions of August 12, 1949.[95]

The phrase 'taking place between armed forces or other organized armed groups under responsible command' set the most critical threshold for determining the kind of situations that were deemed to merit inclusion within the scope of the draft Protocol. The meaning of this formula for the recognition of non-international armed conflict was explained in the following way by Bujard:

[Non-international armed conflict] was defined in the second part of paragraph 1 as the opposition of armed forces capable of concerted military action under responsible command. In response to a request by certain experts, a distinction had been made between the expression 'armed forces', which applied to the armed forces of the established Government, and the expression 'organized armed groups under responsible command', which applied to armed forces organized by insurgents for the purpose of the struggle. That

[93] *Ibid.*, p. 203. [94] *Ibid.*, p. 202.
[95] Draft Protocol, *Official Records*, vol. I, part three, p. 33.

distinction implied no difference in the degree of organization: insurgent armed forces had to have an organic structure, in other words, they must be endowed with a system of competence and responsibility and subjected to a system of internal discipline as implied by article 36 – measures for execution – which stipulated that each party to the conflict should take measures to ensure observance of the Protocol by its military and civilian agents and persons subject to its authority.[96]

For the ICRC, this definition of non-international armed conflict implied a broad field of application for the draft Protocol.[97] Nevertheless, it is worth noting that it restricted the applicability of the instrument to situations where the organisation of insurgents, acting under 'responsible command', would be similar to that of conventional armed forces. It also did not allow for the application of the Protocol to situations of hostilities between organised armed groups. Irrespective of their intensity, such situations would not be covered by the draft Protocol's material field of application. It is fortunate therefore that the ICRC included in the form of draft Article 1(3) a clause noting that the field of application of common Article 3 would not be affected by the Protocol. The Head of the ICRC Legal Division commented at the Diplomatic Conference that:

> The great advantage of this system was that it left intact the guarantee in Article 3 common to the Conventions of basic humane treatment to victims in all cases of non-international armed conflict. Its disadvantage was that it created a somewhat complicated conventional situation by establishing two instruments applicable to non-international armed conflicts. However, in most cases Article 3 common to the Geneva Conventions of 1949 and Protocol II could be applied simultaneously.[98]

Delegates who expressed support for the ICRC draft of Article 1 included the representatives of the Netherlands,[99] Belgium,[100] Switzerland,[101] Italy[102] and the United Kingdom.[103] Ambassador R. Fack, Head of the Dutch delegation during the second session of the Diplomatic Conference, made the following assessment of the provision:

> Article 1 was the heart of draft Protocol II and the text proposed by the ICRC was to be commended. It was true that the wording of paragraph 2 might be

[96] *Official Records*, vol. VIII, CDDH/I/SR.22, p. 204. [97] *Ibid.*, p. 203.
[98] *Ibid.*, p. 204.
[99] *Official Records*, vol. VIII, CDDH/I/SR.23, p. 222.
[100] *Official Records*, vol. VIII, CDDH/I/SR.22, p. 208.
[101] *Official Records*, vol. VIII, CDDH/I/SR.23, p. 219. [102] *Ibid.*, p. 223.
[103] *Official Records*, vol. VIII, CDDH/I/SR.24, p. 236.

subject to various interpretations, but that could not be avoided in a world where there was often a clash between matters of international concern and matters essentially within the domestic jurisdiction of States. It was therefore inevitable that the State concerned would exercise its own judgment with regard to applicability. His delegation's interpretation of article 1 was that draft Protocol II would not be applicable in situations of conflict that were being dealt with by police forces using normal police methods and equipment, but that it would become applicable as soon as the authorities were forced to seek substantial assistance from military units or to hand full responsibility for dealing with the conflict over to the armed forces. His delegation did not consider that it would be applicable in cases of incidental terrorist activities, but thought that it would apply in cases of armed action and activity that obviously involved more than incidental occurrences.[104]

François Pictet of the Swiss delegation also voiced the support of his government for Article 1, stating that 'the combination of negative and positive criteria in that definition made it both flexible and precise'.[105] Expressing similar views on the provision, Luigi Ferrari-Bravo of the Italian delegation and Jean de Breucker of the Flemish delegation both voiced opposition to any restriction on the scope of draft Protocol II.[106]

3.2.1.3 Views of delegates concerning state sovereignty and the threat of external interference

A large majority of delegates at the Diplomatic Conference expressed either reservations or outright opposition to the ICRC draft of Article 1. Some delegations adopted the position that it could provide an opportunity for external interference in the internal affairs of sovereign states. For the delegation of the German Democratic Republic (GDR), draft Article 1 undermined the distinction between international and non-international armed conflict and thus also respect for state sovereignty and territorial integrity in international humanitarian law:

Draft Protocol II was obviously meant ... to cover only a particular category of non-international armed conflicts, a certain group being selected from those covered by the broad scope of Article 3. That meant a complete change from the system of the four Geneva Conventions, in which the distinction was made between international and non-international armed conflicts. It was a very important distinction, based on respect for State sovereignty and territorial integrity.

[104] *Official Records*, vol. VIII, CDDH/I/SR.23, p. 222. [105] *Ibid.*, p. 219.
[106] *Ibid.*, pp. 223 and 208.

> The effort was now being made to distinguish between three categories of armed conflict – first, international armed conflict covered by draft Protocol I; second non-international armed conflict covered by draft Protocol II; and, third, non-international armed conflict covered by Article 3 common to the four Geneva Conventions of 1949.
>
> [The GDR delegation] considered that the introduction of new categories and difficult distinctions was not calculated to strengthen the development of international humanitarian law. Instead, it might encourage interference in the internal affairs of States.[107]

In order to avoid problems arising from the creation of a new category of armed conflict, the GDR delegation proposed an amendment binding the Protocol's field of application to that of common Article 3. It was suggested that the first paragraph of Article 1 be redrafted as follows: '[t]he present Protocol which specifies and supplements Article 3 common to the four Geneva Conventions of August 12, 1949, shall apply to all armed conflicts which in conformity with common Article 3 have not an international character and take place between armed forces or organized armed groups under responsible command.'[108]

The fear of external interference was raised by several delegations from the 'Third World' as grounds for objecting to Article 1 of the draft Protocol. The concerns expressed were similar to many that had been voiced during the drafting of the Geneva Conventions at the Diplomatic Conference of 1949.[109] Commenting on the applicability of the draft Protocol to situations of non-international armed conflict, Graefrath of the GDR delegation stated that the wording of Article 1 was dangerous, 'for it was aimed at the internationalisation of internal conflicts, and would thus encourage interference in the domestic affairs of States. The aim of draft Protocol II was no doubt to ensure the greater protection of victims of non-international armed conflicts, but whether or not the Protocol was applied would depend on the authorities of the State on whose territory the armed conflict occurred.'[110]

In stating that the applicability of the draft Protocol would be decided by the authorities of a state, the very basis for the inclusion of a definition of non-international armed conflict was undermined. The rationale for the 'material field of application' in Article 1 was to avoid situations where the Protocol's relevance was considered a

[107] *Official Records*, vol. VIII, CDDH/I/SR.22, pp. 206–7.

[108] *Official Records*, vol. IV, CDDH/I/88, p. 8.

[109] See section 2.2 of Chapter 2.

[110] *Official Records*, vol. VIII, CDDH/I/SR.22, p. 207.

matter of discretion for the state authorities. This did not discourage states from proposing amendments with a contrary purpose. The Romanian delegation, for example, submitted that Article 1(1) apply 'in cases where the State, on whose territory the events are taking place, recognizes the existence of the conflict, its character and its constituent elements'.[111]

As the terms providing the threshold of applicability for the draft Protocol had not previously been used in the Geneva Conventions, questions were raised concerning their meaning. Expressing concern over the ambiguity of draft Article 1(1), Martin Herrero of the Spanish delegation stated that his government 'was not completely satisfied with the present wording of article 1 which it found rather confused, and would therefore submit an amendment in the Working Group. The terms "responsible command" and "armed forces" should be defined. His delegation understood the latter to mean the regular armed forces of a State.'[112]

With regard to the concept of 'responsible command', the Spanish delegation proposed the inclusion of a clause stating that it be 'effectively exercised in such a way as to guarantee its readiness and ability to observe and enforce observance of the rules of humanitarian law in force'.[113] Like that submitted by the Romanian delegation, this proposal sought to adjust the threshold of applicability contained in draft Article 1 to allow scope for its comfortable interpretation by state authorities. Emphasising the need to secure a threshold that would not impinge on the internal affairs of state, Aureliu Cristescu of Romania stated that his delegation:

> Attached considerable importance to the field of application of draft Protocol II, since the sovereignty of States was involved. There was a fundamental difference between international and non-international armed conflicts, and it would be a mistake automatically to transpose the provisions of draft Protocol I to draft Protocol II. In the spirit of cooperation, his delegation was prepared to consider the establishment of rules for non-international armed conflicts, provided that every care was taken to ensure respect for the principles of national sovereignty and non-intervention in a State's internal affairs. He agreed with the statements made at an earlier meeting by the representatives of India and Indonesia that the type of armed conflict in question was not easy to define. He also shared the view expressed by the Australian representative that additional criteria to those proposed in the ICRC text should

111 *Ibid.* 112 *Ibid.*, p. 209.
113 *Official Records*, vol. IV, CDDH/I/33, p. 7.

be considered, such as, for example, the duration and proportions of the armed conflict.[114]

While various delegations put forward a number of proposals in favour of narrowing the scope of draft Article 1,[115] some expressed reservations about the Protocol in its entirety. Questioning the need for an instrument of international humanitarian law relating to situations of non-international armed conflict, P.R. Sood of the Indian delegation stated that '[t]he definition of non-international armed conflicts was still vague and no convincing arguments had been put forward to justify the need for draft Protocol II, the provisions of which would not be acceptable to his delegation'.[116]

The statement of Sood reflected a position of strong opposition towards the draft Protocol. A sentiment reflected in the statements of many 'Third World' delegations, it indicated a fear that the adoption of the Protocol would undermine state sovereignty and provide a pretext for external interference in the internal affairs of states.

Given the number of objections to either the scope of draft Protocol II or indeed the principle of its existence, there existed doubts at the Diplomatic Conference concerning the future of this instrument. The fear of external interference at the Conference was no doubt exacerbated by the climate of internal relations shaped by the Cold War. The means which were employed to allay the objections of delegations such as India, Nigeria, Romania, Spain, the German Democratic Republic and the Philippines will be explored later in this chapter. Before doing so, the section that follows examines proposals put forward to address the complicated situation introduced by draft Article 1 by harmonising the threshold contained therein with that of common Article 3.

3.2.1.4 Proposals for the harmonisation of thresholds in draft Protocol II and common Article 3

It was clear to delegates at the Diplomatic Conference that the definition of non-international armed conflict contained in draft Article 1 would effectively limit the application of the Protocol to situations of a higher threshold of application than that of common Article 3. The

114 *Official Records*, vol. VIII, CDDH/I/SR.23, p. 221.

115 See *Official Records*, vol. IV, CDDH/I/26, CDDH/I/30, CDDH/I/32, CDDH/I/33, CDDH/I/79, pp. 6–8.

116 *Official Records*, vol. VIII, CDDH/I/SR.23, p. 224. For a statement on the matter by Indian Ambassador B.C. Mishra, see also *Official Records*, vol. V, CDDH/SR.29, p. 345.

issue of harmonising the applicability of the draft Protocol with that already assumed for 'armed conflicts not of an international character' was discussed at length. Hans Wilhelm Longva of the Norwegian delegation put forward an amendment to change the text of Article 1 to ensure the draft Protocol would cover all situations of non-international armed conflict covered by common Article 3: 'The present Protocol shall apply in situations referred to in Article 3 common to the Geneva Conventions of 12 August 1949 for the Protection of War Victims.'[117] The following grounds for objecting to draft Article 1 were stated by the representative of the Norwegian delegation:

With regard to draft Protocol II, article 1, he was concerned, as were other representatives, that it might increase the categories of armed conflicts from two to three. His delegation had therefore submitted an amendment designed to harmonize the wording of article 1 with the text of Article 3 common to the four Geneva Conventions; it did not affect the substance of article 1. In his view, there could not be an armed conflict in the sense of Article 3 common to the four Conventions except in cases where hostilities broke out between armed forces or other organized groups under responsible command.[118]

The statement by the Norwegian delegate indicates a rather loose interpretation of the formula provided by the ICRC. It is clear from the remarks referred to earlier by the ICRC delegate that the threshold proposed for the Protocol was distinctly higher than that of common Article 3 due to the terms contained in draft Article 1 which stipulated its application to armed conflicts 'taking place between armed forces or other organized armed groups under responsible command'. The remarks of the Norwegian representative are peculiar for his delegation in that they veer towards a more restrictive interpretation than normally adopted by Norway at the Diplomatic Conference.

Another delegate advocating the harmonisation of the threshold contained in draft Protocol II with that of common Article 3 was Professor Karl-Joseph Partsch of the Federal Republic of Germany:

The question whether the draft Protocol II should be more closely connected with Article 3 common to the Geneva Conventions was more a technical than a political question. If draft Protocol II was to be regarded as independent of the protection given by Article 3 common to the Conventions, there might be a field of application that it did not cover. The idea behind the concept of draft Protocol II was to broaden protection and not to limit it by new definitions

[117] *Official Records*, vol. IV, CDDH/I/218, p. 9.
[118] *Official Records*, vol. VIII, CDDH/I/SR.23, p. 217.

of non-international armed conflicts. As long as there was no difference between a non-international armed conflict according to Article 3 common to the Geneva Conventions and the new definition in draft Protocol II, article 1, paragraph 1, both concepts could be merged.[119]

The idea of merging the thresholds contained in draft Protocol and common Article 3 found support among only a small minority of those present at the Diplomatic Conference. The British Head of delegation, John Redvers Freeland, argued against the initiative on the grounds that a new threshold of application in draft Article 1 was needed to secure better implementation: 'It was right to divorce Article 1 from Article 3 common to the Geneva Conventions of 1949. That article should continue to stand on its own for those unable to accept Protocol II, but the vagueness of its scope, and its non-application in the past, made a new start essential.'[120]

Despite the pragmatism shown by the ICRC in its formulation of Article 1, the approach employed proved in some respects short-sighted. Objections similar to those raised at the Diplomatic Conference in 1949 emerged again, voiced by states fearful of any measure that might impact on their sovereignty. Given the significance of draft Article 1 in terms of setting the Protocol's field of application, it was of course foreseeable that the definition of non-international armed conflict contained therein would be subject to amendments that would seek to either narrow or expand its scope. Proposals for the harmonisation of thresholds in draft Protocol II and common Article 3 had little hope of success due to the positions adopted by delegates referred to in the previous section. The majority of participants at the Conference were more interested in limiting the scope of draft Article 1 than in considering its expansion to include all situations of non-international armed conflict covered by common Article 3. The breadth of division that existed between delegations on the field of application for draft Protocol II is reflected in the final debate on the issue prior to the adoption of the draft Article 1 at the fourth session of the Diplomatic Conference in 1977.

3.2.1.5 The adoption of Article 1 of draft Protocol II at the Diplomatic Conference

The views expressed by delegates during the final plenary discussions on draft Article 1 offer considerable insight into state practice

[119] *Ibid.*, p. 221.
[120] *Official Records*, vol. VIII, CDDH/I/SR.24, p. 237.

relating to the recognition of non-international armed conflict and the application of international humanitarian law. No single trend of state policy emerges from this debate; the statements of delegates highlight a spectrum of different positions. After considerable debate the Diplomatic Conference approved draft Article 1 with 58 delegations voting in favour,[121] 5 against[122] and 29 abstaining.[123] While the Conference adopted the provision as a whole, it did so without the support of over a third of the delegations present. Indeed, some of the delegations that voted in favour of draft Article 1 also asserted that the interpretation of the Protocol's applicability would be the sole right of the state authorities engaged in non-international armed conflict. An example of this position is provided in the explanation of vote given by the delegation of Saudi Arabia. After voting in favour of draft Article 1, the Legal Adviser of its Ministry of Foreign Affairs, Abdul Majid Nematallah, stated that:

> [H]e wished to make it clear that any definition of the terms of the article was solely the concern of the State on whose territory the armed conflict was taking place. Decision by any other country would constitute an infringement of that State's sovereignty. He reserved his Government's right to enter a reservation on the article.[124]

Associating his delegation with the position expressed by the Saudi Arabian delegate, Mohamad Hassan Mokhtar of the United Arab Emirates stated that 'he had voted in favour of Article 1 for purely

[121] *Official Records*, vol. VII, CDDH/SR.49, p. 70. The following delegations voted in favour: Yugoslavia, Afghanistan, Federal Republic of Germany, Saudi Arabia, Australia, Austria, Belgium, Bulgaria, Canada, Cyprus, Cuba, Denmark, Egypt, United Arab Emirates, Ecuador, Spain, United States of America, Finland, France, Ghana, Greece, Guatemala, Honduras, Hungary, Iran, Ireland, Israel, Italy, Socialist People's Libyan Arab Jamahiriya, Japan, Jordan, Kuwait, Liechtenstein, Luxembourg, Monaco, Mongolia, New Zealand, Pakistan, Netherlands, Peru, Poland, Portugal, Qatar, Republic of Korea, German Democratic Republic, Democratic People's Republic of Korea, Byelorussian Soviet Socialist Republic, Ukrainian Soviet Socialist Republic, Romania, United Kingdom, Holy See, Senegal, Sweden, Switzerland, Czechoslovakia, Tunisia, Union of Soviet Socialist Republics, Venezuela.

[122] *Ibid.* The following delegations voted against: Argentina, United Republic of Cameroon, Chile, India, Syrian Arab Republic.

[123] *Ibid.* The following delegations abstained: Democratic Yemen, Zaire, Algeria, Brazil, Colombia, Ivory Coast, Indonesia, Iraq, Kenya, Lebanon, Madagascar, Morocco, Mauritania, Mexico, Mozambique, Nicaragua, Nigeria, Norway, Oman, Uganda, Panama, Philippines, United Republic of Tanzania, Swaziland, Sudan, Sri Lanka, Thailand, Turkey, Uruguay.

[124] *Ibid.*, p. 79.

humanitarian reasons, but wished to make it clear that his Government would not adhere to any provision that affected its sovereignty'.[125]

Adopting a position similar to that of Saudi Arabia and the United Arab Emirates, the Brazilian delegation's explanation of its abstention also asserts that recognition of draft Protocol II's applicability was to be solely a matter for the government of the state hosting the conflict:

When Article 1 was adopted by consensus in Committee I during the second session of the Conference, the Brazilian delegation stated that the conditions laid down in the article to define its material field of application could be recognized only by the Government of the State on whose territory the conflict was allegedly taking place. These were indeed distinctive factors the verification of which could not be a matter either for the dissent armed forces or for third States.[126]

While India and Chile voted against the adoption of draft Article 1 on the grounds that it threatened state sovereignty,[127] Syria and Cameroon did so on the grounds that terms contained in the provision set an excessively high threshold for the implementation of the Protocol. Prior to a roll-call vote being requested on draft Article 1, the Syrian representative, Abdul-Latif Abdine, noting that there was no consensus on the provision, stated that:

The concept of 'armed conflicts' was very restrictive and the requirement that the armed groups should exercise such control over a part of the State's territory as to enable them to carry out sustained and concerted military operations was useless. Moreover, it opened the door to conflicting interpretations which would make it impossible to implement draft Protocol II. In his delegation's opinion, that Protocol should apply to all organized armed groups with the exception of common law bandits, without the requirement that they should exercise control over a part of the territory. That would be more in keeping with the general and universal character of humanitarian law. Such factors as the scale of the conflict did not constitute valid criteria for depriving revolutionaries of protection.[128]

Associating the position of his delegation with that of Syria, Remy Mbaya of the United Republic of Cameroon also criticised the restrictive nature of the threshold contained in draft Article 1:

He had voted against the article in the light of the very pertinent comment of the representative of the Syrian Arab Republic. The wording in question had restrictive implications which were unacceptable because they represented a retrogressive step in comparison with existing law. Moreover, there was a

[125] *Ibid.*, p. 73. [126] *Ibid.*, p. 76. [127] *Ibid.*, p. 72.
[128] *Ibid.*, p. 67.

danger that the movements concerned would enjoy the protection of draft Protocol II only if they exercised effective control over a part of the national territory.[129]

The views expressed by the different delegations after voting on draft Article 1 show considerable divergences of interpretation. Prior to the vote on Article 1 the Canadian Head of Delegation, David Miller, had expressed his hope that the provision would be adopted by consensus.[130] While the text before the plenary had been previously adopted by consensus in Committee I of the Diplomatic Conference, the aspiration for this to happen again clearly proved unrealistic. Having voted in favour of Article 1, the Canadian delegate stated:

> Like any compromise, the text is subject to certain interpretations not always of the same nature. Some delegations argue that because of the number of qualifications contained in it, only conflicts of a very high threshold such as civil wars are covered. Others, like my delegation, underline that these qualifications are a reflection of the factual and practical circumstances that would in fact have to exist if a Party to the conflict could be expected to implement the provisions of the Protocol. Furthermore, we do not agree that this necessarily means that these conditions could exist only in civil war situations. In our view, dissident armed forces or other organized armed groups would need to have a responsible command, to exercise control over some territory, and to have sustained military operations in order, practically speaking, to implement the Protocol. The key to the height of threshold we suggest lies in the expression 'to implement this Protocol'.[131]

While the explanations of voting provided by various delegations offer valuable insight into the positions of each state relating to the recognition of non-international armed conflict, they exhibit little common ground in terms of overall state practice. As alluded to in the statement of the Canadian delegate, the provision was formulated in such a way as to accommodate different interpretations. The interpretations referred to in this section offer some indication of the breadth of division that existed among delegations in relation to the threshold contained in draft Article 1. As a consequence of their contradictory nature, it is impossible to trace any common understanding of the threshold contained in this provision among delegates at the Diplomatic Conference.

[129] *Ibid.*, p. 70. [130] *Ibid.*, p. 66. [131] *Ibid.*, p. 77.

3.2.2 The threshold for the application of Additional Protocol II

As indicated by the divergent views that were expressed by delegates at the Diplomatic Conference, the interpretation of the threshold contained in Article 1 of Additional Protocol II is problematic. It is clear that it applies to situations of armed conflict that possess a higher degree of intensity than those of common Article 3 but the characterisation of such situations according to the conditions contained in the provision is exacerbated by the terms of their expression. The section that follows investigates the meaning of the criteria contained in Article 1(1), probing in particular the interpretation provided by the Commentary of the ICRC. Case law and state practice relating to the threshold of Additional Protocol II will also be examined.

3.2.2.1 The material field of application in Article 1(1)

In stipulating the material field of application for Additional Protocol II, Article 1(1) states it will apply to situations of armed conflict that take place in the territory of a High Contracting Party 'between its armed forces and dissident armed forces or other organized armed groups which, under responsible command, exercise such control over a part of its territory as to enable them to carry out sustained and concerted military operations and to implement this Protocol'.[132] While considerably higher than that originally proposed by the ICRC, the threshold nevertheless preserves the principle of recognising the applicability of international humanitarian law in situations of non-international armed conflict on the basis of objectively verifiable criteria. According to the ICRC Commentary on the Additional Protocols, Article 1(1)

> lays down a number of objective criteria for determining the field of application of the Protocol. Its application should not depend on the discretionary judgment of the parties. The Protocol applies automatically as soon as the material conditions as defined in the article are fulfilled. The aim of this system is that the protection of the victims of armed conflict should not depend on an arbitrary decision of the authorities concerned – this is one of the cornerstones of international humanitarian law and already applied to Articles 2 and 3 common to the 1949 Conventions.[133]

[132] For excerpts from the *travaux préparatoires* of Article 1, see Levie (ed.), *Law of Non-international Armed Conflict*, pp. 21–90. See also Eide, 'New Humanitarian Law', pp. 299–300.

[133] ICRC, *Commentary on the Additional Protocols*, p. 1351, para. 4459.

One of the key criteria listed in Article 1(1) is that the organised armed groups engaged in hostilities possess 'responsible command'.[134] A fundamental requirement for the implementation of the Protocol by insurgent armed groups, it presupposes a level of organisation sufficient to engage in hostilities and maintain an internal system of discipline: 'The existence of a responsible command implies some degree of organisation of the insurgent armed group or dissident armed forces, but this does not necessarily mean that there is a hierarchical system of military organisation similar to that of regular armed forces. It means an organisation capable, on the one hand, of planning and carrying out sustained and concerted military operations, and on the other, of imposing discipline in the name of a de facto authority.'[135]

A criterion closely related to that of responsible command is that of control over territory. The capacity to maintain control of territory, by virtue of the level of organisation required, provides evidence of responsible command. The extent of the control required, however, is subject to interpretation. In practical terms, the ICRC Commentary states that there must be some degree of stability in the control maintained over territory:

> In many conflicts there is considerable movement in the theatre of hostilities; it often happens that territorial control changes hands rapidly. Sometimes domination of a territory will be relative, for example, when urban centres remain in government hands while rural areas escape their authority. In practical terms, if the insurgent armed groups are organized in accordance with the requirements of the Protocol, the extent of territory they can claim to control will be that which escapes the control of the government armed forces. However, there must be some degree of stability in the control of even a modest area of land for them to be capable of effectively applying the rules of the Protocol.[136]

Perhaps the most significant of the criteria contained in Article 1(1) is the requirement of sustained and concerted military operations. This sets a particularly high threshold for the application of the Protocol:

> 'Sustained' (in French the reference is to 'opérations continues') means that the operations are kept going or kept up continuously. The emphasis is therefore on

[134] The application of the 'responsible command' concept in the situations of non-international armed conflict will be explored in some depth in Chapter 4, at section 4.5.

[135] ICRC, *Commentary on the Additional Protocols*, p. 1352, para. 4463.

[136] *Ibid.*, pp. 1352–3, para. 4467.

continuity and persistence. 'Concerted' (in French: 'concertées') means agreed upon, planned and contrived, done in agreement according to a plan. Thus we are talking about military operations conceived and planned by organized armed groups. The criteria of duration and intensity were not retained as such in the definition because they would have introduced a subjective element. The applicability of the rules of protection of the Protocol must not in fact depend on the subjective judgment of the parties. On the other hand, the criterion whether military operations are sustained and concerted, while implying the element of continuity and intensity, complies with an objective assessment of the situation. At the beginning of a conflict military operations rarely have such a character; thus it is likely that only common Article 3 will apply to the first stage of hostilities.[137]

In determining the applicability of Additional Protocol II to the situation in Rwanda, the International Criminal Tribunal for Rwanda (ICTR) utilised the definition contain in Article 1(1) of the instrument, applying four conditions contained therein. In doing so, the Chamber adopted an approach in line with that of the ICRC Commentary in its interpretation of the Protocol's threshold of application:

> The armed forces opposing the government must be under responsible command, which entails a degree of organisation within the armed group or dissident armed forces. This degree of organisation should be such so as to enable the armed group or dissident forces to plan and carry out concerted military operations, and to impose discipline in the name of a *de facto* authority. Further, these armed forces must be able to dominate a sufficient part of the territory so as to maintain sustained and concerted military operations and to apply Additional Protocol II. In essence, the operations must be continuous and planned. The territory in their control is usually that which has eluded the control of the government forces.[138]

It is clear that a high intensity of hostilities is required for the fulfilment of the criteria contained in Article 1(1). The existence of sustained

[137] *Ibid.*, p. 1353, para. 4469.

[138] *Prosecutor* v. *Akayesu* (Case No. ICTR-96–4), Trial Chamber Judgment, 2 September 1998, paras. 625–6. This interpretation of the concept of 'armed forces' in Article 1(1) of Additional Protocol II was also used in the ruling of the Swiss Tribunal militaire d'appel in the *Niyonteze* case:

> The notion of 'armed forces' in Art. 1(1) of Protocol II, must be seen in its widest sense, to include all armed forces described in domestic legislation. 'Responsible command' implies some degree of organisation within the armed groups or dissident armed forces, but this does not necessarily mean that there is a hierarchical system of military organisation similar to that of regular armed forces. It means an organisation capable of, on the one hand, planning and carrying out sustained and concerted military

and concerted military operations in particular rules out all situations of low-intensity armed conflict. While the authors of the Commentary express firmly the position that the fulfilment of the conditions contained in Article 1(1) must not depend on the subjective judgment of parties to the conflict, it is not clear how otherwise to determine the applicability of the Protocol in the course of an armed conflict.[139]

The ICRC Commentary on the Additional Protocols states that Article 1, determining the material field of application, constitutes 'the keystone of the instrument. It is the result of a delicate compromise, the product of lengthy negotiations, and the fate of the Protocol as a whole depended on it until it was finally adopted in the plenary meetings of the Conference'.[140] In considering the nature of the threshold contained in Article 1(1) it is important to take into consideration the manner in which it was drafted and the depth of division that existed over the issue of extending international humanitarian law to situations of non-international armed conflict. While the provision arguably secures the *principle* that the application of the Protocol is not a matter of discretion, it is clear that the detailed definition contained therein allows plenty of scope for the convenient interpretation of its terms by state parties.

The narrower scope of Additional Protocol II set by the objective criteria in Article 1(1) may be viewed in a negative light for two reasons. First, all situations of armed conflict that do not reach a threshold of intensity approaching that of a civil war are excluded from its application. Given the rudimentary nature of the rules contained in the Protocol, and the clear potential for their applicability in situations short of civil war, this is an unfortunate restriction on the protection provided by the instrument.[141] Second, situations of high-intensity

> operations – operations that are kept up continuously and that are done in agreement according to a plan – and on the other, of imposing discipline.

Switzerland, Tribunal militaire d'appel (Military Appeals Chamber) 1A, decision of 26 May 2000 in the *Niyonteze* case, chapter 3, section C. Unoffical translation printed in Sassoli and Bouvier (eds.), *How Does Law Protect in War?*, vol. II, p. 2250.

139 Provost, *International Human Rights*, p. 264.

140 ICRC, *Commentary on the Additional Protocols*, p. 1348, para. 4446.

141 This point is made by Eide:

> With regard to the provisions concerning humane treatment of persons in the power of a party to the conflict, it would seem very strange if any State claimed that it would go below the level of protection contained in these provisions because the conflict had not reached the level provided for in Art. 1. In fact, it must be immaterial what level the conflict has reached – these

armed conflict between organised armed groups, not involving the armed forces of a *de jure* government, are also excluded.[142] As it is often in situations of non-international armed conflict where state structures have disintegrated that international humanitarian law is needed most, the omission of armed conflicts between organised armed groups is regrettable.

The restrictive definition of non-international armed conflict contained in Article 1(1) is perhaps the greatest failing of the instrument, imposing a threshold similar in certain respects to that stipulated by the recognition of belligerency in traditional international law. According to René Provost, 'Protocol II can be considered a regression, given that it requires basically the same conditions as did the recognition of belligerency, but without triggering the full application of all humanitarian rules for international armed conflicts.'[143] Rwelamira goes so far as to state that 'Protocol II has in effect restated the general rule of international law relating to the status of belligerency'.[144]

The comments of Provost and Rwelamira are not, however, entirely accurate. It ought to be acknowledged that although there are similarities, the grounds for the application of Additional Protocol II are not identical to those required by the recognition of belligerency. As noted by Yair M. Lootsteen, 'the criteria established in Protocol II, while establishing a threshold that is considerably higher than mere civil unrest, is lower than state-to-state warfare'.[145] Before recognition of belligerency may occur, insurgents must be in command of an administration similar to that of a government. This requirement is not included in Additional Protocol II. According to Lootsteen, the main difference in the conditions required for the recognition of belligerency is in the scale of insurgent organisation and control over territory:

> The belligerency requirements are more stringent than those in the Protocol in that they lend themselves to a group of rebels who have more than mere

> provisions contain nothing more than what follows from the general law of human rights, which today must be considered part of *jus cogens*.

Asbjörn Eide, 'New Humanitarian Law', p. 299.

[142] The authors of the ICRC Commentary on the Additional Protocols recognise that such situations may constitute armed conflict: 'A situation of armed conflict may also exist in which armed factions fight against each other without intervention by the armed forces of the established government.' Pilloud *et al.*, *Commentary*, p. 1319, fn. 2.

[143] Provost, *International Human Rights*, p. 264.

[144] Rwelamira, 'Significance and Contribution', in Swinarski (ed.) *Études*, pp. 234–5.

[145] Lootsteen, 'Concept of Belligerency', at 130.

military control over part of the state. The belligerency conditions … require that rebels establish some semblance of government or administration in the area under their control. The substantive distinction lies in the fact that upon attaining the objective criteria of belligerency, the insurgents achieve many of the characteristics of an independent state – they become in effect a *de facto* state.[146]

The threshold determining the application of Additional Protocol II is thus lower than that required for the recognition of belligerency. The scope of the Protocol, albeit restrictive in comparison with that of common Article 3, requires a lower threshold of armed conflict than that stipulated in traditional international law.

3.2.2.2 Internal disturbances and tensions in Article 1(2)

While Article 1(1) provides a positive definition of non-international armed conflict, Article 1(2) of the Protocol provides a negative definition. This provision states that the protocol 'shall not apply to situations of internal disturbances and tensions, such as riots, isolated and sporadic acts of violence and other acts of a similar nature, as not being armed conflicts'.[147] According to the ICRC Commentary on Additional Protocol II, the application of the term 'armed conflict' requires 'the existence of open hostilities between armed forces which are organized to a greater or lesser degree'.[148] Thus:

[i]nternal disturbances and tensions, characterized by isolated or sporadic acts of violence, do not therefore constitute armed conflict in a legal sense … non-international armed conflict seems to be a situation in which hostilities break out between armed forces or organized armed groups within the territory of a single state. Insurgents fighting against the established order would normally seek to overthrow the government in power or alternatively to bring about a secession so as to set up a new state.[149]

The meaning of the 'internal disturbances and tensions' remains unclear. The ICRC Commentary on the Additional Protocols acknowledges that:

No real definitions are given. The concept of internal disturbances and tensions may be illustrated by giving a list of examples of such situations without any

[146] *Ibid.*

[147] See generally Asbjörn Eide, 'Internal Disturbances and Tensions', in UNESCO, *International Dimensions*; Gasser, 'Code of Conduct', 51; Meron *et al.* 'Combating Lawlessness', 215.

[148] ICRC, *Commentary on the Additional Protocols*, p. 1319, para. 4341. The threshold for the existence of armed conflict will be explored in detail in Chapter 4.

[149] ICRC, *Commentary on the Additional Protocols*, pp. 1319–20, para. 4341.

attempt to be exhaustive: riots, such as demonstrations without a concerted plan from the outset; isolated and sporadic acts of violence, as opposed to military operations carried out by armed forces or armed groups; other acts of a similar nature, including, in particular, large scale arrests of people for their activities or opinions.[150]

The provision in Article 1(2) providing for the exclusion of internal disturbances and tensions was retained from the earlier draft of the Protocol that had same threshold of application as common Article 3.[151] According to the ICRC Commentary on the Protocol, the purpose of this provision 'was to define the lower threshold of the concept of armed conflict, assuming that the field of application of common Article 3 and the Protocol would be identical. The paragraph was not questioned and was retained and adopted without lengthy debates'.[152]

Given the list of objective criteria in Article 1(1), it would appear unnecessary to include a further provision excluding situations of internal disturbance. The inclusion of Article 1(2) is significant as it demarcates the lower threshold of non-international armed conflict and thus the applicability of common Article 3. Commenting on the distinction between situations of non-international armed conflict and internal disturbances, Dietrich Schindler lists the following four conditions as determining the existence of armed conflict:

In the first place, the hostilities have to be conducted by force of arms and exhibit such intensity that, as a rule, the government is compelled to employ its armed forces against insurgents instead of mere police forces. Secondly, as to the insurgents, the hostilities are meant to be of a collective character, that is, they have to be carried out not only by single groups. In addition, the insurgents have to exhibit a minimum amount of organisation. Their armed forces should be under responsible command and be capable of meeting humanitarian requirements. Accordingly, the conflict must show certain similarities to a war without fulfilling all conditions necessary for the recognition of belligerency.[153]

It is clear, however, that the distinction between situations of internal disturbance and non-international armed conflict is not always so apparent. The conditions outlined by Schindler approximate those contained in Article 1(1) of Additional Protocol II. Situations of low-intensity armed conflict outside the remit of the Protocol, necessitating

150 *Ibid.*, p. 1354, para. 4474.

151 *Official Records*, vol. I, part 3: ICRC, 'Draft Additional Protocols to the Geneva Conventions of 1949', 1973, p. 33.

152 ICRC, *Commentary on the Additional Protocols*, p. 1354, para. 4473.

153 Schindler, 'Different Types of Armed Conflicts', at 147.

the application of common Article 3, are often more difficult to differentiate.[154]

Although Additional Protocol II delineates more substantively than common Article 3 the context of application, it nevertheless faces the same obstacle in its implementation: the non-recognition by a state of the existence of armed conflict. In this way, 'the first line of defence against international humanitarian law is to deny that it applies at all'.[155]

3.2.3 *Applicability of Additional Protocol II*

The fear of external interference in internal affairs is no doubt one of the reasons why state practice relating to the implementation of Additional Protocol II is so scarce.[156] The complicated nature of the threshold contained in Article 1(1) is arguably the issue that has most weakened the applicability of this instrument. The Analytical Report of the Secretary-General on Minimum Humanitarian Standards,[157] comments on the threshold contained in Article 1 stating that it 'would appear to limit the application of Protocol II to situations at or near the level of a full-scale civil war, and certainly few Governments are prepared to admit the application of the Protocol to situations of lesser intensity'.[158] The high intensity of hostilities required by Article 1(1) clearly limits considerably the scope of applicability, yet the restrictions inherent in the Protocol's field of application are only one aspect of the problem. In the absence of an impartial mechanism to determine the relevance of the Protocol to particular situations, an issue of more serious concern is the reluctance of states parties to the Protocol to recognise its applicability. The Analytical Report of the Secretary-General states that:

[154] See Bond, *Rules of Riot*, p. 52. See Chapter 4, for conditions determining the lower threshold for the application of common Article 3.

[155] Baxter, 'Some Existing Problems', in *The Concept of International Armed Conflict: Further Outlook* (Proceedings of the International Symposium on Humanitarian Law, Brussels, 1974), at 2.

[156] See Moir, *Law of Internal Armed Conflict*, pp. 119–32. For a survey of state practice relating to Additional Protocol II, see Cho, 'International Humanitarian Law', pp. 32–41. See also Sassoli and Bouvier (eds.), *How Does Law Protect in War?*, vol. I, p. 262.

[157] Minimum Humanitarian Standards: Analytical Report of the Secretary-General Submitted pursuant to Commission on Human Rights Res. 1997/21, UN Doc. E/CN.4/1998/87, 5 January 1998. See generally Petrasek, 'Moving Forward', 557; Momtaz, 'Minimum Humanitarian Rules', 455.

[158] Minimum Humanitarian Standards, para. 79.

Since neither the Protocol nor any other agreement allows for an impartial outside body to decide on whether the criteria are met to apply the Protocol, it is largely left to the goodwill of the Government concerned. This goodwill is often lacking – admitting the application of the Protocol is seen as conferring international legitimacy on the opposition forces (even though such an interpretation is specifically ruled out by another provision of the Protocol), and/or an implicit admission on the Government's part of its lack of effective control in the country.[159]

Recognition of the Protocol's applicability by states engaged in non-international armed conflict is rare. When recognised as such in international fora, situations of non-international armed conflict are generally characterised by third states, international organisations or UN bodies such as the Security Council or the General Assembly. An example of characterisation by a third state is provided by the Swiss Federal Department of Foreign Affairs in its Note of 20 January 1986 on the situation in El Salvador:

[T]he material field of application of the Protocol is defined by using purely objective criteria. As is the case with the Geneva Conventions, both with regard to international armed conflicts and non-international armed conflicts such as those referred to in Article 3 common to the four Conventions, where the objective conditions laid down are satisfied application of the Protocol is triggered automatically – the parties to the conflict do not have to carry out an assessment of the situation as it is in the territory of the State in which they are in conflict.[160]

The Swiss Directorate for Public International Law applied the conditions contained in Article 1(1) of Additional Protocol II to the situation in El Salvador and deemed that they were 'objectively satisfied' by the facts on the ground.[161] While it is not uncommon for individual states to qualify the status of situations for their own purposes, such acts rarely (if ever) occur in isolation from developments within the United Nations.[162] As no impartial body exists for determining the applicability of the Additional Protocol, the implementation of its provisions is

[159] *Ibid.*

[160] Note from the Directorate for Public International Law, in Sassoli and Bouvier (eds.), *How Does Law Protect in War?*, vol. II, p. 1384. Originally printed in *Annuaire Suisse de Droit International*, 1987, pp. 185–7.

[161] Note from the Directorate for Public International Law, in Sassoli and Bouvier (eds.), *How Does Law Protect in War?*, vol. II, p. 1385.

[162] In support of its qualification of the situation in El Salvador, the Directorate for Public International Law noted that 'The General Assembly, the Economic and Social Council and the United Nations Commission on Human Rights have, on several occasions, been concerned at the situation in El Salvador and specifically

dependent upon the will of the state hosting hostilities to recognise the existence of non-international armed conflict within its own territory. From a humanitarian perspective, this is clearly an unsatisfactory state of affairs. As noted in the Analytical Report of the Secretary-General, '[t]he result is that there are many situations of internal violence – including ones leading to thousands of deaths – where there are no clear treaty rules in place to regulate important aspects of the behaviour of the armed forces and armed groups involved. It is revealing to note that there are occasions where the Security Council has determined that an internal situation amounts to a threat to international peace and security (so as to initiate action under the Charter), but where it is unclear as to whether Protocol II would apply.'[163]

Article 1(1) is thus arguably the greatest weakness of Additional Protocol II. It is possible for state parties to avoid the applicability of this instrument by contending that one or more of the conditions contained in Article 1 are unfulfilled. The Analytical Report of the Secretary-General goes on to state that:

> Clearly, from the point of view of the actual or potential victims, this is an unsatisfactory state of affairs. Civilians and civilian objects should be clearly protected against direct and indiscriminate attack in all circumstances. Weapons or methods of warfare the use of which is prohibited in international armed conflicts should also generally be prohibited in situations of internal violence and conflict. Likewise, obligations on armed forces to take precautions in attack so as to reduce the risk of civilian casualties, and detailed rules regarding facilitating and protecting the work of humanitarian agencies providing relief to the civilian population should apply regardless of the nature or scale of the conflict. It seems illogical, and indeed morally indefensible, to suggest that armed forces are free to engage in behaviour against citizens of their own country which would be outlawed were they involved in military operations abroad. Likewise, why should armed groups be held internationally accountable for arbitrarily expelling people from their homes, for example, only when the conflict they are engaged in meets the high threshold established in Protocol II?[164]

The arbitrary nature of the threshold contained in Article 1(1), and its impact on the effectiveness of Additional Protocol II, is also highlighted by Adam Roberts and Richard Guelff:

called for compliance with the Geneva Conventions and the two Additional Protocols.' *Ibid.*

163 Minimum Humanitarian Standards, para. 80. Examples cited by the Report include Res. 794 (1992) of 3 December 1992, 814 (1993) of 26 March 1993 and 837 (1993) of 6 June 1993 on Somalia; and Res. 813 (1993) of 26 March 1993 on Liberia.

164 Minimum Humanitarian Standards, para. 81.

The application of Protocol II in conflicts has been problematical. A number of states parties to the agreement experienced armed conflicts with a substantial element of civil war. These included Colombia, El Salvador, Guatemala, Liberia, Rwanda, Sierra Leone, USSR/Russia, and the former Yugoslavia. In some cases the conflict pre-dated the state becoming a party to the agreement. While the application of the Protocol has been recognized by some of the parties involved, these conflicts have raised questions regarding the extent to which 1977 Geneva Protocol II may be effective in practice.[165]

In assessing the applicability of Additional Protocol II, it is important to bear in mind the object and purpose of the instrument. The third preambular paragraph emphasises 'the need to ensure better protection for the victims of [armed conflicts not of an international character]'. While it is clear that the effectiveness of Additional Protocol II as a tool for the protection of the victims of non-international armed conflict is undermined by the conditions contained in Article 1(1), it is foreseeable that the customary status of provisions may lessen the influence of the threshold. It is noteworthy that the ICRC Study *Customary International Humanitarian Law* includes most of the humanitarian standards contained in Additional Protocol II in its list of customary rules applicable to *all* situations of non-international armed conflict.[166] If the customary status of these rules is accepted, the threshold contained in Article 1(1) loses much of its relevance for the applicability of these standards.

While the scope of Article 1(1) is significantly narrower that than of 'armed conflict not of an international character', the substantive content of Additional Protocol II represents an advancement in expanding the body of international humanitarian law that governs situations of non-international armed conflict. The limitations inherent in Article 1 do not detract from the customary status of the humanitarian provisions contained in the Protocol. As Article 1(1) states that the instrument 'develops and supplements' common Article 3 'without modifying its existing conditions of application', Additional Protocol II does not impact on the field of application associated with 'armed conflict not of an international character'. In this regard, it is worth recalling the words of a delegate at the 1949 Diplomatic Conference that 'half a loaf is better than no bread'.[167]

[165] Roberts and Guelff, *Documents*, p. 482.

[166] See Henckaerts and Doswald-Beck (eds.), *Customary International Humanitarian Law*.

[167] *Final Record*, vol. II-B, Minutes, 29 July 1949, p. 335.

3.3 Concluding observations

The distinctions introduced by Article 1(1) of Additional Protocol II and Article 1(4) are products of a diplomatic conference where the status of national liberation movements was prioritised above the development of international humanitarian law applicable to situations of non-international armed conflict. Article 1(4) of Additional Protocol I clearly boosted the status of such movements at the Conference. The recognition of wars of national liberation as international armed conflicts helped strengthen the international standing of organisations such as the African National Congress, the Angola National Liberation Front, the Mozambique Liberation Front and the Palestine Liberation Organisation. It is clear from the *Official Records of the Diplomatic Conference* that the initiative to include wars of national liberation within the scope of international armed conflict was motivated by considerations of an intrinsically political character as opposed to an appreciation of the need to expand the protection provided by international humanitarian law to the victims of such conflicts. The move to internationalise wars of national liberation at the Diplomatic Conference formed part of a broader political campaign to secure the legitimacy of such movements before the international community. The appropriateness of using the Diplomatic Conference as a venue to address the issue is questionable.

The impact of Article 1(4) on the recognition of Additional Protocol I's applicability by *de jure* governments militarily engaged in the suppression of insurgents is not favourable. For a government to admit the applicability of Additional Protocol I in the context of Article 1(4) would be for it also to implicitly acknowledge the legitimacy of the national liberation movement's campaign and the illegitimacy of its own position in suppressing such dissent. As this is not to the advantage of the state either legally or politically, the provision has the effect of discouraging any formal recognition of the Protocol's applicability by governments engaged in hostilities with national liberation movements.

The creation of a new threshold of application by Article 1(1) of Additional Protocol II was also in many ways a regressive development – rather than bolstering the implementation of international humanitarian law, the heightened threshold serves to strengthen the discretionary power of states to deny the Protocol's applicability. It is dependent upon a higher intensity of armed conflict than that required by common Article 3 and thus is only applicable to 'situations at or near the level of a full-scale civil war'.[168]

Despite the ICRC's intention of providing an objective basis for the application of Additional Protocol II, the problem of characterisation is one that still affects the implementation of this instrument. As pointed out by Rwelamira, '[i]ndividual states are [...] left with a *carte blanche* to decide when the Protocol [...] should be invoked'.[169] The conditions of responsible command, control over territory, the existence of sustained and concerted military operations, and the ability to implement the Protocol, provide ample opportunity for states to contend the non-applicability of the instrument. It is important to recognise that this threshold of application is peculiar to the Protocol and does not reflect customary international law. Many of the norms codified in this instrument have crystallised into customary standards applicable in all situations of non-international armed conflict. If acknowledged as such, the threshold contained in Article 1(1) loses much of its significance for the application of these standards.

The impact of Article 1(4) of Additional Protocol I and Article 1(1) of Additional Protocol II on the applicability of international humanitarian law should not be overstated. While the cohesiveness of this body of law is not helped by these provisions, they should not be interpreted as a fragmenting of applicability. They do not affect the lower threshold for the application of international humanitarian law to situations of non-international armed conflict. If the customary status of the rules contained in the Additional Protocols is recognised, the issue of applicability need only depend on the existence of a state of armed conflict. The chapter that follows investigates this lower threshold for application of international humanitarian law, focusing on characteristics distinguishing situations of non-international armed conflict.

168 Minimum Humanitarian Standards, para. 74.
169 Rwelamira, 'Significance and Contribution', p. 236.

PART II • THE ANATOMY OF NON-INTERNATIONAL ARMED CONFLICT IN INTERNATIONAL HUMANITARIAN LAW

4 The threshold of non-international armed conflict

This chapter examines the threshold distinguishing situations of non-international armed conflict from situations of internal disturbances in light of recent developments. An argument is advanced in support of a particular approach to the application of this threshold in the characterisation of non-international armed conflict. The definition of non-international armed conflict provided in the case law of the International Criminal Tribunal for the former Yugoslavia (ICTY) forms a central tenet of this argument.

The chapter begins with an analysis of the concept of armed conflict developed in the case law of the ICTY. After unpacking the cardinal elements of this concept, and illustrating examples of how it has been applied, the geographical and temporal scope of non-international armed conflict is examined. The development of international humanitarian law to include conflict between non-state actors is also scrutinised as an integral feature of the concept. Another aspect that will be addressed is the question as to whether a state of armed conflict presupposes the existence of responsible command. In summing up the essential features of the non-international armed conflict threshold, the chapter will conclude with some remarks on its future development.

4.1 *Tadić*: a formula for the characterisation of armed conflict

On 2 October 1995 the Appeals Chamber in the *Tadić* case issued its Decision on the Defence Motion for Interlocutory Appeal on Jurisdiction (*Tadić* Jurisdiction Decision).[1] The context of this decision was the trial of Duško Tadić, a Bosnian Serb charged with

[1] *Tadić* Jurisdiction Decision.

crimes against humanity, grave breaches of the Geneva Conventions and violations of the customs of war under Articles 2, 3 and 5 of the ICTY Statute.[2] The Decision addressed, *inter alia*, a challenge that the Tribunal lacked subject-matter jurisdiction to try Tadić for war crimes.[3] Before allegations relating to violations of the laws and customs of war under Article 3 of the ICTY Statute could be considered, the Tribunal first needed to determine the existence of armed conflict. This preliminary issue concerned the status of the situation in Bosnia and Herzegovina from around 24 May until 30 August 1992, the period of time during which it was alleged Tadić committed war crimes including murder, forcible sexual intercourse and abuse of prisoners.[4]

The defence for Tadić contended that 'there did not exist a legally cognizable armed conflict – either internal or international – at the time and place that the alleged offences were committed'.[5] This argument was based on the fact that 'the conflict in the Prijedor region (where the alleged crimes are said to have taken place) was limited to a political assumption of power by the Bosnian Serbs and did not involve armed combat (although movements of tanks are admitted)'.[6] The Appeals Chamber rejected the argument of the appellant on the grounds that 'the temporal and geographical scope of both internal and international armed conflicts extends beyond the exact time and place of hostilities'.[7] The significance of this position will be returned to later in this chapter.[8] At this juncture, attention will be focused on the concept of armed conflict propounded in this decision: '[A]n armed conflict exists whenever there is a resort to armed force between States or protracted armed violence between governmental authorities and organized armed groups or between such groups within a State'.[9]

This description of armed conflict represents a very significant development of international humanitarian law. As noted by Professor Christopher Greenwood,

[2] *Prosecutor* v. *Tadić* (Case No. IT-94-1-AR72), Second Amended Indictment, 14 December 1995.

[3] *Tadić* Jurisdiction Decision, para. 8.

[4] *Tadić* Second Amended Indictment.

[5] *Tadić* Jurisdiction Decision, para. 8. [6] *Ibid.*

[7] *Ibid.* para. 67. [8] See sections 4.2 and 4.3.

[9] *Tadić* Jurisdiction Decision, para. 70.

The definitions of international and internal armed conflict are of considerable importance. Neither term is defined in the Geneva Conventions or other applicable agreements. Whereas there is an extensive literature on the definition of 'war' in international law, armed conflict has always been considered a purely factual notion and there have been few attempts to define or even describe it.[10]

According to Sonja Boelaert-Suominen, a legal adviser at the Office of the Prosecutor:

The seemingly innocuous description by the Appeals Chamber of what constitutes an armed conflict was innovative in various respects. First, it covers a variety of hypotheses and caters explicitly for conflicts between non-state entities. Second, whilst it sets a low threshold for the application of humanitarian law in general, it is particularly important for its consequences in relation to internal armed conflicts. The definition of armed conflict suggested by the Appeals Chamber covers not only the classic examples of (a) an armed conflict between two or more states and (b) a civil war between a state on the one hand, and a non-state entity on the other. It clearly encompasses a third situation, (c) an armed conflict in which no government party is involved, because two or more non-state entities are fighting each other.[11]

The latter part of the definition, referring to 'protracted armed violence between governmental authorities and organized armed groups or between such groups within a State', is particularly significant for its development of the threshold associated with 'armed conflict not of an international character'.[12] The wording has been credited to the Presiding Judge, Professor Antonio Cassese.[13]

The definition clarifies the threshold distinguishing situations of non-international armed conflict in international humanitarian law. It distinguishes broadly the conditions determining the existence of armed conflict, as distinct from situations of internal disturbance. The definition indicates a threshold that is clearly lower than that required by Article 1(1) of Additional Protocol II. As noted by Peter Rowe, '[t]his definition conflates the issue of the degree of intensity of armed action required for an armed conflict to exist and the nature of such a conflict. In the latter context it is wider than Additional Protocol II, which does not encompass an armed conflict between organized groups within a State'.[14]

[10] Greenwood, 'Development of International Law' at 114.

[11] Boelaert-Suominen, 'Yugoslav Tribunal', at 632–3.

[12] For an analysis of the original field of application associated with common Article 3, see Chapter 2, at section 2.2.4.

[13] Rowe, 'International Criminal Tribunal for Yugoslavia', at 697.

[14] *Ibid.*

The definition was applied for the first time in *obiter dicta* by the ICTY to the situation in the Prijedor region of Bosnia and Herzegovina.[15] In doing so, the *Tadić* Appeals Chamber considered grounds for asserting the existence of 'a legally cognizable armed conflict',[16] triggering the application of international humanitarian law:

> Applying the foregoing concept of armed conflicts to this case, we hold that the alleged crimes were committed in the context of an armed conflict ... There has been protracted, large-scale violence between the armed forces of different States and between governmental forces and organized insurgent groups. Even if substantial clashes were not occurring in the Prijedor region at the time and place the crimes allegedly were committed – a factual issue on which the Appeals Chamber does not pronounce – international humanitarian law applies. It is sufficient that the alleged crimes were closely related to the hostilities occurring in other parts of the territories controlled by the parties to the conflict.[17]

The definition propounded in the *Tadić* Jurisdiction Decision on 2 October 1995 has since been widely utilised as a formula for the characterisation of non-international armed conflict. In addition to being applied consistently in the case law of the ICTY,[18] the definition has

[15] The definition of armed conflict was introduced by the Appeals Chamber as an *obiter dictum*. An *obiter dictum* is 'a judicial comment made while delivering a judicial opinion, but one that is unnecessary to the decision in the case and therefore not precedential (although it may be considered persuasive)', Bryan A. Garner, *Black's Law Dictionary* (8th edn; St. Paul: West Publishing, 2004), p. 1102.

[16] *Tadić* Jurisdiction Decision, para. 66. [17] *Ibid.*, para. 70.

[18] See *Ibid.*; *Prosecutor* v. *Tadić* Trial Chamber Judgment, 7 May 1997, ICTY Case No. IT-94-1-AR72, para. 561; *Prosecutor* v. *Delalic, Mucic, Delic and Landzo*, Trial Chamber Judgment, 16 November 1998, ICTY Case No. IT-96-21-T, para. 183; *Prosecutor* v. *Furundzija*, Trial Chamber Judgment, 10 December 1998, ICTY Case No. IT-95-17/1, para. 59; *Prosecutor* v. *Kordic and Cerkez*, Trial Chamber Judgment, 26 February 2001, ICTY Case No. IT-95-14/2-T, para. 24; *Prosecutor* v. *Kordic and Cerkez*, Appeals Chamber Judgment, 17 December 2004, ICTY Case No. IT-95-14/2-T, para. 336; *Prosecutor* v. *Kunarac, Kovac and Vukovic*, Trial Chamber Judgment, 22 February 2001, ICTY Case No. IT-96-23, para. 402; *Prosecutor* v. *Kunarac, Kovac and Vukovic*, Appeals Chamber Judgment, 12 June 2002, ICTY Case No. IT-96-23, para. 56; *Prosecutor* v. *Naletilic and Martinovic*, Trial Chamber Judgment, 31 March 2003, ICTY Case No. IT-98–34-T, para. 177; *Prosecutor* v. *Stakić*, Case No. IT-97-24-T, Judgment, Trial Chamber II, 31 July 2003, para. 568; *Prosecutor* v. *Slobodan Milošević*, Third Chamber Decision on Motion for Judgment of Acquittal (*Milošević* Rule 98bis Decision), ICTY Case No. IT-02-54-T, 16 June 2004, para. 16; *Prosecutor* v. *Blagojevic and Jokic*, Case No. IT-02-60-T, Judgment, Trial Chamber I, 17 January 2005, para. 536; *Prosecutor* v. *Strugar*, Case No. IT-01-42-T, Judgment, Trial Chamber II, 31 January 2005, para. 215; *Prosecutor* v. *Limaj, Bala, and Musliu*, Case No. IT-03-66-T, Judgment, 30 November 2005, para. 84; *Prosecutor* v. *Orić*, Judgment, Case No. IT-03-68-T, Trial Chamber II, 30 June 2006, para. 254; *Prosecutor*

also been employed in the reports of independent experts,[19] international commissions of enquiry[20] and various manuals on the law of armed conflict.[21] It has furthermore been utilised in the case law of the ICTR,[22] the ICJ,[23] the International Criminal Court (ICC)[24] and the Special Court for Sierra Leone.[25] The incorporation of this threshold

v. *Haradinaj et al.*, Judgment, Trial Chamber I, ICTY Case No. IT-04-84-T, 3 April 2008, paras. 37–49; *Prosecutor* v. *Boškoski and Tarčulovski*, Judgment, Trial Chamber II, Case No. IT-04-82-T, 10 July 2008, para. 175.

19 For examples, see Report of the Special Rapporteur on the Human Rights Situation in the Sudan, Sima Samar, UN Doc. E/CN.4/2006/111, 11 January 2006, para. 8; Report of the Independent Expert on the Protection of Human Rights and Fundamental Freedoms while Countering Terrorism, Robert K. Goldman, UN Doc. E/CN.4/2005/103, 7 February 2005, p. 30, fn. 14; Terrorism and Human Rights: Final Report of the Special Rapporteur, Kalliopi K. Koufa, E/CN.4/Sub.2/2004/40, 25 June 2004, p. 30, fn. 23; Report of the Special Rapporteur of the Commission on Human Rights on the Situation of Human Rights in the Palestinian Territories Occupied by Israel since 1967, E/CN.4/2002/32, 6 March 2002, para. 18; Report of the Special Rapporteur of the Commission on Human Rights on the Situation of Human Rights in the Palestinian Territories Occupied by Israel since 1967, A/56/440, 4 October 2001, para. 13; Report on the Situation of Human Rights in Somalia, prepared by the Independent Expert of the Commission on Human Rights, Mona Rishmawi, pursuant to Commission Resolution 1996/57 of 19 April 1996, E/CN.4/1997/88, 3 March 1997, para 54.

20 Report of the Commission of Inquiry on Lebanon pursuant to Human Rights Council Resolution S-2/1, UN Doc. A/HRC/3/2, 23 November 2006, para. 51; Report of the International Commission of Inquiry on Darfur to the United Nations Secretary-General pursuant to Security Council Resolution 1564 of 18 September 2004, 25 January 2005, para. 74. See also Report of the Sierra Leone Truth and Reconciliation Commission, vol. 1, 5 October 2004, para. 57 (available at www.trcsierraleone.org. Last visited: 3 April 2008); Report of the Commission for Reception, Truth and Reconciliation Timor-Leste, 31 October 2005, para. 141 (available at www.etan.org/news/2006/cavr.htm).

21 See, e.g. UK Ministry of Defence, *Manual*, 2004, p. 29; Canadian Department of National Defence, *Prisoner of War Handling Detainees and Interrogation and Tactical Questioning in International Operations*, Joint Doctrine Manual; Ottawa: Department of Defence, 2004, section 1–7, fn. 21; International Institute of Humanitarian Law, *The Manual on the Law of Non-International Armed Conflict with Commentary* (Sanremo: IIHL, 2006), p. 2.

22 *Akayesu*, Judgment, para. 619; *Prosecutor* v. *Rutaganda*, Trial Chamber Judgment, 6 December 1999, ICTR Case No. ICTR-96-3, para. 92.

23 *Democratic Republic of the Congo* v. *Uganda*, ICJ, Case Concerning Armed Activities on the Territory of the Congo, Separate Opinion of Judge Simma, 19 December 2005, para. 23. Available at www.icj-cij.org/icjwww/idocket/ico/ico_judgments/ico_judgment_opinions_simma_20051219.pdf, last visited: 3 April 2008.

24 *Prosecutor* v. *Lubanga* (Case No. ICC-01/04-01/06), Decision on the confirmation of charges, 29 January 2007, para. 233.

25 *Prosecutor* v. *Fofana et al.*, Decision on Appeal against 'Decision on Prosecution's Motion for Judicial Notice and Admission of Evidence', 16 May 2005, Appeals Chamber Decision of the Special Court for Sierra Leone. Separate Opinion of Justice Robertson, para. 32.

into the Rome Statute of the International Criminal Court has been cited as indicative of its customary status.[26]

While the concept of non-international armed conflict created by the definition is distinctly broader in scope than that considered by the drafters of the Geneva Conventions, it is arguably now the most authoritative formulation of the threshold associated with common Article 3. The section that follows examines how the definition has been interpreted in the case law of the ICTY. In doing so, it explores conditions associated with the existence of armed conflict in international humanitarian law.

4.1.1 *Two aspects of non-international armed conflict determining the applicability of international humanitarian Law: the organisation of parties and the intensity of hostilities*

In its judgment on the merits, the *Tadić* Trial Chamber interpreted the definition expounded in the Jurisdiction Decision as a 'test' for the existence of armed conflict and hence also for applicability of common Article 3.[27] The definition 'focuses on two aspects of a conflict; the intensity of the conflict and the organisation of the parties to the conflict'.[28] The Trial Chamber went on to say that in 'an armed conflict of an internal or mixed character, these closely related criteria are used solely for the purpose, as a minimum, of distinguishing an armed conflict from banditry, unorganized and short-lived insurrections, or terrorist activities, which are not subject to international humanitarian law'.[29]

The two aspects of non-international armed conflict stated by the *Tadić* Trial Chamber – the *intensity* of the conflict and the *organisation* of parties to the conflict – provide grounds for the characterisation of a state of armed conflict (and thus also for the application of common Article 3). The Trial Chamber in the *Delalic* case highlighted this interpretation of non-international armed conflict, stating that 'in order to distinguish from cases of civil unrest or terrorist activities, the emphasis is on the protracted extent of the armed violence and the extent of organisation of the parties involved'.[30] This approach was echoed by the *Kordic and Cerkez* Appeals Chamber which stated that 'the requirement of *protracted* fighting is significant in excluding mere cases of civil unrest or single acts of terrorism'.[31]

26 Bothe, 'War Crimes' in Cassese *et al. Rome Statute*, p. 423. The incorporation of the *Tadić* definition into the Rome Statute of the International Criminal Court will be examined in detail in Chapter 6.

27 *Tadić*, Trial Chamber Judgment, para. 562. 28 *Ibid.*

29 *Ibid.* 30 *Delalic et al.*, Trial Chamber Judgment, para. 184.

31 *Kordic and Cerkez*, Appeals Chamber Judgment, para. 341 (emphasis in original).

In interpreting the definition of non-international armed conflict provided by the *Tadić* Jurisdiction Decision, the International Criminal Tribunal for Rwanda (ICTR) employed an approach in line with that of the ICTY. Applying it to the situation in Rwanda, the tribunal held that it was 'necessary to evaluate both the intensity and organisation of the parties to the conflict'.[32]

These two aspects of non-international armed conflict provide a basis for determining the existence of armed conflict and thus also the applicability of international humanitarian law. However, as noted by Idi Gaparayi, an Associate Legal Officer at the ICTY, '[d]etermining what counts as "protracted" armed violence and as a "well-organized" armed group requires a case-specific analysis of the facts'.[33] The sections that follow will examine the terms contained in the *Tadić* definition, focusing in particular on the meaning of 'organized armed group' and 'protracted armed violence'. In doing so, a framework for the analysis of facts on a case-by-case basis will be developed.

4.1.1.1 The organisation of parties

The organisational requirement for the characterisation of armed conflict has been highlighted on a number of occasions by the International Committee of the Red Cross (ICRC). The Seville Agreement on the Organisation of the International Activities of the Components of the International Red Cross and Red Crescent Movement states that 'an armed conflict exists when the armed action is taking place between two or more parties and reflects a minimum of organization'.[34] The importance of organisation was also emphasised by the ICRC in the analysis of situations that are unclear in status.

> Common Article 3 does not define the term 'party to the conflict'. In the case of an international armed conflict, the parties thereto in principle can only be States, but the situation in non-international armed conflicts is less clear, as in

[32] *Akayesu*, Judgment, para. 620.

[33] Gaparayi, 'Milošević Trial', at 753. A similar point was made by the ICTR Trial Chamber in which it stated that 'whether a conflict meets the criteria of Common Article 3 is to be decided on a case by case basis'. *Prosecutor* v. *Musema*, Judgment and Sentence, Trial Chamber I, Case No. ICTR-96-13-A, 27 January 2000, para. 251.

[34] The Seville Agreement, formally known as 'The Agreement on the Organisation of the International Activities on the Components of the International Red Cross and Red Crescent Movement', was an internal agreement within the Red Cross Movement concerning the division of operations between the ICRC and the International Federation of Red Cross and Red Cresent Societies. See 'Agreement on the Organisation of the International Activities of the Components of the International Red Cross and Red Crescent Movement' (1998) 322 *International Review*

such cases at least one party to the conflict is not a State. The general consensus of expert opinion is that armed groups opposing a government must have a minimum degree of organization and discipline – enough to enable them to respect international humanitarian law – in order to be recognized as a party to the conflict.[35]

Similarly, the commentary, *Elements of War Crimes under the Rome Statute of the International Criminal Court*, indicates the parties should be 'organized to a greater or lesser extent' in order for a situation to qualify as one of armed conflict.[36] While the *Tadić* Jurisdiction Decision did not define what constitutes an 'organized armed group',[37] indicators to this effect have been provided by subsequent case law. The Decision on Motion for Judgment of Acquittal (*Milošević* Rule 98bis Decision) rendered in the case of *Prosecutor* v. *Milošević* highlights conditions indicative of the level of organisation required for an armed group to qualify as 'organized' under the *Tadić* definition.[38]

The context of the Rule 98bis Decision concerned the trial of Slobodan Milošević for crimes including violations of the laws or customs of war allegedly committed in Kosovo.[39] As violations of the laws or customs of war cannot occur in the absence of armed conflict, the Trial Chamber examined the situation in Kosovo at the time the alleged violations took place to see if the requirements of the *Tadić* test were fulfilled. In order for the situation to qualify as a legally cognisable armed conflict, hostilities are required to be of sufficient intensity and the parties to the conflict must be organised to a greater or lesser extent. For the *Milošević* Trial Chamber, the latter required an evaluation of the Kosovo Liberation Army (KLA) as an organised armed group. In assessing the level of organisation in the KLA, the Trial Chamber found 'a sufficient body of evidence pointing to the KLA being an organized military force, with an official joint command structure, headquarters,

of the Red Cross 159. Available online at www.icrc.org/web/eng/siteeng0.nsf/iwpList74/02CED570ABFDD384C12/56B66005C9C6. Last visited: 3 April 2008.

[35] ICRC, 'Armed Conflicts Linked to the Disintegration of State Structures: Preparatory Document drafted by the International Committee of the Red Cross for the First Periodical Meeting on International Humanitarian Law, Geneva, 19–23 January 1998'; 23 January 1998. Available at www.icrc.org/web/eng/siteeng0.nsf/html/57JPLQ.

[36] Dörmann *et al.*, *Elements of War Crimes*, p. 442.

[37] This point is also made by Sonja Boelaert-Suominen. See 'Yugoslav Tribunal' at 635.

[38] See generally Idi Gaparayi, 'Milošević Trial', at 752.

[39] *Prosecutor* v. *Milošević, et al.*, Second Amended Indictment, Case No. IT-99-37-PT, 16 October 2001. Available at www.un.org/icty/indictment/english/mil-2ai011029e.htm. Last visited: 3 April 2008.

designated zones of operation, and the ability to procure, transport, and distribute arms'.[40]

The reasoning used in the *Milošević* Rule 98bis Decision was cited in the Judgment of Trial Chamber II in the case of *Prosecutor* v. *Limaj*.[41] In determining the existence of armed conflict during an earlier period in Kosovo, the *Limaj* Trial Chamber applied the *Tadić* test using an approach similar to that of the *Milošević* Trial Chamber.[42] The degree of organisation in the KLA was assessed along with the intensity of hostilities prior to May 1998.[43]

The Judgment of the *Limaj* Trial Chamber detailed how the KLA qualifies as 'an organised armed group' within the meaning of the *Tadić* formula.[44] In assessing the level of organisation in this armed group, considerable emphasis was placed on the role of the General Staff as the main governing body of the KLA.[45] The functions of this body included the appointment of zone commanders,[46] the supply of weapons,[47] the issuance of political statements and communiqués,[48] the distribution of KLA Regulations to units,[49] the authorisation of military action[50] and the assignment of tasks to individuals within the organisation.[51] According to the Trial Chamber, the organised nature of the KLA was also shown in how members of the General Staff were involved in the negotiations with representatives of the European Community and foreign missions based in Belgrade.[52] Diplomatic relations with the KLA developed to the extent that:

> [B]y July 1998 the KLA had become accepted by international representatives, and within Kosovo, as a key party involved in political negotiations to resolve the Kosovo crisis. This discloses and confirms that by that time the KLA had achieved a level of *organizational stability and effectiveness*. In particular this gave it the recognized ability to speak with one voice and with a level of persuasive authority on behalf of its members. Both the KLA's need for secrecy and the existence of an established hierarchy in its ranks is apparent from the

[40] *Prosecutor* v. *Slobodan Milošević*, Trial Chamber Decision, para. 23.

[41] *Limaj et al.*, Judgment, para. 90. [42] *Ibid.*

[43] The time frame was earlier than that of *Milošević*. The charges brought against Milošević concerned the commission of crimes 'beginning on or about 1 January 1999 and continuing until 20 June 1999'. *Prosecutor* v. *Milošević et al.*, Second Amended Indictment, para. 17.

[44] *Limaj et al.*, Judgment, paras. 94–134. [45] *Ibid.*, para. 94.

[46] *Ibid.*, para. 96. [47] *Ibid.*, para. 100.

[48] *Ibid.*, para. 101. [49] *Ibid.*, para. 98.

[50] *Ibid.*, para. 46. [51] *Ibid.*, para. 46.

[52] *Ibid.*, para. 125.

circumstance that individuals involved in negotiations with foreign missions were referred to by a number, apparently corresponding to their level in the KLA hierarchy. Further, from the course of these discussions it appears that the KLA was able to formulate and declare a change of military tactics and also conditions for refraining from further military action. This is indicative that at the time the KLA had the ability to coordinate military planning and activities and to determine a unified military strategy, as well as the ability to conduct military operations of a larger scale.[53]

The level of organisation within the KLA was thus also evidenced by its operational effectiveness. The ability to coordinate a unified military strategy through a chain of command was clearly important in this regard. The Trial Chamber highlighted the role of the command structure utilised by the KLA in overall functioning of the organisation:

[T]he KLA had a General Staff, which appointed zone commanders, gave directions to the various units formed or in the process of being formed, and issued public statements on behalf of the organization. Unit commanders gave combat orders and subordinate units and soldiers generally acted in accordance with these orders. Steps have been established to introduce disciplinary rules and military police.[54]

The ability to recruit, train and equip new members was also cited as evidence of the level of organisation within the KLA.[55] The possession of weapons, including artillery mortars and rocket launchers, was further evidence relevant to this requirement.[56] In the utilisation of these weapons, the intensity of hostilities was emphasised by the Trial Chamber as an additional indicator of the KLA's level of organisation:

By the end of May 1998 KLA units were constantly engaged in armed clashes with substantial Serbian forces in areas from the Kosovo–Albanian border in the west, to near Prishtina/Pristina in the east, to Prizren/Prizren and the Kosovo–Macedonian border in the south and the municipality of Mitrovice/Kosovka Mitrovica in the north. The ability of the KLA to engage in such varied operations is a further indicator of its level of organization.[57]

Evaluating the evidence, the *Limaj* Trial Chamber concluded that 'before the end of May 1998 the KLA sufficiently possessed the characteristics of an organized armed group, able to engage in an internal armed conflict'.[58] Accordingly, the first requirement of the *Tadić* test was fulfilled. The Trial Chamber's analysis of the KLA as an 'organised armed group' reveals a

[53] *Ibid.*, para. 129. Emphasis added.
[54] *Ibid.*, para. 171. [55] *Ibid.* [56] *Ibid.* [57] *Ibid.*, para. 172. [58] *Ibid.*, para. 134.

number of indicators relevant to the application of the *Tadić* definition. It is important however to appreciate, in view of the complex nature of non-international armed conflict, that each situation has to be considered on a case-specific analysis of facts.[59] The requirement of sufficient intensity is closely related to that of organisation and will now be examined in the interpretation of the term 'protracted armed violence'.

4.1.1.2 The intensity of hostilities

Similar to the organisational requirement, the threshold of 'protracted armed violence' requires the interpretation of facts on a case-specific basis. As noted in *Rutaganda*, 'the definition of an armed conflict *per se* is termed in the abstract, and whether or not a situation can be described as an "armed conflict", meeting the criteria of Common Article 3, is to be decided upon on a case-by-case basis'.[60] The need to proceed to consider each situation on its merits is also highlighted by the Inter-American Commission on Human Rights in the *Tablada* case:

> The most difficult problem regarding the application of Common Article 3 is not at the upper end of the spectrum of domestic violence, but rather at the lower end. The line separating an especially violent situation of internal disturbances from the 'lowest' level Article 3 armed conflict may sometimes be blurred and, thus, not easily determined. When faced with making such a determination, what is required in the final analysis is a good faith and objective analysis of the facts in each particular case.[61]

It is useful to consider the terms of the *Tadić* definition as a means of clarifying this threshold for the application of international humanitarian law. It is clear that the intensity required for the existence of armed conflict is above that of internal disturbances and tensions. It is also clear that hostilities need not reach the magnitude of 'sustained and concerned military operations'. The issue is one of clarifying the threshold of intensity that is required for the characterisation of a situation as one of armed conflict. This degree of intensity hinges on the interpretation of the word 'protracted'. The level of armed violence associated with this term determines the applicability of international humanitarian law when the organisational requirement of an armed

[59] *Rutaganda*, Judgment, para. 93. [60] *Ibid.*

[61] Report No. 55/97 Case 11.137, Juan Carlos Abella Argentina [1]/November 18, 1997, para. 153. Available at www.cidh.oas.org/annualrep/97eng/Argentina11137.htm. See also *Akayesu*, Judgment, para. 603.

group is also met. On the use of the term 'protracted', Sonja Boelaert-Suominen comments that

> the decision of the Appeals Chamber seems to indicate that this implies a time element. The case-law of the Tribunal indicates that the terms 'protracted armed violence' should be interpreted in a flexible manner and that 'protracted' does not carry the same meaning as 'sustained'. Accordingly, there is no requirement that military operations be carried out in a sustained or continuous manner.[62]

Similarly, Bahia Thahzib-lie and Olivia Swaak-Goldman state that:

> [T]he protracted requirement is met when the hostilities are extended over time and include events attributable to the conflict. Whether or not hostilities are 'protracted' is assessed by reference to the entire period from the initiation of hostilities to the cessation of hostilities. While an examination of the 'protracted' nature of hostilities might be fairly straightforward in a more classic non-international armed conflict, it is more problematic if several non-State parties are involved. The extent to which hostilities originating from several different non-State parties can be aggregated in considering whether hostilities are protracted will depend on the relationship between the non-State parties.[63]

Thus to the extent that the protracted element is considered, it must be loosely interpreted. It should not be read to require that hostilities be carried out in a sustained or continuous manner. Rather, it should be judged by reference to the entire period of hostilities.

The level of armed violence required for the application of common Article 3 must be high enough to exclude isolated or sporadic acts of violence, but low enough to include situations of internal conflict where hostilities are not necessarily carried out on a continuous basis. The degree of intensity required for the existence of armed conflict was examined in the *Milošević* Rule 98bis Decision. The intensity requirement was assessed focusing on the length or protracted nature of the conflict and the seriousness of armed clashes,[64] the spread of clashes over the territory,[65] the increase in number of governmental

[62] 'Yugoslav Tribunal', at 634.

[63] Thahzib-lie and Swaak-Goldman, 'Determining the Threshold', in Lijnzaad *et al.*, *Making the Voice of Humanity Heard*; Leiden/Boston: Martinus Nijhoff Publishers, 2004, p. 248.

[64] *Milošević*, Trial Chamber Decision on Motion for Judgment of Acquittal (*Milošević* Rule 98bis Decision) Case No. IT-02-54-T, 16 June 2004, para. 28.

[65] *Ibid.*, para.29.

forces sent to Kosovo[66] and the type of weaponry used.[67] In clarifying the threshold for the application of international humanitarian law to the situation, the Trial Chamber made two significant points in response to submissions by *amici curiae*. The *amici curiae*, Steven Kay and Timothy McCormack, submitted that the KLA did not act under an organised civil authority and that, as a consequence, the situation fell short of the threshold of armed conflict.[68] In responding to this claim, the Trial Chamber asserted it did not 'accept existence of a civilian authority as a requirement for the existence of an armed conflict'.[69] In another submission, the *amici curiae* contended that the KLA did not exercise sufficient control over territory.[70] In response, the Trial Chamber stated that it did not 'accept that such control of territory is a requirement for the existence of an armed conflict'.[71] While holding that control over territory and the existence of organised civil authority were not necessary for the characterisation of a situation as one of armed conflict, the Chamber nevertheless noted these conditions did in fact exist in Kosovo during the period relevant to the indictment.[72]

In assessing the intensity of armed violence during a different period of the conflict in Kosovo, the *Limaj* Trial Chamber used a similar approach to that employed by the *Milošević* Trial Chamber.[73] The seriousness of armed clashes,[74] the mobilisation of troops by the government,[75] the kind of weaponry utilised,[76] the destruction of property,[77] the displacement of local population[78] and the existence of casualties[79] were highlighted as conditions indicative of the intensity of hostilities.

In assessing the intensity of hostilities, the Trial Chamber emphasised the level of armed violence between the parties to the conflict and the irrelevance of the purpose for which the parties were fighting:

> The two forces were substantially engaged in their mutual military struggle. While the Serbian forces were far more numerous and better trained and equipped, it appears they were ill-prepared to deal effectively with small guerrilla type forces that would not engage them in prolonged fixed

[66] *Ibid.*, para. 30. [67] *Ibid.*, para. 31.

[68] *Milošević*, Trial Chamber Decision, para. 34. [69] *Ibid.*

[70] *Ibid.*, para. 36. Mr. Steven Kay, QC, and Professor Timothy L.H. McCormack acted as *amici curiae*.

[71] *Ibid.*, para. 36. [72] *Ibid.*, paras. 34, 36.

[73] 'First Trial', at *Prosecutor* v. *Milošević*, Trial Chamber Decision, paras. 26–32.

[74] *Limaj et al.*, Judgment, paras. 135–43 . [75] *Ibid.*, para. 150.

[76] *Ibid.*, para. 166. [77] *Ibid.*, para. 142.

[78] *Ibid.*, paras. 142, 167. [79] *Ibid.*, para. 134.

engagements. Serbian military intelligence may also have overestimated the strength and capability of the KLA at the time so that the Serbian forces were arraigned in greater number and with greater military resources than was warranted by the actual KLA forces. In this respect, as revealed by the evidence, many combat operations were carried out in the area of Drenica where the KLA developed earlier and was probably best organised. But, most importantly in the Chamber's view, the determination of the existence of an armed conflict is based solely on two criteria: the intensity of the conflict and organisation of the parties, the purpose of the armed forces to engage in acts of violence or also achieve some further objective is, therefore, irrelevant.[80]

This statement by the Trial Chamber indicates the irrelevance of *jus ad bellum* in determining the existence of armed conflict. This is an important point to note. Governments have been known to deny the applicability of international humanitarian law on the grounds of not recognising the cause of an organised armed group.[81] It should be emphasised in relation to such cases that the existence of armed conflict is determined on the basis of objective criteria and not the subjective judgement of either party to the conflict. As noted by the ICTR Trial Chamber in *Akayesu*:

It should be stressed that the ascertainment of the intensity of a non-international conflict does not depend on the subjective judgment of the parties to the conflict. It should be recalled that the four Geneva Conventions, as well as the two Protocols, were adopted primarily to protect the victims, as well as potential victims, of armed conflicts. If the application of international humanitarian law depended solely on the discretionary judgment of the parties to the conflict, in most cases there would be a tendency for the conflict to be minimized by the parties thereto. Thus, on the basis of objective criteria, both Common Article 3 and Additional Protocol II will apply once it has been established there exists an internal armed conflict which fulfils their respective pre-determined criteria.[82]

The predetermined criteria relating to common Article 3 are the level of organisation possessed by parties to the conflict and the intensity of hostilities. In relation to the requirement of intensity, it is important to consider the evolution that has taken place in international humanitarian law since the drafting of the Geneva Conventions, in particular since the establishment of the international criminal tribunals for Rwanda and the former Yugoslavia, and to bear in mind that the

[80] *Ibid.*, para. 170. [81] See Chapter 2, at section 2.4.
[82] *Akayesu*, Judgment, para. 603.

characterisation of situations should be approached on a case-by-case basis.

Some studies stipulate a *numerical* threshold of deaths for the recognition of a situation as one of armed conflict. The *Yearbook* of the Stockholm International Peace Research Institute sets a numerical threshold of 1,000 battle-related deaths,[83] while the Uppsala Department of Peace and Conflict Research sets a threshold of twenty-five battle-related deaths.[84] Such numerically defined thresholds would arguably be inappropriate in a legal context for a number of reasons. First, the focus of these thresholds is solely on the number of deaths and the criterion of organisation on the part of non-state actors is overlooked. Second, the number of deaths that occur in the vast majority of armed conflicts represent only a subset of the total number of victims. Third, the stipulation of a numerical threshold would set an unwarranted restriction on the application of common Article 3 and other rules of customary international humanitarian law. The protection that might otherwise be provided by international humanitarian law would no longer apply to many situations, in particular in the early stages of hostilities or in cases of low-intensity armed conflict. As noted by Jean Pictet, '[t]he respect due to the human personality as such is not measured by the number of victims'.[85]

As a condition for determining the existence of armed conflict, the intensity of hostilities is an important consideration for the application of international humanitarian law. While conditions evidencing the intensity of non-international armed conflict are often similar to those of international armed conflict, it is worth noting that the threshold for the application of international humanitarian law to the former is distinctly different from that of the latter. A state of international armed conflict can be said to exist in the absence of hostilities in cases of military occupation. A situation where two or more states are considered 'at war' also qualifies as international armed conflict in the absence of hostilities. Article 2 common to the four Geneva Conventions of 1949 defines the terms of their applicability to such situations. It states that each Convention shall apply to

> all cases of declared war or of any other armed conflict which may arise between two or more of the High Contracting Parties, even if the state of war is not recognized by one of them.

83 SIPRI *Yearbook 2006*.

84 See Wallensteen and Sollenberg, 'Armed Conflict'. See also www.pcr.uu.se/research/UCDP/definition_of_armed_conflict.htm.

85 Pictet, *Commentary II*, p. 27.

> The Convention shall also apply to all cases of partial or total occupation of the territory of a High Contracting Party, even if the said occupation meets with no armed resistance.

As a declaration of war in itself is sufficient to bring into force the Geneva Conventions, it is clear that the requirement of intensity need not be relevant to determining the status of an armed conflict initiated in this way. It is noteworthy also that the second paragraph of Article 2 stresses that the Conventions apply to all cases of occupation 'even if the said occupation meets with no armed resistance'.[86]

Considering that the existence of hostilities is not a prerequisite for international armed conflict, it is clear that the threshold of applicability associated with such situations is distinctly different to that of non-international armed conflict. Any analogy between the two thresholds therefore needs to be carefully qualified. While there is considerable overlap in the customary international law standards applicable to international and non-international armed conflicts, it is important to recognise how such situations are characterised. The former generally manifests itself as 'a resort to armed force between States' while the latter may be characterised according to the level of organisation of armed groups and the intensity of hostilities. As noted in Chapter 2, common Article 3 provides no indication of the degree of intensity required for a situation to qualify as 'armed conflict not of an international character'. At the time of drafting, the material field of application associated with this provision was that of civil war, i.e. an armed conflict of dimensions similar to that of a conventional international war but taking place within the borders of a sovereign state. This concept of non-international armed conflict is now of less contemporary relevance. It bears little resemblance to the current threshold of application of common Article 3. The category of situations that qualify as 'armed conflict not of an international character' has broadened considerably since 1949. The lowering of the threshold of intensity required for the existence of armed conflict has resulted in the extension of the protection provided by international humanitarian law. The definition of non-international armed conflict as 'protracted armed violence between governmental authorities and organized armed groups'

[86] The Elements of Crimes states that 'the term "international armed conflict" includes military occupation.' ICC, Elements of Crimes, UN Doc. PCNICC/2000/1/Add.2 (2000), fn. 34.

has broadened the scope of 'armed conflict not of an international character'. It also implicitly reaffirmed the exclusion of situations of internal disturbance and tensions from the remit of common Article 3. The section that follows will examine applications of the *Tadić* definition in order to illustrate further how the test may be interpreted and to show also its currency as a formula for the characterisation of non-international armed conflict.

4.1.2 Application of the Tadić *formula for the characterisation of armed conflict*

The *Tadić* formula has been applied to various situations to confirm the existence of armed conflict for the application of international humanitarian law. As this standard for the characterisation of armed conflict was first developed in the jurisprudence of the ICTR and the ICTY, it is useful to probe further the case law of these institutions before observing its application in other contexts.

The *Tadić* definition of non-international armed conflict was first applied in the case law of the ICTR when dealing with allegations of violations of international humanitarian law committed by Jean Paul Akayesu.[87] While the UN Security Council had already characterised the situation in Rwanda as one of non-international armed conflict,[88] the ICTR Trial Chamber found it necessary to establish the applicability of common Article 3 and Additional Protocol II individually.[89] The Tribunal determined the applicability of war crimes provisions in the ICTR Statute through the utilisation of the ICRC Commentary on Common Article 3, the ICRC Commentary on Additional Protocol II and the *Tadić* definition of non-international armed conflict. In order to distinguish the situation from ones constituting internal disturbance and tensions, the Chamber stated that it would be 'necessary to evaluate both the intensity and organisation of the parties to the conflict'.[90] Applying this approach to the situation in Rwanda, the Trial Chamber found that there had been:

> A civil war between two groups … Both groups were well-organized and considered to be armies in their own right. Further, as pertains to the intensity of conflict, all observers to the events, including UNAMIR and UN Special

[87] *Akayesu*, Judgment, para. 619. [88] *Ibid.*, para. 605.
[89] *Ibid.*, para. 607.
[90] *Ibid.*, 620. The Trial Chamber described de facto armed conflict as 'the existence of hostilities between armed forces organised to a greater or lesser extent', *ibid.*

rapporteurs, were unanimous in characterizing the confrontation between the two forces as a war, an internal armed conflict. Based on the foregoing, the Chamber finds there existed at the time of the events alleged in the Indictment an armed conflict not of an international character as covered by Common Article 3 of the 1949 Geneva Conventions.[91]

After confirming the application of common Article 3, the Trial Chamber went on to state that the situation also met the requirements of Article 1(1) of Additional Protocol II:

In addition to the requirements of Common Article 3 being met, that the material conditions listed above relevant to Additional Protocol II have been fulfilled. It has been shown that there was a conflict between, on the one hand, the RPF [Rwandan Patriotic Front], under the command of General Kagame, and, on the other, the governmental forces, the FAR [Rwandan Armed Forces]. The RPF increased its control over the Rwandan territory from that agreed in the Arusha Accords to over half of the country by mid-May 1994, and carried out continuous and sustained military operations until the cease fire on 18 July 1994 which brought the war to an end. The RPF troops were disciplined and possessed a structured leadership which was answerable to authority. The RPF had also stated to the International Committee of the Red Cross that it was bound by the rules of International Humanitarian law. The Chamber finds the said conflict to have been an internal armed conflict within the meaning of Additional Protocol II. Further, the Chamber finds that conflict took place at the time of the events alleged in the Indictment.[92]

The *Tadić* definition of non-international armed conflict was utilised again before the ICTR in the *Rutaganda* case.[93] Here the approach employed in *Akayesu* was referred to: '[I]n dealing with this issue, the *Akayesu Judgment* suggested an "evaluation test", whereby it is necessary to evaluate the intensity and the organisation of the parties to the conflict to make a finding on the existence of an armed conflict. This approach also finds favour with the Trial Chamber in this instance.'[94] A similar line of reasoning was followed by the ICTR Trial Chamber in *Musema*:

The expression 'armed conflicts' introduces a material criterion: the existence of open hostilities between armed forces which are organized to a greater or

[91] *Ibid.*, para. 621. [92] *Ibid.*, para. 627.
[93] *Rutaganda*, Judgment, 6 December 1999, para. 93. [94] *Ibid.*

lesser degree. Internal disturbance and tensions, characterized by isolated or sporadic acts of violence, do not therefore constitute armed conflicts in the legal sense, even if the government is forced to resort to police forces or even armed units for the purpose of restoring law and order. Within these limits, non-international armed conflicts are situations in which hostilities break out between armed forces or organized armed groups within the territory of a single State.

Having defined the term in an abstract manner, to the Chamber it is apparent that whether a conflict meets the criteria of Common Article 3 is to be decided on a case by case basis.

In dealing with this issue, the Akayesu Judgment suggested an 'evaluation test' whereby the Trial Chamber evaluated the intensity and organization of the parties to the conflict to make a finding on the existence of an armed conflict not of an international character.

This approach, followed as well in the Rutaganda Judgment, finds favour with the Trial Chamber of this instance.[95]

The approach employed by the ICTR is naturally in line with that of its sister institution the ICTY.[96] The *Tadić* definition has been employed consistently in the case law of the ICTY[97] and has been described in a recent judgment as 'well-settled in the jurisprudence of the Tribunal'.[98] The first context of its application, discussed earlier in the chapter, was to a situation in Bosnia and Herzegovina.[99] The status

95 *Musema*, Judgment and Sentence, paras. 248–51.

96 The principle of *stare decisis* applies to decisions of both tribunals. *Stare decisis* is 'the doctrine of precedent, under which it is necessary for a court to follow earlier judicial decisions when the same points arise again in litigation'. Bryan A. Garner, *Black's Law Dictionary* (8th edn; St. Paul: West Publishing, 2004), p. 1443.

97 This was noted in *Limaj et al.*, Judgment, para. 84.

98 *Orić*, Judgment, para. 254.

99 The *Tadić* Trial Chamber confirmed the existence of armed conflict in the region but did not rule on its classification as either internal or international:

> Having regard then to the nature and scope of the conflict in the Republic of Bosnia and Herzegovina and the parties involved in that conflict, and irrespective of the relationship between the Federal Republic of Yugoslavia (Serbia and Montenegro) and the Bosnian Serb forces, the Trial Chamber finds that, at all relevant times, an armed conflict was taking place between the parties to the conflict in the Republic of Bosnia and Herzegovina of sufficient scope and intensity for the purposes of the application of the laws or customs of war embodied in Article 3 common to the four Geneva Conventions of 12 August 1949, applicable as it is to armed conflicts in general, including armed conflicts not of an international character.
> *Tadić*, Trial Chamber Judgment, para. 568.

of situations in this state was also examined in *Celebici*,[100] *Orić*[101] and *Hadžihasanović*.[102]

In addition to Bosnia and Herzegovina, the *Tadić* definition of non-international armed conflict was furthermore applied to determine the status of situations in Croatia.[103] Decisions from the *Milošević* and *Limaj* cases relating to situations in Kosovo have thus far however

[100] The object of *Celebici* Trial Chamber's deliberations concerned allegations of war crimes committed in the municipality of Konjic. The existence of armed conflict in this region was confirmed mainly by reference to the intensity of hostilities:

> The level of the fighting in Bosnia and Herzegovina as a whole, as in Konjic itself, was clearly intense and consequently attracted the concern of the United Nations Security Council and General Assembly, along with other international organizations. Acting under Chapter VII of the United Nations Charter, the Security Council passed numerous resolutions in relation to the conflict and consistently called upon all of the parties involved to put an end to their military operations.
>
> In Konjic, the TO and MUP were joined for a short period by the HVO as part of a Joint Command established and organized to fight the Serb forces. At the very least, these forces representing the 'governmental authorities' were engaged against the forces of the Bosnian Serbs – the JNA and VRS joined by local volunteers and militias – who themselves constituted 'governmental authorities' or 'organized armed groups'. This finding is without prejudice to the possibility that the conflict may in fact have been international and the parties involved States and their representatives.
>
> The Trial Chamber must therefore conclude that there was an 'armed conflict' in Bosnia and Herzegovina in the period relevant to the Indictment and notes that, regardless of whether or not this conflict is considered internal or international, it incorporated the municipality of Konjic. Thus, the first fundamental precondition is met for the application of international humanitarian law, including those norms of the law incorporated in Articles 2 and 3 of the Statute, to the present case, providing there is shown to be a sufficient nexus between the alleged acts of the accused and this armed conflict.

Delalic et al., paras. 190–2.

[101] *Prosecutor* v. *Orić*, Judgment, Trial Chamber II, Case No. IT-03-68-T, 30 June 2006, para. 259.

[102] See section 4.2.1.

[103] The characterisation of the situation in Croatia was dealt with in the judgments of both Trial Chamber and the Appeal Chamber in the *Kunarac* case. The ruling of the Trial Chamber on the status of the situation as one of armed conflict was upheld by the Appeal Chamber. Both chambers refer to the *Tadić* definition of non-international armed conflict in discussions relating to the applicability of Article 3 of the ICTY Statute. *Kunarac et al.*, Trial Chamber Judgment, para 402; *Kunarac et al.*, Appeals Chamber Judgment, 1 para. 56. These rulings will be discussed further at section 4.2, relating to the geographical scope of internal armed conflict.

The status of the situation in Croatia was also dealt with in the *Furundzija* case. Here the *Tadić* definition of non-international armed conflict was applied in determining the existence of armed conflict between the Croatian Defence Council (HVO) and the Army of Bosnia and Herzegovina (ABiH) during May

carried more important elucidations of the threshold for non-international armed conflict. As illustrated above at section 4.1.1, the content of these decisions is of particular significance to the interpretation of the twin criteria associated with the *Tadić* definition.

In addition to its use by the ICTR and the ICTY, the *Tadić* definition of non-international armed conflict has also been applied to determine the status of situations in a number of other contexts. These situations include Palestine,[104] the Sudan,[105] Somalia,[106] Sierra Leone,[107] Lebanon[108] and East Timor.[109]

The Special Rapporteur of the Commission on Human Rights on the situation of human rights in the Palestinian territories, John Dugard, used the definition on a number of occasions in evaluating the status of the situation in the Occupied Palestinian Territories of the Middle East.[110] In a report issued on the 4 October 2001 he stated that the situation could be characterised, 'on an irregular and sporadic basis', as an armed conflict due to the 'frequent exchanges of gunfire between the Israel Defence Forces and Palestinian gunmen'.[111]

Mona Rishmawi, an Independent Expert of the Commission on Human Rights, applied the *Tadić* definition to the situation in Somalia in order to determine the existence of armed conflict and thus the applicability of international humanitarian law. Accordingly, she held

1993. The Trial Chamber's findings, however, dealt briefly with the matter. It did not elaborate on how the formula was applied or why evidence presented by the prosecutor met the requirements for the existence of armed conflict. *Prosecutor* v. *Furundzija*, Trial Chamber Judgment, 10 December 1998, Case No. IT-95-17/1, para. 59.

104 Report of the Special Rapporteur, para. 13; Report of the Special Rapporteur, E/CN.4/2002/32, para. 18.

105 For examples, see Report of the Special Rapporteur, UN Doc. E/CN.4/2006/111, para. 8; Report of the International Commission of Inquiry on Darfur to the United Nations Secretary-General Pursuant to Security Council Resolution 1564 of 18 September 2004, 25 January 2005, para. 74.

106 Report on the Situation of Human Rights in Somalia, E/CN.4/1997/88, para 54.

107 See also Report of the Sierra Leone Truth and Reconciliation Commission, vol. 1, 5 October 2004, para. 57 (available at www.trcsierraleone.org. Last visited: 3 April 2008).

108 Report of the Commission of Inquiry on Lebanon pursuant to Human Rights Council Resolution S-2/1, UN Doc. A/HRC/3/2, 23 November 2006, para. 51.

109 Report of the Commission for Reception, Truth, and Reconciliation Timor-Leste, 31 October 2005, para. 141 (available at www.etan.org/news/2006/cavr.htm.

110 Report of the Special Rapporteur, E/CN.4/2002/32, 6 para. 18; Report of the Special Rapporteur, A/56/440, para. 13.

111 Report of the Special Rapporteur, E/CN.4/2002/32, para. 18; Report of the Special Rapporteur, A/56/440, para. 13.

that 'as long as the faction leaders, the militias and other irregular armed forces continue their conflict in Somalia and until a peaceful settlement is reached, international humanitarian law related to internal armed conflict applies in the whole territory of Somalia irrespective of whether the specific area is engulfed in active fighting'.[112]

In explaining the work of the Sierra Leone Truth and Reconciliation Commission in relation to violations of international humanitarian law, the report of the Commission cites the definition of armed conflict provided by and states:

With regard to its work the Commission has assumed the existence of armed conflict throughout the timeframe defined in section 6(1) of the Act. It seems appropriate to consider that international humanitarian law continued to apply within Sierra Leone subsequent to the Lomé Peace Agreement and probably until 18 January 2002, when the conflict was officially declared to have come to an end.[113]

The Report of the International Commission of Inquiry on Darfur to the United Nations Secretary-General referred to the formula provided by the *Tadić* Jurisdiction Decision in its evaluation of the situation's status. In matching the facts of the situation to this formula,[114] the Commission recognised the situation as one of non-international armed conflict rendering common Article 3 applicable:

The conflict in Darfur opposes the Government of the Sudan to at least two organized armed groups of rebels, namely the Sudan Liberation Movement/Army (SLM/A) and the Justice and Equality Movement (JEM). As noted above, the first two groups of insurgents took up arms against the central authorities

[112] Report on the Situation of Human Rights in Somalia, E/CN.4/1997/88, para. 55.

[113] Report of the Sierra Leone Truth and Reconciliation Commission, vol. 1, para. 57.

[114] It should be noted however that the approach adopted by the Commission on Inquiry is not entirely consistent with the jurisprudence of the ICTY. The Report of the Commission on Inquiry refers to the 'existence of organised armed groups fighting against the central authorities' as a requirement of 'internal armed conflict under common Article 3 of the Geneva Conventions'. In doing so, it overlooks the possibility of a state of armed conflict occurring between organised armed groups without the involvement of state authorities. The Report also refers to 'control by rebels over part of the territory' as a requirement for the charartcrisation of a situation as one of non-international armed conflict. This appears to set a much higher threshold for the application of international humanitarian law than that which would normally be required for the application of common Article 3. See Report of the International Commission of Inquiry on Darfur, 25 January 2005, para. 75.

in or around 2002. However, the scale of rebel attacks increased noticeably in February 2003. The rebels exercise *de facto* control over some areas of Darfur. The conflict therefore does not merely amount to a situation of internal disturbances and tensions, riots, or isolated and sporadic acts of violence. Rather, the requirements of (i) existence of organized armed groups fighting against the central authorities, (ii) control by rebels over part of the territory and (iii) protracted fighting, in order for this situation to be considered an internal armed conflict under common Article 3 of the Geneva Conventions are met.[115]

A further example of the application of the *Tadić* definition by a fact-finding body is provided in the Report of the Commission of Inquiry on Lebanon relating to the 'grave situation of human rights in Lebanon caused by Israeli military operations'.[116] The Report of the Commission states that:

It is well established in international humanitarian law that for the existence of an armed conflict the decisive element is the factual existence of the use of armed force. That aside, there is authority for the proposition that an armed conflict exists whenever there is a resort to armed force between States or protracted armed violence between governmental authorities and organized armed groups or between such groups within a State. International humanitarian law applies as soon as an armed conflict arises and it binds all the parties thereto to fully comply with it. On the basis of the factual circumstances of the conduct of the hostilities that took place, including the intensity of the violence and the use of armed force, the Commission is of the view that the existence of an armed conflict during the relevant period has been sufficiently established.[117]

The different contexts to which the *Tadić* definition has been applied indicate the authoritative standing it has acquired as a formula for the characterisation of non-international armed conflict in international humanitarian law. It is worth noting, in addition to the sources referred to in this section, that the definition has also been incorporated into the Rome Statute of the International Criminal Court. This will be returned to later in Chapter 5. The section that follows will examine the geographical scope of the *Tadić* definition of non-international armed conflict.

[115] *Ibid.*

[116] Report of the Commission of Inquiry on Lebanon pursuant to Human Rights Council Resolution S-2/1, UN Doc. A/HRC/3/2, 23 November 2006, para. 51.

[117] *Ibid.*

4.2 The geographical scope of non-international armed conflict

In considering grounds for recognising the existence of armed conflict in Prijedor the *Tadić* Appeals Chamber held, in accordance with the definition of non-international armed conflict referred to above, that 'the temporal and geographical scope of both internal and international armed conflicts extends beyond the exact time and place of hostilities'.[118] International humanitarian law thus pertains not only to those areas where actual fighting is taking place: it applies to the entire territory of the state involved in armed conflict. This position clearly strengthens the reach of international humanitarian law. It is expressed consistently in the jurisprudence of the Tribunal.[119] The Trial Chamber in the *Blaskic* case referred to the definition of armed conflict provided by the *Tadić* Jurisdiction Decision as a 'criterion' applicable

> to all conflicts whether international or internal. It is not necessary to establish the existence of an armed conflict within each municipality concerned. It suffices to establish the existence of the conflict within the whole region of which the municipalities are a part.[120]

Similarly, in *Kordic and Cerkez* the Trial Chamber stated that

> in order for norms of international humanitarian law to apply in relation to a particular location, there need not be actual combat activities in that location. All that is required is a showing that a state of armed conflict existed in the larger territory of which a given location forms a part.[121]

In the *Kunarac* case, the Trial Chamber applied the *Tadić* definition of non-international armed conflict to determine the existence of armed conflict between Bosnian Serbs and Bosnian Muslims in the municipalities of Foca, Gacko and Kalinovik.[122] In doing so it held that a state

[118] *Tadić* Jurisdiction Decision, para. 67.

[119] See *Delalic et al.*, Trial Chamber Judgment, para. 185; *Prosecutor* v. *Blaskic*, Trial Chamber Judgment, 3 March 2000, ICTY Case No. IT-95-14, para. 64; *Kunarac et al.*, Trial Chamber Judgment, paras. 402 and 567; *Naletilic and Martinovic*, Trial Chamber Judgment, para. 177; *Kordic and Cerkez*, Appeals Chamber Judgment, para. 319.

[120] *Blaskic*, Trial Chamber Judgment, para. 64.

[121] *Kordic and Cerkez*, Trial Chamber Judgment, para. 27. The findings of the Trial Chamber on this point were supported in the Judgment of the Appeals Chamber. *Kordic and Cerkez*, Appeals Chamber Judgment, para. 319.

[122] *Kunarac et al.*, Trial Chamber Judgment, paras. 402 and 567. Similar to the *Furundzija* Trial Chamber's finding, the finding of the *Kunarac* Trial Chamber does not elaborate on its application of the *Tadić* formula.

of armed conflict existed in the region relevant to the indictment and emphasised that international humanitarian law applies continuously to the whole of the territory under the control of one of the parties, whether or not actual combat takes place there.[123] While the defence conceded the existence of an armed conflict in Foca, this finding was appealed on the grounds that the Trial Chamber had erred, *inter alia*, in establishing the existence of armed conflict in Gacko and Kalinovik.[124] In responding to this challenge, the Appeals Chamber stated pointedly that:

> [T]he Prosecutor did not have to prove that there was an armed conflict in each and every square inch of the general area. The state of armed conflict is not limited to the areas of actual military combat but exists across the entire territory under the control of the warring parties. The Appeals Chamber finds that ample evidence was adduced before the Trial Chamber to demonstrate that an armed conflict was taking place in the municipalities of Gacko and Kalinovik at the relevant time.[125]

The language used by the Appeals Chamber in this case places emphasis on the broad geographical scope of international humanitarian law. The position originally expressed in the *Tadić* Jurisdiction Decision is reproduced in the *Kunarac* Appeal Chamber's Judgment:

> There is no necessary correlation between the area where the actual fighting is taking place and the geographical reach of the laws of war. The laws of war apply in the whole territory of the warring states or, in the case of internal armed conflicts, the whole territory under the control of a party to the conflict, whether or not actual combat takes place there, and continue to apply until a general conclusion of peace or, in the case of internal armed conflicts, until a peaceful settlement is achieved. A violation of the laws or customs of war may therefore occur at a time when and in a place where no fighting is actually taking place. As indicated by the Trial Chamber, the requirement that the acts of the accused must be closely related to the armed conflict would not be negated if the crimes were temporally and geographically remote from the actual fighting. It would be sufficient, for instance, for the purpose of this requirement, that the alleged crimes were closely related to hostilities occurring in other parts of the territories controlled by the parties to the conflict.[126]

[123] *Kunarac et al.*, Trial Chamber Judgment, para. 568.

[124] *Kunarac et al.*, Appeals Chamber Judgment, para. 49.

[125] *Ibid.*, para. 56. [126] *Ibid.*, para. 57.

The prosecution of war crimes is thus dependent upon: (a) the existence of armed conflict; and (b) a nexus to armed conflict.[127] The broad interpretation given to the geographical scope of armed conflict is not without significance. In so far as it avoids fragmentation of status, it facilitates a greater degree of clarity and cohesiveness in the application of international humanitarian law to situations of non-international armed conflict. The Trial Chamber in the *Delalic* case states that 'whether or not the conflict is deemed to be international or internal, there does not have to be actual combat activities in a particular location for the norms of international humanitarian law to be applicable'.[128] The continuity of applicability is preserved by this position preventing interpretations of the law that would arbitrarily deprive victims of the protection it provides.

4.3 The temporal scope of non-international armed conflict

The Tribunal's position concerning the temporal scope of armed conflict confirms the constant applicability of international humanitarian law to situations of protracted armed violence where hostilities are not necessarily to be characterised as continuous.[129] Indeed, the use of the term 'protracted' in the Tribunal's definition of non-international armed conflict implies that hostilities need not require, unlike Additional Protocol II, the use of 'sustained and concerted' military operations.[130] As interruptions in fighting do not suspend the obligations of the parties under international humanitarian law, the

[127] The existence of a nexus to the armed conflict is an important requirement for the prosecution of war crimes. In order to hold a person responsible for such offences, the acts of the accused must be closely related to the hostilities. *Delalic et al.*, Trial Chamber Judgment, para. 185; *Naletilic and Martinovic*, Trial Chamber Judgment, para. 177. While the geographical scope of the armed conflict concept is to be broadly interpreted, the nexus requirement ensures a degree of balance in the applicability of international humanitarian law. As noted by the *Naletilic* Trial Chamber:

> Once it is established that an armed conflict occurred in a territory, the norms of international humanitarian law apply. It is not necessary to further establish that actual combat activities occurred in a particular part of the territory. The existence of an armed conflict nexus is established if the alleged crimes 'were closely related to the hostilities'.

Naletilic and Martinovic, Trial Chamber Judgment, para. 177.

[128] *Delalic et al.*, Trial Chamber Judgment, para. 185.

[129] See Zimmermann, 'War Crimes', in O. Triffterer (ed.), *Commentary on Statute of the International Criminal Court* (Verlagsgesellschaft: Baden-Baden, 1999), p. 285.

[130] See Zimmermann, 'War crimes'.

use of 'protracted' in the Tribunal's definition allows for a broad interpretation of the non-international armed conflict threshold. Given its breadth, a question may be raised concerning the parameters of reasonable interpretation. As discussed earlier, implicit in the term 'protracted armed violence' is that the hostilities in question must possess a certain degree of intensity. It also implies the conflict must be of a certain duration. The duration required, like the aspect of intensity, is subject to interpretation and should be assessed on the basis of a case-specific analysis of facts. According to the jurisprudence of the Inter-American Commission on Human Rights however it would appear that if the other characteristics of armed conflict are fulfilled the temporal aspect need not exceed a couple of days. As the findings of the Commission are relevant to subsequent discussion, it is useful here to look at the *La Tablada* case in order to explore its interpretation of the temporal aspect of non-international armed conflict.

According to the decision of the Inter-American Commission on Human Rights in the *La Tablada* case, 'Common Article 3 is generally understood to apply to low intensity and open armed confrontations between relatively organized armed forces or groups that take place within the territory of a particular State.'[131] On the threshold determining the existence of armed conflict, the Commission held that:

> In contrast to these situations of domestic violence, the concept of armed conflict, in principle, requires the existence of organized armed groups that are capable of and actually do engage in combat and other military actions against each other. In this regard, Common Article 3 simply refers to, but does not actually define 'an armed conflict of a non-international character'. However, Common Article 3 is generally understood to apply to low intensity and open armed confrontations between relatively organized armed forces or groups that take place within the territory of a particular State. Thus, Common Article 3 does not apply to riots, mere acts of banditry or an *unorganised* and short-lived rebellion. Article 3 armed conflicts typically involve armed strife between governmental armed forces and organized armed insurgents. It also governs situations where two or more armed factions confront one another without the intervention of governmental forces where, for example, the established government has dissolved or is too weak to intervene. It is important to understand that application of Common Article 3 does *not* require the existence of large-scale and generalized hostilities or a situation comparable

[131] Case 11.137 (*La Tablada*), Juan Carlos Abella Argentina, Report N° 55/97 of the Inter-American Commission on Human Rights, 18 November 1997, para. 152. Available at www.cidh.oas.org/annualrep/97eng/Argentina11137.htm.

to a civil war in which dissident armed groups exercise control over parts of national territory.[132]

The issue before the Commission concerned an attack on a military base in Argentina. In order to determine the applicability of international humanitarian law, the Commission had to evaluate the status of the situation and decide on its characterisation as one of either armed conflict or internal disturbance.

The Commission believes that before it can properly evaluate the merits of the petitioner's claims concerning the recapture of the La Tablada base by the Argentine military, it must first determine whether the armed confrontation at the base was merely an example of an 'internal disturbance or tensions' or whether it constituted a non-international or internal armed conflict within the meaning of Article 3 common to the four 1949 Geneva conventions ('Common Article 3'). Because the legal rules governing an internal armed conflict vary significantly from those governing situations of internal disturbances or tensions, a proper characterization of the events at the La Tablada military base on January 23 and 24, 1989 is necessary to determine the sources of applicable law. This, in turn, requires the Commission to examine the characteristics that differentiate such situations from Common Article 3 armed conflicts in light of the particular circumstances surrounding the incident at the La Tablada base.[133]

The Commission drew on the concept of internal disturbances and tensions outlined by the ICRC Commentary on Additional Protocol II to elucidate the distinction demarcating the applicability of international humanitarian law in situations of non-international armed conflict:

- riots, that is to say, all disturbances *which from the start are not directed by a leader and have no concerted intent*;
- isolated and sporadic acts of violence, *as distinct from military operations carried out by armed forces or organized armed groups*;
- other acts of a similar nature which incur, in particular, mass arrests of persons because of their behaviour or political opinion.[134]

Despite its brevity, spanning only two days, the Commission considered the event to rise above the threshold of internal disturbances to merit the application of international humanitarian law:

Based on a careful appreciation of the facts, the Commission does not believe that the violent acts at the La Tablada military base on January 23 and 24, 1989

[132] *La Tablada*, para. 152. [133] *Ibid.*, para. 148.
[134] *Ibid.*, para. 149. Emphasis added by Commission.

can be properly characterized as a situation of internal disturbances. What happened there was not equivalent to large scale violent demonstrations, students throwing stones at the police, bandits holding persons hostage for ransom, or the assassination of government officials for political reasons – all forms of domestic violence not qualifying as armed conflicts.

What differentiates the events at the La Tablada base from these situations are the concerted nature of the hostile acts undertaken by the attackers, the direct involvement of governmental armed forces, and the nature and level of the violence attending the events in question. More particularly, the attackers involved carefully planned, coordinated and executed an armed attack, i.e., a military operation, against a quintessential military objective – a military base. The officer in charge of the La Tablada base sought, as was his duty, to repulse the attackers, and President Alfonsín, exercising his constitutional authority as Commander-in-Chief of the armed forces, ordered that military action be taken to recapture the base and subdue the attackers.

The Commission concludes therefore that, despite its brief duration, the violent clash between the attackers and members of the Argentine armed forces triggered application of the provisions of Common Article 3, as well as other rules relevant to the conduct of internal hostilities.[135]

This decision of the Inter-American Commission of Human Rights sets a low temporal requirement for the application of international humanitarian law in situations of non-international armed conflict. While the definition of armed conflict requires the existence of 'protracted' hostilities, it appears from the *La Tablada* case that this temporal element need not exceed a couple of days. This is a significant clarification of the law of armed conflict for the reason that it precludes expansive interpretations of the time required for a situation to merit the application of international humanitarian law. According to the reasoning of the Commission, the application of international humanitarian law to situations of non-international armed conflict may be asserted where the material conditions manifesting a state of armed conflict are met despite being brief in duration.

If applied to the definition of non-international armed conflict propounded by the ICTY, the position of the Inter-American Commission on Human Rights would appear to infer that a situation of 'protracted armed violence' need not be measured in terms of weeks or months in order for it to be characterised as an armed conflict. The fact that the La Tablada incident lasted only thirty hours is indicative of the broad temporal scope that is sometimes assumed for application of international humanitarian norms in situations of non-international

[135] *Ibid.*, paras. 154–6.

armed conflict.[136] The temporal element should not however be considered independently of other conditions governing the applicability of international humanitarian law. As noted earlier, all aspects are interrelated and must be considered on a case-by-case basis.

4.4 The existence of armed conflict between non-state actors

The application of international humanitarian law to hostilities between non-state armed groups was not an issue considered by the drafters of the Geneva Conventions of 1949. As illustrated in Chapter 2, the term indicating common Article 3's field of application, 'armed conflict not of an international character',[137] was understood by delegates at the Diplomatic Conference as referring to situations akin to civil war.[138] Civil wars, by definition, required the participation of an armed force representing a *de jure* government.[139] As the prevailing standard was that of belligerency,[140] the idea that common Article 3 would also cover conflicts between non-state actors without the involvement of a *de jure* government would have appeared somewhat incongruous to the drafters of the Geneva Conventions. International humanitarian law has however developed to cover such situations. As noted by A.P.V. Rogers:

> The existence of an armed conflict does not necessarily mean that there is an armed contention between the state and an insurgent faction. There can be an armed conflict between factions within a state. Some light has been thrown on these issues by the important ruling on jurisdiction of the Appeals Chamber of the International Criminal Tribunal for the Former Yugoslavia in the *Tadić* case.[141]

The definition of non-international armed conflict as 'protracted armed violence between governmental authorities and armed groups *or between such groups*' by the *Tadić* Appeals Chamber confirms the applicability of international humanitarian law to conflicts lacking any involvement of governmental authorities. The approach taken by the Appeals Chamber

[136] This is viewed by some authors as a positive development of the law. For Bahia Thahzib-lie and Olivia Swaak-Goldman, the protracted requirement does not 'immunise acts committed in the early stages of a conflict'. 'Determining the Threshold', p. 248.

[137] As noted by Sonja Boelaert-Suominen, 'the ICRC commentary to Common Article 3, and especially the criteria suggested by the ICRC for its application, do not cater for the hypothesis of conflicts between non-State entities'. 'Yugoslav Tribunal' at 633.

[138] See Chapter 2, at section 2.1.2.

[139] See Chapter 2, at section 2.1.1

[140] On the doctrine of belligerency, see Chapter 1, at section 1.4.

[141] Rogers, *Law on the Battlefield*, p. 218.

on this issue indicates an important development of international humanitarian law. Support for this development is evidenced not only by the extensive utilisation of the *Tadić* definition of non-international armed conflict, but also by the incorporation of the definition's terms into the Rome Statute of the International Criminal Court.

It is noteworthy that the position taken by the ICRC prior to *Tadić* was to encourage the application of international humanitarian law in such situations. In its Commentary on Additional Protocol II, the ICRC notes the rejection of its proposal for the Protocol to apply to armed conflict between non-state armed groups:

> In its draft the ICRC had provided that the Protocol would be applicable in the case of several factions confronting each other without involvement of the government's armed forces, for example, if the established government had disappeared or was too weak to intervene. Such a situation, it appeared to the Conference, was merely a theoretical textbook example and the provision was dropped, even though the ICRC had already been confronted with this type of situation.[142]

The ICRC Commentary goes on to say that as a consequence of this, the definition of non-international armed conflict contained in Additional Protocol II 'does not cover such cases and only common Article 3 will apply to them'.[143] The Commentary was published in 1987, eight years before the *Tadić* Jurisdiction Decision. The position expressed in the Commentary on the applicability of common Article 3 to conflicts between non-state actors indicates the ICRC's interest in the formal extension of international humanitarian law to cover such situations. A position paper issued by the ICRC in January of 1998 argued for a similar approach to the issue of common Article 3's applicability:

> Given the humanitarian purpose of common Article 3, its scope of application must be as wide as possible and should not be limited by unduly formal requirements. It is revealing in this respect that various recent UN Security Council resolutions have called upon 'all parties to the conflict' to respect international humanitarian law, and this also in the context of such 'anarchic conflicts' as those in Somalia and Liberia ... In [these] cases the Security Council implicitly stated that hostilities linked to the disintegration of the State constituted an armed conflict.[144]

While noting positions adopted by the UN Security Council on 'anarchic conflicts', the ICRC also conceded that the majority of expert opinion did

142 ICRC, *Commentary on the Additional Protocols*, para. 4461. 143 *Ibid.*
144 ICRC, 'Armed conflicts linked to the disintegration of State structures'.

not support this approach to the application of international humanitarian law: 'With regard to the term "armed conflict", expert opinion has also and almost exclusively taken into account conflicts between a government and a rebel party, but not conflicts between different factions in a country.'[145]

The subsequent incorporation of the *Tadić* definition into Article 8(2)(f) of the Rome Statute of the International Criminal Court suggests a general acceptance of the fact that a state of armed conflict can now exist between organised armed groups without any involvement of state authorities.[146] This development of international humanitarian law ensures that the victims of conflicts between non-state armed groups need not be excluded from the protection it provides on account of the non-involvement of state authorities.

Common Article 3 is now a recognised applicable standard in situations of guerrilla warfare where hostilities take place between organised armed groups without the involvement of governmental authorities. To characterise such situations as manifestations of armed conflict would have appeared controversial in the past because of non-involvement of *de jure* state authorities. The definition of non-international armed conflict provided by the *Tadić* Jurisdiction Decision has been a catalyst in remedying this. It is important to recognise the influence of this decision on the development and interpretation of the law.[147] The formula it provides for the characterisation of non-international armed conflict addresses what was one of the most significant lacunae of international humanitarian law, the material conditions governing its applicability. The section that follows investigates the existence of 'responsible command' as an additional condition of the characterisation of armed conflict. In doing so, attention is focused on its effect on the threshold of non-international armed conflict in international humanitarian law.

4.5 The question of responsible command

4.5.1 Does the concept of non-international armed conflict presuppose the existence of responsible command?

In the case of *Prosecutor* v. *Hadžihasanović* the ICTY affirmed for the first time the applicability of the doctrine of command responsibility to

[145] *Ibid.* [146] See Zimmermann, 'War Crimes', p. 286.

[147] See Greenwood, 'Development of International Law'. See also Boelaert-Suominen, 'Yugoslav Tribunal', 619.

situations of non-international armed conflict.[148] In doing so, however, the Tribunal asserted the existence of 'responsible command' to be an integral part of the concept of non-international armed conflict. The notion of responsible command employed in this context is taken from Article 1(1) of Additional Protocol II. As illustrated in Chapter 3, this provision sets a high threshold for the application of international humanitarian law.[149] Decisions issued in the *Hadžihasanović* case relating to the doctrine of command responsibility are explored in this section as a means of examining how such an interpretation of responsible command affects the threshold for the characterisation of non-international armed conflict.

The doctrine of command responsibility, expressed in Article 7(3) of the Statute of the ICTY,[150] allows a commander to be held criminally responsible for the illegal acts of a subordinate 'if he knew or had reason to know that the subordinate was about to commit such acts or had done so and [...] failed to take the necessary and reasonable measures to prevent such acts or to punish the perpetrators thereof'.[151] On 16 July 2003 the ICTY Appeals Chamber in the *Hadžihasanović* case issued a decision affirming the applicability of this doctrine to crimes committed in situations of non-international armed conflict.[152] The decision

[148] See *Prosecutor* v. *Hadžihasanović, Alagić and Kubura*, Case No. IT-01-47-PT, Trial Chamber, Decision on Joint Challenge to Jurisdiction, 12 November 2002; *Prosecutor* v. *Hadžihasanović, Alagić and Kubura*, Case No. IT-01-47-AR72, Appeals Chamber, Decision on Interlocutory Appeal Challenging Jurisdiction in Relation to Command Responsibility, 16 July 2003. Available at www.un.org/icty.

[149] See Chapter 3, at section 3.2.2.

[150] Statute of the ICTY, updated November 2003. Available at www.un.org/icty/basic/statut/stat11-2003.htm (last visited: 3 April 2008).

[151] The doctrine of command responsibility is also expressed in Article 38 of the Rome Statute of the International Criminal Court (37 ILM 999, 1998):

(a) A military commander or person effectively acting as a military commander shall be criminally responsible for crimes within the jurisdiction of the Court committed by forces under his or her effective command and control, or effective authority and control as the case may be, as a result of his or her failure to exercise control properly over such forces, where:
   (i) That military commander or person either knew or, owing to the circumstances at the time, should have known that the forces were committing or about to commit such crimes; and
   (ii) That military commander or person failed to take all necessary and reasonable measures within his or her power to prevent or repress their commission or to submit the matter to the competent authorities for investigation and prosecution.

[152] *Hadžihasanović et al.*

of the Appeals Chamber upheld a previous ruling on the matter by the *Hadžihasanović* Trial Chamber.[153] The decisions of both Chambers in this case are, for a number of reasons, of particular significance to the development of international humanitarian law. First, prior to the *Hadžihasanović* case, the ICTY had never explicitly ruled on the question of whether, under customary international law, a commander could be held criminally responsible for the illegal acts of his or her subordinates in a situation of non-international armed conflict. Second, in linking the doctrine of command responsibility to the existence of 'responsible command', the tribunal has equated the latter concept to the 'organised' nature of armed groups. The implication of doing so is that the term 'organised armed group' may now not be applied without assuming also the existence of responsible command. Third, the *Hadžihasanović* case contributes further to the existing overlap in the norms applicable in internal and international armed conflict in international humanitarian law.

In so far as this development of the law ensures a greater degree of accountability for violations of humanitarian norms, the Tribunal's affirmation of the doctrine's applicability in non-international armed conflict is to be welcomed. It is unfortunate, however, that the approach adopted in doing so confuses the threshold for the application of international humanitarian law in such situations.

4.5.2 The existence of responsible command as a condition for the characterisation of armed conflict: Prosecutor *v.* Hadžihasanović

As highlighted previously, the threshold for the application of international humanitarian law in the *Tadić* definition of non-international armed conflict is significantly lower than that stipulated in Additional Protocol II.[154] Article 1(1) of the Protocol states that it applies to armed conflicts

> which take place in the territory of a High Contracting Party between its armed forces and dissident armed forces or other organized armed groups which, *under responsible command*, exercise such control over a part of its territory as to enable them to carry out sustained and concerted military operations and to implement this Protocol.[155]

[153] *Hadžihasanović, et al.* Trial Chamber,

[154] See Zimmermann, 'War Crimes' p. 285.

[155] Protocol Additional to the Geneva Conventions of 12 August 1949 and Relating to the Protection of Victims of Non-International Armed Conflicts, 12 December 1977, art. 1, 1125 UNTS 609. Emphasis added.

In the *Hadžihasanović* case, the Tribunal uses the concept of responsible command contained in Article 1(1) of Additional Protocol II to illustrate the applicability of the command responsibility doctrine in situations of non-international armed conflict. In doing so, however, the Tribunal confuses the matter by referring to the standard of responsible command contained in the Additional Protocol as being applicable in *all* situations of non-international armed conflict.

4.5.2.1 The meaning of responsible command

The *Hadžihasanović* Trial Chamber cites the ICRC Commentary on Protocol II to clarify how it understands the meaning of responsible command:

> The existence of a responsible command implies some degree of organization of the insurgent armed group or dissident armed forces, but this does not necessarily mean that there is a hierarchical system of military organization similar to that of regular armed forces. *It means an organization capable, on the one hand, of planning and carrying out sustained and concerted military operations, and on the other, of imposing discipline in the name of a de facto authority.*[156]

Utilising this interpretation of the term, the Trial Chamber states that 'responsible command means an organisation that is both capable of planning and carrying out sustained and concerted military operations, *and* imposing discipline in the name of the *de facto* force or government'.[157] The Chamber also refers to the ICRC Commentary on common Article 3 to support the principle of responsible command as a standard applicable in all situations of armed conflict:

> As the ICRC Commentary on Common Article 3 states, when discussing the criteria for an 'armed conflict' (to distinguish an armed conflict from acts of banditry or an 'unorganized and short-lived insurrection'), the Party in revolt against the *de jure* government 'possesses an organized military force, an authority responsible for its acts, acting within a determinate territory and having the means of respecting and ensuring respect for the Convention.'[158]

4.5.2.2 Questions concerning the use of criteria indicating the existence of armed conflict from the ICRC Commentary on common Article 3

The fact that the ICRC included the above criterion among others referred to as being 'in no way obligatory' for the application of

[156] As cited in *Hadžihasanović et al.*, Trial Chamber, Pilloud *et al.*, *Commentary*, p. 1352. Emphasis added by Trial Chamber.

[157] *Hadžihasanović et al.*, Trial Chamber, para. 161. [158] *Ibid.*

common Article 3 is not mentioned by the Trial Chamber.[159] Regardless of this omission, the appropriateness of referring to the criteria listed in the ICRC Commentary must be questioned as the contemporary concept of non-international armed conflict differs considerably from that employed at the time of the drafting of the Geneva Conventions.

Some scholars of international law see the list of conditions posited in the ICRC Commentary as a useful tool for determining the existence of armed conflict. For example, Derek Jinks states that 'the criteria are best understood as independently sufficient grounds to establish the existence of an "armed conflict"'.[160] The weight generally given to the ICRC criteria in interpreting grounds for recognising the existence of armed conflict is further evidenced by their use in decisions of the ICTR and the ICTY.[161]

As illustrated in Chapter 2,[162] the term 'armed conflict not of an international character' was understood by delegates at the Diplomatic Conference to have a meaning synonymous with that of 'civil war'. As common Article 3 is now applicable in situations that fall short of civil war, a lower threshold for the application of international humanitarian law clearly needs to be recognised. The approach employed by the Trial Chamber in referring to the ICRC Commentary is thus not helpful. As noted by René Provost:

> The criteria put forward by the ICRC in its commentary, however convenient, can be seriously misleading. The criteria were elaborated in the context of an attempt to define armed conflict not of an international character to which the Conventions as a whole would be applicable. A decision was made at the Conference not to make the Conventions applicable to a narrow type of internal conflict, but rather to adopt a widely applicable but substantively limited regime. There is therefore no justification for the adoption of the elements of a restrictive definition of internal armed conflict in the context of Article 3.[163]

The Appeals Chamber, taking a similar approach to that of the Trial Chamber in citing ICRC Commentary,[164] also neglects to mention the

159 Pictet, *Commentary I*, p. 49.

160 Jinks, 'September 11', at 31. See also Lt. Colonel H. Wayne Elliott on use of the criteria as a basis for determining the existence of armed conflict in Chechnya, 'Chechnya and the Laws of War', available at www.crimesofwar.org/expert/chech-eliot.html.

161 E.g. *Akayesu*, Judgment, paras. 619 and 562.

162 See Chapter 2, at section 2.1.2.

163 Provost, *International Human Rights*, p. 266.

164 See *Hadžihasanović et al.*, Appeals Chamber, para. 15:

> Responsible command was an integral notion of the prohibition imposed by Article 3 common to the 1949 Geneva Conventions against the doing of certain

criteria as being 'in no way obligatory' for the application of common Article 3. Affirming the command responsibility doctrine to be a corollary of responsible command in non-international armed conflict,[165] the Appeals Chamber furthermore utilises Article 1(1) of Additional Protocol II in the same way as the Trial Chamber.[166] The approach adopted by both Chambers in their interpretation of command responsibility implies a threshold of application higher than that associated with common Article 3.

4.5.2.3 The requirement of 'sustained and concerted' military operations

By stating that the existence of armed conflict presupposes the existence of responsible command and that responsible command in turn presupposes 'sustained and concerted' military operations, the minimum threshold for the application of international humanitarian law is raised, requiring a higher intensity of hostilities. The ICRC Commentary on Additional Protocol II interprets the requirement of 'sustained and concerted military operations' as follows:

> 'Sustained' (in French the reference is to 'opérations continues') means that the operations are kept going or kept up continuously. The emphasis is therefore on continuity and persistence. 'Concerted' (in French: 'concertées') means agreed upon, planned and contrived, done in agreement according to a plan. Thus we are talking about military operations conceived and planned by organized armed groups.[167]

By inserting the Additional Protocol II notion of responsible command into the non-international armed conflict concept the Tribunal effectively narrows the latter to exclude situations where hostilities are of a lower level of intensity. It is important to emphasise that not all situations of armed conflict involve 'sustained and concerted' military operations.[168] The condition of 'sustained and concerted' military

things in the course of an internal armed conflict. Referring to the criteria for determining whether there was an 'armed conflict not of an international character' within the meaning of that provision, the *ICRC Commentary* spoke, authoritatively, of a revolting party possessing 'an organized military force, an authority responsible for its acts, acting within a determinate territory and having the means of respecting and ensuring respect for the' convention.

165 *Ibid.*, para. 14. 166 *Ibid.*, para. 15.

167 Pilloud *et al.*, *Commentary*, p. 1353.

168 Commenting on the definition of armed conflict provided by the *Tadić* Jurisdiction Decision, Zimmermann states 'it has to be noted, that unlike in the case of sustained armed violence, the operations need not be kept going continuously by the

operations, according to its use in the *Hadžihasanović* case,[169] is only applicable to hostilities reaching a high level of intensity. Hostilities that lack 'sustained and concerted' military operations may also be said to lack responsible command. In the absence of responsible command, according to the standard employed by the Tribunal, it is not possible to characterise a situation as one of armed conflict. The implication of not recognising an armed conflict on such grounds is that the application of international humanitarian law becomes restricted to situations where hostilities have already reached a high threshold of intensity.

4.5.2.4 Responsible command, command responsibility and the organisational requirement for armed groups engaged in non-international armed conflict

In supporting the Trial Chamber's affirmation of the applicability of the command responsibility doctrine in non-international armed conflict, the Appeals Chamber states that '[r]esponsible command was an integral notion of the prohibition imposed by Article 3 common to the 1949 Geneva Conventions against the doing of certain things in the course of an internal armed conflict'.[170] Referring to the existence of an organised military force as a prerequisite for the existence of armed conflict, the Chamber states that this in turn presupposes the existence of responsible command: 'It is evident that there cannot be an organised military force save on the basis of responsible command.'[171] Interpreting the organised nature of an armed group as evidence of responsible command, the Appeals Chamber states that

> [t]he relevant aspects of international law unquestionably regard a military force engaged in an internal armed conflict as organized and therefore as being under responsible command. In the absence of anything to the contrary, it is the task of a court to interpret the underlying State practice and *opinio juris* (relating to the requirement that such a military force be organized) as bearing its normal meaning that military organization implies responsible command and that responsible command in turn implies command responsibility.[172]

conflicting parties'. He also affirms that 'there is no need that the relevant military actions must be concerted and thus be planned and contrived.' 'War crimes' p. 285.

169 See *Hadžihasanović et al.*, para. 161; and *Hadžihasanović et al.*, Appeals Chamber, para. 15.

170 *Hadžihasanović et al.*, Appeals Chamber, para. 15.

171 *Ibid.*, para. 16. 172 *Ibid.*, para. 17.

4.5.3 Responsible command as a condition for the characterisation of non-international armed conflict in international humanitarian law

The position expressed by the *Hadžihasanović* Appeals Chamber clearly implies a higher threshold for the application of international humanitarian law than that of the *Tadić* definition of non-international armed conflict. As the concept of responsible command in *Hadžihasanović* is taken from Additional Protocol II, and as the interpretation of this concept is tied to Article 1(1) of the instrument, it follows as a logical consequence that the material field of application for non-international armed conflict is higher than that ordinarily assumed for the application of common Article 3. This threshold necessarily excludes all situations of non-international armed conflict where an organised armed group is not capable 'on the one hand, of planning and carrying out sustained and concerted military operations, and on the other, of imposing discipline in the name of a *de facto* authority'.[173] Considering how these terms narrow the scope of applicability, it would arguably be of benefit to distinguish between situations of internal armed conflict where the Additional Protocol II concept of responsible command applies and all other situations of non-international armed conflict.

Situations of non-international armed conflict without responsible command include cases where hostilities are protracted but of low intensity, lacking sustained and concerted military operation. Armed conflicts taking place between organised armed groups without the involvement of governmental authorities, referred to above at section 4.4, would also lack responsible command. In cases of armed conflict between governmental authorities and organised armed groups, the latter party would furthermore be required to represent a de facto authority for the concept of responsible command to apply.

Given the high threshold of application associated with Additional Protocol II, and the much lower threshold associated with common Article 3, it is important for responsible command not to be viewed as a condition determining the existence of armed conflict. Without making explicit this distinction, the concept of responsible command may serve to restrict unduly the application of international humanitarian law to situations not reaching the threshold of Additional Protocol II.

The approach taken by the *Hadžihasanović* Appeals Chamber in its interpretation of responsible command places considerable weight on

[173] As cited in *Hadžihasanović et al.*, Trial Chamber, para. 87. Pilloud *et al.*, *Commentary*, p. 1352.

the ICRC Commentary on common Article 3.[174] As emphasised above, the concept of non-international armed conflict has developed significantly since the drafting of the Geneva Conventions. The threshold of application currently associated with common Article 3 is considerably different to that indicated in the ICRC Commentary. The definition of non-international armed conflict provided by *Tadić* is a clear illustration of this. Drawing on the terms of this definition, Sonja Boelaert-Suominen comments that 'it can be safely concluded that the threshold suggested by the ICRC Commentary has failed to crystallise into customary international law. In particular, there is no requirement in the ICTY judgments that the non-State entities should somehow exert control over part of a territory, or that such armed forces have a responsible command.'[175]

Expressing a similar position to Boelaert-Suominen, Bahia Thahzib-lie and Olivia Swaak-Goldman also hold that the existence of responsible command should not be considered a requirement for the characterisation of non-international armed conflict:

> [F]or common Article 3 to apply, the hostilities must meet a minimum level of intensity and must arguably be sufficiently protracted. The hostilities must be conducted between parties that are sufficiently organised ... although not necessarily under responsible command and willing to respect the laws of war.[176]

The reasoning of the *Hadžihasanović* Appeal Chamber has been criticised for its approach to the interpretation of responsible command in non-international armed conflict. Professor Christopher Greenwood comments that

> [T]he reasoning leaves open some large questions. Despite what it said about the need to be satisfied that state practice recognized the principle, the decision cites almost no state practice and concedes that 'domestically, most States have not legislated for command responsibility to be the counterpart of responsible command in internal conflict.' It does not explain why the concept of responsible command, which imposes duties on belligerents, automatically entails criminal responsibility for individuals. Nor does it explain why it is illogical for one concept of customary international humanitarian law to be applicable in international but not internal conflicts, while, nevertheless, conceding that not all of the principles of that law extend to both types of conflict.

[174] *Hadžihasanović*, Appeals Chamber, para. 15.
[175] See Boelaert-Suominen, 'Yugoslav Tribunal', at 633–4.
[176] Thahzib-lie and Swaak-Goldman, 'Determining the Threshold', p. 253.

Indeed, one might argue that a different approach to command responsibility might be appropriate in a non-international armed conflict, because the armed forces involved in such conflicts are often less structured and well organized (particularly on the non-governmental side) than in international hostilities.[177]

In so far as the responsible command concept presupposes the threshold of application associated with Additional Protocol II, the question as to whether it may be considered a prerequisite for the characterisation of non-international armed conflict must be answered in the negative. As the application of common Article 3 is not dependent on the existence of a de facto authority, sustained and concerted military operations or the involvement of governmental authorities, it would arguably be inappropriate to limit the reach of this provision by adding such conditions to its threshold of application. If responsible command is to be proposed as a condition for the characterisation of non-international armed conflict, it would first need to be redefined in terms that are consistent with the existing threshold of common Article 3. In the absence of such a development there are no grounds to depart from the prevailing standard.

4.6 Concluding observations

The approach first adopted in *Tadić* has developed into the prevailing standard for distinguishing the status of situations for the application of international humanitarian law. As such it has arguably impacted positively in the elucidation of the conditions signifying the existence of armed conflict. According to the jurisprudence of the ICTY and ICTR, the two factors distinguishing a state of armed conflict from internal disturbance are the level of organisation within armed groups and the intensity of hostilities. This approach provides a broad interpretation of non-international armed conflict, allowing reasonable breadth for the application of international humanitarian law to such situations.

The adaptation of the definition in the Rome Statute, and its application by various international bodies, illustrate the authority of the standard for the characterisation of armed conflict. It is important to recognise however that the utility of the formula is premised on the coherence of its interpretation. If it continues to be interpreted in the broad terms used in the earlier jurisprudence of the ICTY and ICTR,

[177] Greenwood, 'Command Responsibility', at 601.

the formula's future application will cover situations of low intensity armed conflict and will be capable of adapting to new forms of non-international warfare. However, if interpreted as requiring the existence of responsible command, as implied in the *Hadžihasanović* case, then it is foreseeable that its future application will be limited to situations of high-intensity armed conflict. The notion of 'responsible command' employed in this case is essentially an Additional Protocol II concept, requiring a higher threshold of application than common Article 3. It presupposes the existence of 'sustained and concerted' military operations and does not allow for the existence of armed conflict if the hostilities are of consistent low intensity.

It is important furthermore to recognise that the definition of non-international armed conflict is not to be interpreted on the basis of the criteria put forward by the ICRC in its Commentary on common Article 3. These criteria imply a threshold for the application of international humanitarian law higher than that required by the contemporary concept of non-international armed conflict. Derived from proposals discussed at the Diplomatic Conference of 1949, the criteria refer to situations displaying the characteristics of civil war. As the notion of non-international armed conflict has evolved considerably since the drafting of the ICRC Commentary, it needs to be recognised that the contemporary threshold for the application of international humanitarian law is lower than that which was assumed during the drafting of common Article 3. The *travaux préparatoires* of the Rome Statute provides further evidence of this and will be discussed in the chapter that follows.

5 The concept of non-international armed conflict in the Rome Statute of the International Criminal Court

As illustrated in the previous chapter, the concept of non-international armed conflict evolved in the final decade of the twentieth century to cover situations which had hitherto not been included within its scope. The jurisprudence of the International Criminal Tribunals for Rwanda (ICTR) and the former Yugoslavia (ICTY) was pivotal in this regard, setting new parameters for non-international armed conflict in international humanitarian law. While the concept of non-international armed conflict contained in the Rome Statute of the International Criminal Court (ICC) is partly derived from that propounded in the case law of these tribunals, its threshold of applicability is however less clear.[1] This chapter looks at possible lines of interpretation applicable to non-international armed conflict in the Statute and in doing so sets out an argument for an understanding of the threshold contained in Article 8(2)(f) as one equivalent to that of Article 3 common to the four Geneva Conventions of 1949.

In adopting this approach, an argument will be advanced for the interpretation of the threshold contained in Article 8(2)(f) of the Rome Statute as one applicable to all situations of non-international armed conflict within the Court's jurisdiction. The scope of applicability defined by this provision is held to be distinctly broader than that of Article 1(1) of Additional Protocol II. It is also contended that there exist reasons, despite a difference in wording, to view the threshold contained in this provision as equivalent to that propounded in the *Tadić* Jurisdiction Decision. The first of the four parts of this chapter explores the background to the

An earlier version of this chapter was published in the *Journal of Conflict and Security Law*. See Cullen, 'Definition of Non-International Armed Conflict'.

[1] For an early decision of the court providing an interpretation of 'conflict not of an international character', see *Lubanga*, Decision on the Confirmation of Charges, paras. 229–37.

Rome Conference and highlights the evolution that took place in the various meetings of the Preparatory Committee on the Establishment of the International Criminal Court. The second part analyses the debate at the Rome Conference relating to the question of subject-matter jurisdiction over war crimes committed in situations of non-international armed conflict. This section examines the views of the delegates relating to the threshold for the application of provisions specific to armed conflicts not of an international character. The third part puts forward an interpretation of the threshold contained in Article 8(2)(f) as one applicable to all situations of non-international armed conflict subject to the Court's jurisdiction. In doing so, the definition of non-international armed conflict contained in this provision is held to be equivalent to that contained in common Article 3. The chapter concludes by placing emphasis on the position of victims in the interpretation of the war crimes provisions in the Rome Statute.

5.1 The question of subject-matter jurisdiction over war crimes in non-international armed conflicts prior to the Rome Conference

In the years preceding the Rome Conference, the reports of the Preparatory Committee show some reluctance on the part of states to include in the Statute crimes relating to non-international armed conflict. The original draft Statute produced in 1994 by the International Law Commission (ILC) did not include jurisdiction over war crimes committed in such situations.[2] This was primarily because of the fact that at the time of its formulation, the war crimes concept was generally only deemed relevant to situations of international armed conflict. This area of international law however evolved swiftly. Some months after the presentation of ILC's draft Statute to the UN General Assembly, the UN Security Council adopted a resolution approving the Statute of the International Criminal Tribunal for Rwanda.[3] The report of the UN Secretary-General on the Rwanda Tribunal notes the expansive approach taken by the Council to this area of international humanitarian law:

[2] Report of the ILC on its Forty-Sixth Session, Draft Statute for an International Criminal Court, 2 May–22 July, 1994 (GA, 49th Sess., Supp. No. 10, A/49/10, 1994).

[3] UNSCR 955 Establishing the International Tribunal for Rwanda, UN Doc. S/RES/955 (1994), 8 November 1994.

[T]he Security Council has elected to take a more expansive approach to the choice of the applicable law than the one underlying the Statute of the Yugoslav Tribunal, and included within the subject-matter jurisdiction of the Rwanda Tribunal regardless of whether they were considered part of customary international law or whether they have customarily entailed the individual criminal responsibility of the perpetrator of the crime. Article 4 of the Statute, accordingly, includes violations of Additional II Protocol, which, as a whole, has not yet been universally recognized as part of customary international law, for the first time criminalizes common article 3 of the four Geneva Conventions.[4]

Despite the adoption of the Statute for the ICTR,[5] and the emergence of jurisprudence from the ICTY,[6] states involved in the drafting of the Statute remained divided on the inclusion of jurisdiction over war crimes committed in non-international armed conflict. According to the report issued by the *Ad Hoc* Committee on the Establishment of an International Criminal Court in 1995:

There were different views as to whether the laws and customs applicable in armed conflict, including treaty crimes, should include those governing non-international armed conflicts, notably common Article 3 of the 1949 Geneva Conventions and Additional Protocol II thereto. Those who favoured the inclusion of such provisions drew attention to the current reality of armed conflicts, the statute of the ad hoc Tribunal for Rwanda and the recent decision of the ad hoc Tribunal for the former Yugoslavia recognizing the customary-law status of common Article 3. However other delegations expressed serious reservations concerning the possibility of covering non-international armed conflicts and questioned the consistency of such an approach with the principle of complementarity. As regards Additional Protocol II, the view was expressed that that instrument as a whole had not achieved the status of customary law and therefore was binding only on States party thereto. The view was also expressed that non-international armed conflicts should not fall within the jurisdiction of the Court either with respect to common Article 3 or Additional Protocol II.[7]

Subsequent to the report of the *Ad Hoc* Committee, the Preparatory Committee on the Establishment of the International Criminal Court was set up.[8] The first Report of the Preparatory Committee, issued after sessions held in March to April and August of 1996, recorded a distinct

[4] Report of the Secretary-General Pursuant to Paragraph 5 of Security Council Resolution 955 (1994), UN Doc. S/1995/134, 13 February 1995, para. 12.

[5] UNSCR 955. [6] See *Tadić* Jurisdiction Decision.

[7] Report of the *Ad Hoc* Committee on the Establishment of an International Criminal Court; GA, 50th Sess., Supp. No. 22, A/50/22, 1995, para. 74.

[8] UN General Resolution 50/46 Establishment of an International Criminal Court, UN Doc. A/RES/50/46, 11 December 1995.

lack of consensus on the question of whether the draft Statute should include subject-matter jurisdiction over war crimes committed in non-international armed conflicts. Under the heading of 'character of the armed conflict' the Report states:

> There were different views as to whether this category of crimes should include violations committed in international or non-international armed conflicts. Some delegations expressed the view that it was important to include violations committed in internal armed conflicts given their increasing frequency in recent years, that national criminal justice systems were less likely to be able to adequately address such violations and that individuals could be held criminally responsible for such violations as a matter of international law, with references being made to the Statute of the Rwanda Tribunal and the decision of the Yugoslavia Tribunal Appeals Chamber in the *Tadić* case. Other delegations expressed the view that violations committed in internal armed conflicts should not be included, that the inclusion of such violations was unrealistic and could undermine the universal or widespread acceptance of the Court, that individual criminal responsibility for such violations was not clearly established as a matter of existing law, with attention being drawn to the absence of criminal offence or enforcement provisions in Additional Protocol II, and that customary law had not changed in this respect since the Rwanda Tribunal Statute.[9]

Despite a divergence of views on the matter, the Preparatory Committee decided to include some provisions relating to armed conflicts not of an international character during the session that took place in February of 1997.[10] Among the offences listed in this draft were 'serious violations of Article 3 common to the four Geneva Conventions of 1949'.[11] The terms of its application to non-international armed conflicts however were not defined. This was partially addressed at a subsequent session of the Preparatory Committee, when the decision was taken to include the wording of Article 1(2) of Additional Protocol II in a *chapeau* covering the sections relating to non-international armed conflict: 'Sections C and D of this [provision] apply to armed conflicts not of an international character and thus do not apply to situations of internal disturbances and tensions, such as riots, isolated and sporadic acts of violence or other acts of a similar nature.'[12] While this clause

[9] Report of the Preparatory Committee on the Establishment of an International Criminal Court, vol. I (Proceedings of the Preparatory Committee During March–April and August 1996), GA, 51st Sess., Supp. No. 22, A/51/22, 1996, para. 78.

[10] Decisions Taken by the Preparatory Committee at its Session Held 11–21 February 1997, A/AC.249/1997/L.5, 1997.

[11] *Ibid.*, p. 12.

[12] Decisions Taken by the Preparatory Committee, A/AC.249/1997/L.9/Rev. 1, p. 12.

was retained as part of the draft Statute that was submitted for the consideration of delegates at the Rome Conference,[13] it is noteworthy that, apart from this provision, no threshold relating to situations of non-international armed conflict was included at any stage by the Preparatory Committee. The matter of extending subject-matter jurisdiction to cover war crimes committed in armed conflicts not of an international character was contentious enough for the Committee without having to decide what such situations consisted of. As a consequence, the question of defining the scope of 'armed conflict not of an international character' was left to delegates at the Rome Conference.

5.2 The question of subject-matter jurisdiction over war crimes in non-international armed conflicts at the Rome Conference

Debate at the Rome Conference over the inclusion of provisions relating to situations of non-international armed conflict was no less vigorous than those which took place at the Diplomatic Conferences that drafted the Geneva Conventions of 1949 and Additional Protocols of 1977. The outcome however was distinctively different. The Statute's applicability to situations of non-international armed conflict is much broader in scope than that considered either in the drafting of the Geneva Conventions or the Additional Protocols. This section will examine how this occurred and why the threshold included at Rome Conference extended the concept of non-international armed conflict beyond that of previous instruments.

5.2.1 Report of the Preparatory Committee on the Establishment of an International Criminal Court

After concluding its work on the formulation of 'a widely acceptable consolidated text of a convention for an international criminal court',[14] the Preparatory Committee submitted a draft Statute for the consideration of delegates at the Rome Conference in its report of 15 April 1998.[15] Sections C and D of Article 5 of the draft Statute contained

[13] Report of the Preparatory Committee on the Establishment of an International Criminal Court, Draft Statute & Draft Final Act; A/CONF.183/2/Add.1, 1998, p. 25.

[14] A/CONF.183/2, para. 2. [15] A/CONF.183/2.

provisions relating to non-international armed conflict.[16] The offences listed in section C were taken from common Article 3, while many of those contained in section D were common to Additional Protocol II. As already mentioned, both sections were covered by a *chapeau* stipulating their applicability to 'armed conflicts not of an international character' that explicitly excluded situations of internal disturbances and tensions.

Delegates did not formally discuss the subject of a threshold specific to situations of non-international armed conflict until requested to do so by the Chairman of the Committee of the Whole, Philippe Kirsch, on 8 July 1998.[17] At the time of this request, the *chapeau* covering sections relating to non-international armed conflict provided one threshold of application for the provisions contained therein. It stated that 'Sections C and D of this article apply to armed conflicts not of an international character and thus do not apply to situations of internal disturbances and tensions, such as riots, isolated and sporadic acts of violence or other acts of a similar nature.'[18] This uniform threshold of application for situations of non-international armed conflict was changed in a subsequent discussion paper issued by the Bureau on 10 July 1998.[19] The alteration introduced by the Bureau implied two different categories of armed conflict, stipulating a new threshold covering section D of the draft statute. Included as a means of bridging the gap between states on the issue of the Court's jurisdiction over war crimes committed in non-international armed conflict, the Bureau proposal will be discussed later in this section. Before doing so, the divergent views expressed by delegates on the matter will be examined to show the context in which this initiative was brought forward.

[16] The parts of the draft Statute relating to non-international armed conflict were referred to as 'sections C and D' by delegates at the Rome Conference. This labelling was kept throughout the negotiations until discussions relating to their inclusion were concluded.

[17] As Chairman of the Committee of the Whole, Philippe Kirsch opened discussion on Wednesday, 8 July 1998 by requesting comments on a number of issues including 'sections C and D on armed conflict not of an international character [...] the need for those sections and, if they were included, the threshold for those provisions' (A/CONF.183/C.1/SR.25, para. 2). Implicit in this remark is an assumption of one threshold for both provisions. See Bureau discussion paper A/CONF.183/C.1/L.53, 6 July 1998.

[18] A/CONF.183/C.1/L.53, 6 July 1998.

[19] A/CONF.183/C.1/L.59, 10 July 1998.

5.2.2 *Views of delegations on inclusion of clauses relating to non-international armed conflict*

The incorporation of provisions relating to non-international armed conflict was strongly supported by the majority of delegates for a number of different reasons. As nearly all contemporary armed conflicts were not international in character, it was argued that to exclude such situations would be to leave an unacceptable gap in the protection provided by the Court.[20] The body of international law relating to non-international armed conflict had also clearly developed since the drafting of the Geneva Conventions and Additional Protocols. Speaking on behalf of the United States, Jamison S. Borek emphasised that 'it was essential to cover internal armed conflicts, which were the most frequent and the most cruel. That area of law had been developed and clearly established and must be included in the Statute.'[21] Addressing the Plenary of the Conference as Head of her delegation, the Finnish Minister for Foreign Affairs, Tarja Halonen, stated that 'since conflicts were often civil and internal in nature, and sometimes no effective national systems were available, the mandate of the Court must be extended to such situations'.[22]

Referring to the situation in his own state, Sierra Leone's ambassador to the United Nations, Fode M. Dabor, also expressed a strong position in support of provisions relating to non-international conflict. Dabor 'strongly supported the inclusion of sections C and D since, as was well known, his country was undergoing an internal conflict in

[20] The Head of the New Zealand delegation, Don MacKay, made the following statement on the matter: 'As to whether armed conflicts not of an international character should be covered by the Statute, failure to include such conflicts would leave a huge gap that would be quite unacceptable to the international community.' A/CONF.183/SR.25, para. 19.

[21] A/CONF.183/SR.6, para. 100. The delegation of the United States, led by Ambassador David Scheffer, strongly supported the inclusion of provisions relating to non-international armed conflict in the draft Statute. Professor Theodor Meron, a distinguished adviser to the US government on matters of international humanitarian law, had been instrumental in getting the issue onto the agenda of the US delegation prior to the Conference. Also present at the Conference as a member of this delegation, Meron played an important role in advancing the position of the United States on the inclusion of provisions governing situations of internal armed conflict. Source: Interview with Ambassador David Scheffer, Galway, 13 July 2003.

[22] A/CONF.183/SR.6, para. 34.

which very serious offences had been committed over which the Court should have jurisdiction'.[23]

The strength of support for the retention of sections C and D of the draft Statute, evidenced in the statements made by delegations before the Committee of the Whole and Conference Plenary,[24] secured the place of the provisions despite the opposition expressed by a not insignificant minority of states.[25] Opposition to the inclusion of provisions relating to non-international armed conflict was not, however, as strong or concerted as at previous diplomatic conferences. Views expressed on the matter were generally tempered by an understanding that compromises were needed to achieve general agreement on the Statute as a whole.

Arguments opposing provisions relating to non-international armed conflict were similar in many ways to those raised at the Diplomatic Conferences that drafted the Geneva Conventions of 1949 and Additional Protocols of 1977. Concerns were expressed over the possibility for external interference in the internal affairs of sovereign states and the lack of clarity on how the Court would determine the status of situations.[26] It was furthermore argued that the inclusion of crimes relating to non-international armed conflict in the Statute

[23] A/CONF.183/SR.25, para. 55. Expressing a view similar to that of Sierra Leone, João Soares Da Gama of Guinea-Bissau stated that he 'attached prime importance to the inclusion of sections C and D, since his country continued to suffer from non-international armed conflicts'. A/CONF.183/C.1/SR.28, para. 77.

[24] In addition the United States, Finland, Sierra Leone and Guinea-Bissau, other delegations voicing support for the incorporation of provisions relating to non-international armed conflict included Albania, Andorra, Argentina, Armenia, Australia, Bangladesh, Benin, Bosnia and Herzegovina, Botswana, Brunei Darussalam, Bulgaria, Burkina Faso, Canada, Cape Verde, Chile, Colombia, Congo, Costa Rica, Croatia, Cyprus, Czech Republic, Ecuador, Estonia, Ethiopia, Gabon, Georgia, Hungary, Israel, Japan, Jordan, Lithuania, Malta, Mozambique, Namibia, New Zealand, Nicaragua, Philippines, Republic of Korea, Romania, Russian Federation, San Marino, Senegal, Slovakia, Slovenia, South Africa (speaking on behalf of the Southern African Development Community), Switzerland, Trinidad and Tobago, Uganda, the United Kingdom (speaking on behalf of the EU, the Central and Eastern European countries associated with the EU, the associated country of Cyprus and the European Free Trade Association countries of Iceland and Norway), Venezuela and Zambia.

[25] The minority of delegations opposed to the inclusion of provisions relating to non-international armed conflict included states such as Algeria, Burundi, China, India, Indonesia, Iraq, Libyan Arab Jamahiriya, Nepal, Oman, Pakistan, Saudi Arabia, Syrian Arab Republic, Thailand, Turkey and Vietnam.

[26] For examples see: A/CONF.183/C.1/SR.27, para. 5; and A/CONF.183/C.1/SR.5, para. 107.

would conflict with the principle of complementarity.[27] Overall, however, the views expressed were notably less rigid than those voiced in the drafting of the Geneva Conventions and Additional Protocols. While asserting their opposition to sections C and D, many delegates voiced willingness to compromise if certain conditions narrowing the applicability of these provisions were included. Among the suggestions to this effect was a proposal for the inclusion of the threshold contained in Additional Protocol II.[28] As previously mentioned, the only provision indicating a threshold for non-international armed conflict was the *chapeau* of sections C and D, which stated that these provisions would apply to 'armed conflicts not of an international character and thus do not apply to situations of internal disturbances and tensions, such as riots, isolated and sporadic acts of violence or other acts of a similar nature'. This negative definition of armed conflict was clearly insufficient for the purpose of distinguishing situations of non-international armed conflict. In order to allay the fears of states opposed to clauses concerning non-international armed conflict a positive definition was needed to clarify the terms of applicability.

5.2.3 Bridging the gap: proposals for a threshold for non-international armed conflict

The question of including a new threshold provision relating to situations of non-international armed conflict arose as a means of facilitating consensus on sections C and D. In order to balance the concerns of states opposed to non-international armed conflict clauses with others who had expressed support for the retention of C and D, the Bureau of

[27] See comments made by Mr Perera of the Sri Lankan delegation during the 35th meeting of the Committee of the Whole. A/CONF.183/C.1/SR.35, para. 44.

[28] Speaking on behalf of the Egyptian delegation, Sayed Kassem El Masry stated that 'he did not favour the inclusion of sections C and D, but could consider section C if safeguards such as non-interference in the internal affairs of States, a higher threshold and the guarantees contained in Additional Protocol II to the Geneva Conventions of 1949 were stipulated'. A/CONF.183/C.1/SR.5, para. 115. A similar position was voiced by Bahrain's Minister for Justice and Islamic Affairs, Khalid Bin Abdullah Al-Khalifa:

> He found the thresholds in sections C and D difficult to accept because there was no positive definition of non-international conflicts. An exact definition of internal conflicts would be required, along the lines of Additional Protocol II to the Geneva Conventions of 1949, and great care must be taken not to interfere in the internal affairs of States.

A/CONF.183/C.1/SR.27, para. 21.

the Committee of the Whole formulated a proposal based on the text of Article 1(1) of Additional Protocol II.[29] The new threshold provision, included in a discussion paper circulated by the Bureau,[30] received mixed reviews from delegates.

5.2.3.1 The Bureau proposal

As a way of accommodating views expressed by those opposed to the inclusion of provisions relating to situations of non-international armed conflict, and in particular to concerns voiced about the threshold of applicability, the following text was inserted into the *chapeau* of section D of draft Article 5 *quater*:

> Section D of this article applies to armed conflicts not of an international character and thus does not apply to situations of internal disturbances and tensions, such as riots, isolated and sporadic acts of violence or other acts of a similar nature. It applies to armed conflicts that take place in a territory of a State Party between its armed forces and dissident armed forces or other organized armed groups which, under responsible command, exercise such control over a part of its territory as to enable them to carry out sustained and concerted military operations.[31]

The second sentence of this new provision was taken from Article 1(1) of Additional Protocol II. As explained in Chapter 4, the text of this provision sets a particularly high threshold of application. Stipulating conditions such as the involvement of a State Party in hostilities, control over territory and the existence of 'sustained and concerted military operations', the proposal imposed considerable restrictions on the applicability of the provisions contained in section D. As a consequence, it was strongly resisted by delegations interested in maintaining the previously uniform threshold for the application of sections C and D.

The first delegate to speak in opposition to the new threshold was Professor Gerhard Hafner of the Austrian delegation. Speaking on behalf of the European Union and its Member States, he stated that:

> Article 5 quater, section D, was preceded by a reference to armed conflict between armed forces and dissident armed forces or other organized armed groups. That reference needed also to cover conflicts in which only organized armed groups were engaged, regardless of whether they exercised control over territory.[32]

[29] A/CONF.183/C.1/L.59 (10 July 1998). [30] *Ibid.*
[31] *Ibid.* [32] A/CONF.183/C.1/SR.33, para. 14.

The representatives of Finland,[33] Romania,[34] Lithuania[35] and the Sudan[36] each took the floor to voice their support for the position expressed by the Presidency of the European Union. Speaking as Head of the United States delegation, David Scheffer was also critical of the new threshold introduced in the Bureau discussion paper:

> The United States noted the changes made to the chapeaux of sections C and D in an endeavour to facilitate consensus. It believed, however, that the change raising the threshold of applicability of section D to that of Additional Protocol II to the Geneva Conventions of 1949 should be rejected. The bulk of armed conflicts encountered in the real world were non-international, and that change would send the wrong message to civilian victims of internal armed conflicts.[37]

The view expressed by Scheffer was supported by the German Head of Delegation, Gerd Westdickenberg, who stated that his delegation 'continued to believe that the same standards should apply in section D as in section C of Article 5 *quater*. It thus had reservations regarding the second part of the chapeau prefacing section D.'[38] The remarks of Westdickenberg draw attention to the fact that the new threshold provision proposed by the Bureau introduced a distinction between sections C and D which had hitherto not existed. Previously, one threshold had applied to both sections. While ambiguity existed concerning the scope of this threshold, it was clear that prior to the Bureau's proposal both sections shared the same field of applicability.

Given the the previously uniform threshold for non-international armed conflict, the new heightened threshold for section D posed a problem for many delegates. The Head of the United Kingdom delegation, Franklin Berman, stated that 'it was important to avoid setting a threshold so high as to remove from the Court's jurisdiction the very cases that had given rise to such grave concerns of late'.[39] Likewise, Tuvako Manongi of the Tanzanian delegation stated that the new threshold was too high 'to allow the Court to play any meaningful role in the situations of non-international armed conflict with which the international community was increasingly faced'.[40]

33 A/CONF.183/C.1/SR.35, para. 37. 34 *Ibid.*, para. 77.
35 *Ibid.*, para. 60. 36 A/CONF.183/C.1/SR.34, para. 94.
37 A/CONF.183/C.1/SR.33, para. 24. 38 *Ibid.*, para. 68.
39 A/CONF.183/C.1/SR.33, para. 80.
40 A/CONF.183/C.1/SR.35, para. 49. In addition to the criticisms expressed by representatives of Austria, United States, Germany, the United Kingdom, New Zealand, Norway, South Africa and Tanzania, opposition to the new threshold was furthermore voiced by representatives of Switzerland, Uganda, Samoa, Trinidad and Tobago, Spain, the Russian Federation, Australia, Mexico, the Sudan, Sierra

The Head of the New Zealand delegation, Don McKay, expressed a similar concern to those voiced by the representatives of Britain and Tanzania: 'The fundamental problem raised by article 5 quater was the new chapeau of section D, which would leave very serious gaps in the Statute. It should either be deleted or tightened up.'[41] As the terms of this provision excluded the vast majority of situations that would otherwise qualify as 'armed conflict not of an international character', many delegates viewed it as imposing an excessively restrictive standard for the application of the very basic humanitarian rules contained in section D.[42]

In addition to arguments concerning the restrictive nature of the threshold, its consistency with the current state of international law was also questioned. For Rolf Einar Fife, Head of the Norwegian delegation, 'the new chapeau unduly limited the scope of well-established norms of international law'.[43] Speaking on behalf of South Africa and the member states of the Southern African Development Community, Professor Medard R. Rwelamira stated that he was concerned that 'the new chapeau of section D not only restricted the scope of application but also, by implication, excluded conflicts between organized armed groups'.[44] Given that the concept of armed conflict in international humanitarian law had developed, albeit relatively recently, to include situations of hostilities between organised armed groups, the exclusion of such situations from the Statute appeared unwarranted to many delegates. Furthermore, if an armed group failed to meet criteria such as possessing responsible command or control over territory they would also fail to meet the requirements of section D and the offences listed therein would thus not be within the Court's jurisdiction.[45]

Leone, Italy, Canada, Denmark, Hungary, Estonia, Slovenia, Zimbabwe, Bosnia and Herzegovina, Finland, Romania and Lithuania.

41 A/CONF.183/C.1/SR.34, para. 22.

42 This was also the view of the ICRC. The last speaker to address the Committee of the Whole on the matter was Louise Doswald-Beck of the ICRC:

> With regard to armed conflicts not of an international character, she pointed out that, under the new threshold added to section D, many conflicts, and indeed most internal armed conflicts, would not be covered, and that many atrocities would thus not be triable under the Statute. Furthermore, many of the acts listed in section D were recognized as crimes by customary law. It was therefore most important that section D should not be omitted.

A/CONF.183/C.1/SR.36, para. 52.

43 *Ibid.*, para. 2. 44 A/CONF.183/C.1/SR.34, para. 60.

45 This point was made by Australian representative Geoffrey James Skillen who was opposed to the additional language in the *chapeau* of section D of article 5 *quater*: 'It

While the new threshold of application for section D was considerably higher than that previously assumed by delegates, its inclusion followed a line of reasoning that did not depart from conventional international humanitarian law. The incorporation of language from Article 1(1) of Additional Protocol II into the *chapeau* of section D would have appeared reasonable to the Bureau given that most of the offences listed in this section had been provided for in the Protocol. Nevertheless, as indicated by the statements included above, the new threshold of application was clearly not acceptable to the Conference. While opposition to the new threshold was strong among states that had backed the inclusion of sections C and D, support for the new *chapeau* was also lacking among those delegations opposed to the inclusion of non-international armed conflicts clauses. Despite the high threshold of the new *chapeau*, the deletion of sections C and D continued to be supported by the majority of states who had previously opposed these provisions. States, such as India,[46] Turkey,[47] Algeria,[48] Pakistan,[49] Qatar,[50] Iraq,[51] Libyan Arab Jamahiriya[52] and Oman[53] took the floor during the 34th to the 36th meetings of the Committee of the Whole to voice their resistance to the inclusion of clauses relating to non-international armed conflict.

As an approach that sought to balance the concerns of states opposed to non-international armed conflicts clauses with the position of states favouring the inclusion of such provisions, the Bureau proposal failed to achieve the required consensus. Records of the discussion in the Committee of the Whole show a continued divergence of views on the matter. In an effort to break this impasse, an amendment to the text proposed by the Bureau was submitted by the delegation of a country that was at the time itself engaged in non-international armed conflict.[54]

5.2.3.2 The Sierra Leone proposal

As an alternative to the threshold introduced by the Bureau, a proposal to broaden the scope of applicability stipulated in the *chapeau* was submitted to delegates during the thirty-fifth meeting of the Committee

would not cover conflicts between two or more dissident groups or those in which the dissident group failed to meet the criteria of responsible command or territorial control.' A/CONF.183/C.1/SR.34, para. 107.

[46] A/CONF.183/C.1/SR.33, para. 37. [47] A/CONF.183/C.1/SR.34, para. 48.

[48] A/CONF.183/C.1/SR.35, para. 31. [49] *Ibid.*, para. 54.

[50] *Ibid.*, para. 57. [51] *Ibid.*, para. 64.

[52] A/CONF.183/C.1/SR.36, para. 6. [53] *Ibid.*, para. 20.

[54] A/CONF.183/C.1/L.62 (13 May 1998).

of the Whole. Issued on 13 July 1998, the proposal was put forward on the day the Committee was due to conclude its discussion on the war crimes provisions of the draft Statute. Speaking on behalf of Sierra Leone, Fode M. Dabor urged

> that sections C and D should be included in the new article 5 quater, but it had reservations, for example, regarding the chapeau of section D, which referred to organized armed groups that exercised 'control over a part of [a State party's] territory'. That wording was very restrictive: in his own country, for example, the rebel forces did not occupy a territory. Thus, as presently drafted, section D would exclude the type of internal conflict presently taking place in Sierra Leone. His delegation therefore proposed that the second sentence of the chapeau should be replaced by the text: 'It applies to armed conflicts that take place in a territory of a State when there is protracted armed conflict between governmental authorities and organized armed groups or between such groups.'[55]

The proposed amendment was modelled on language taken from the *Tadić* Jurisdiction Decision of 2 October 1995.[56] Discussed in Chapter 4, this decision defined non-international armed conflict as 'protracted armed violence between governmental authorities and organized armed groups or between such groups within a State'. For the purposes of the Sierra Leone proposal, the word 'violence' was replaced with 'conflict'.[57]

Instead of applying to situations of armed conflict 'that take place in a territory of a State Party between its armed forces and dissident armed forces or other organized armed groups which, under responsible command, exercise such control over a part of its territory as to enable them to carry out sustained and concerted military operations', the amendment suggested a lower threshold of 'protracted armed conflict between governmental authorities and organized armed groups or between such groups'. Conditions such as the existence of responsible command, control over territory and the conduct of sustained and concerted military operations were not included in Sierra Leone's amendment. The requirement of state involvement in hostilities was also no longer considered necessary.

Sierra Leone was not the only state engaged in non-international armed conflict to have a representative voice criticising the threshold contained in the *chapeau* of section D. Other such delegates who had

[55] A/CONF.183/C.1/SR.35, para. 8. [56] *Tadić* Jurisdiction Decision, para. 70.

[57] The significance of the change in wording for the interpretation of Article 8(2)(f) will be discussed later.

expressed opposition towards the Bureau proposal included representatives from Guinea-Bissau,[58] the Sudan[59] and Uganda.[60] Arguing that the Bureau proposal had unduly limited the scope of the Court's jurisdiction in situations of non-international armed conflict, the Head of the Ugandan delegation, Bertazar Katureebe, was supportive of the Sierra Leone amendment:

> Uganda shared other delegations' concern about the watering down of the Court's jurisdiction over situations of internal conflict. As currently worded, the second sentence of the chapeau of article 5 quater, section D, severely limited the Court's scope in that regard. Whether or not the perpetrators controlled territory was immaterial: they might be operating from a neighbouring country, with or without that country's consent, as was currently the case in Uganda. His delegation thus supported the proposal by the representative of Sierra Leone with regard to the chapeau of section D.[61]

Addressing the Committee of the Whole on behalf of the Solomon Islands, Professor Andrew Clapham also expressed support for Sierra Leone's proposal:

> On the question of war crimes in internal armed conflict, his delegation supported the inclusion of sections C and D in article 5 quater. However, the new chapeau of section D did not take account of the sort of contemporary conflict that the Court was designed to address. If the chapeau was retained, it should be amended to cover armed conflict between armed groups, as suggested by the representative of Sierra Leone.[62]

In addition to these statements, delegates from Slovenia[63] and Bosnia and Herzegovina[64] also took the floor to voice support for the Sierra Leone proposal. Given the strong opposition that had been voiced towards the threshold provision derived from Article 1(1) of Additional Protocol II, and the emphasis that had been placed on including armed conflict taking place between armed groups, the proposal presented by Sierra Leone was a more favourable option for securing support of the Conference. It was thus incorporated into the consolidated text of the draft Statute proposed for adoption by the Committee of the Whole on 17 July 1998. Formal consideration of this non-international armed conflict threshold, included as Article 8(2)(f) of the Statute, was concluded at 10.50 p.m. on Monday, 13 July.[65] There is no record of any further

[58] A/CONF.183/C.1/SR.28, para. 77. [59] A/CONF.183/C.1/SR.34, para. 94.
[60] A/CONF.183/C.1/SR.35, para. 23. [61] *Ibid.*
[62] *Ibid.*, para. 79. [63] A/CONF.183/C.1/SR.36, para. 30.
[64] *Ibid.*, para. 42. [65] A/CONF.183/C.1/SR.37, para. 53.

discussion of the matter between this date and that of 17 July when the Statute as a whole was adopted by the Conference. The lack of recorded comment on this provision was due to the timing of Sierra Leone's proposal and the shortage of time available to the Committee of the Whole.[66] The amendment was tabled during the thirty-fifth meeting of the Committee, not long before it was due to conclude consideration of the Bureau's discussion paper.[67] Given the numerous other issues that had to be agreed upon in the final days of the Conference, the Bureau could not afford to reopen the matter.

Despite the lack of substantive comment by delegates on Sierra Leone's proposal, it is clear from the *travaux préparatoires* of the Rome Statute that the provision would never have been included if certain views on the applicable threshold were not accommodated by the Conference. This point will be returned to in the section that follows, which argues for the interpretation of Article 8(2)(f) as a development of Article 8(2)(d).

5.3 Interpreting the threshold contained in Article 8(2)(f)

The language of Article 8(2)(f) does not facilitate straightforward interpretation. While the provision appears to introduce a standard similar to that propounded in the *Tadić* Jurisdiction Decision, it is not immediately clear as to whether the threshold is equivalent to that assumed for the application of common Article 3. There are two reasons for this. First, the phrase 'protracted armed conflict' is used instead of the 'protracted armed violence' formulation that is used in the *Tadić* Jurisdiction Decision. Second, there are two distinct sections in Article 8 listing crimes relating to situations of non-international armed conflict and each is followed by a provision stipulating a threshold of application. Does Article 8(2)(f) thus imply a new category of non-international armed conflict, one that had previously not existed in international humanitarian law, or does it represent another codification of an existing threshold? There exist contending schools of thought on the answer to this question.

Given the lack of consensus on the meaning of Article 8(2)(f), it is important to examine carefully the text of this provision in light of the guidance on interpretation provided by the Vienna Convention

[66] A/CONF.183/C.1/SR.34, para. 1.

[67] The 35th meeting of the Committee of the Whole began at 18.05 on Monday, 13 July 1998. The Committee concluded consideration of the Bureau's discussion paper at 22.50 the same day.

on the Laws of Treaties. Article 31(1) of the Convention states as a general rule of interpretation that 'A treaty shall be interpreted in good faith in accordance with the ordinary meaning to be given to the terms of the treaty in their context and in the light of its object and purpose.' The 'context' of Article 8(2)(f) is discussed below at section 5.3.1, where the intention of the Statute's drafters is considered. At section 5.3.2 the 'ordinary meaning' given to the terms of Article 8(2)(f) is examined, exploring a plain reading of the provision in conjunction with sections (c), (d) and (e). Finally, the customary status of non-international armed conflict offences is highlighted at section 5.3.3, focusing in particular on the interpretation of the threshold contained in 8(2)(f).

5.3.1 *The meaning of the threshold intended by the Rome Conference*

The original context of a provision is particularly important for its interpretation when the meaning of the text can be considered ambiguous. In considering 'context', Article 32 of the Vienna Convention provides that:

> Recourse may be had to supplementary means of interpretation, including the preparatory work of the treaty and the circumstances of its conclusion, in order to confirm the meaning resulting from the application of article 31, or to determine the meaning when the interpretation according to article 31: (a) leaves the meaning ambiguous or obscure; or (b) leads to a result which is manifestly absurd or unreasonable.

The divergence of scholarly opinion on the meaning of Article 8(2)(f) arguably increases the significance of the *travaux préparatoires* of the Rome Statute as a supplementary source of interpretation.[68] However, as noted in the preceding section, the official record of discussion on the final text of this threshold provision is brief and contains no reference as to how states understood Sierra Leone's proposal in relation to the existing threshold of application for common Article 3. In the absence of such explicit clarification, it is useful to recall views expressed by delegates on the concept of non-international armed conflict before the Committee of the Whole. It is clear that the majority of states would have rejected the proposal if it merely submitted a reformulation of the threshold contained in Article 1(1) of Additional Protocol II. It is also clear that the majority of states favoured the inclusion of a threshold that would allow

[68] The different schools of thought on the interpretation of Article 8(2)(f) will be returned to in section 5.3.2.

the provisions contained in section D to apply to situations of armed conflict between organised armed groups.

It is furthermore worth noting that prior to the Bureau's proposal for an additional threshold, delegates had assumed only one threshold of application for war crimes committed in non-international armed conflict. The proposal was shared with delegates only days before the five-week long Conference was due to conclude. Its hasty introduction indicates that the inclusion of an additional non-international armed conflict threshold had not been well thought through.[69] Apart from the many problems associated with the text of Article 1(1) of Additional Protocol II,[70] the drafting history of the Statute shows consistency in positing one threshold for all provisions relating to armed conflict not of an international character. Reports of the Preparatory Committee offer no differentiation of different thresholds of application for non-international armed conflict. It had been assumed that all non-international armed conflict provisions possessed the same field of applicability, i.e., armed conflict not of an international character.

The introduction of a new non-international armed conflict threshold clearly departs from the approach previously adopted by the drafters of the Rome Statute. Considering the context of the Bureau's proposal, i.e. a divergence of positions among states on non-international armed conflict clauses, and the fact that it was raised only four days before the Conference was to close, this initiative was clearly motivated by an interest in securing the general agreement of participants as soon as possible. The fact that no delegate voiced support for the proposal and that a significant number addressed the Committee of the Whole to criticise it, indicates an acute lack of support for the Bureau's idea of including an additional non-international armed conflict threshold.

The lack of support for the Bureau's proposal is significant. Considering how it was received by delegates, it would appear reasonable to exclude the objective of the proposal from the interpretation of the threshold in Article 8(2)(f). The position of the Conference is clear from the Official Records – the same threshold had applied to all offences relating to situations of non-international armed conflict prior to the Bureau's proposal.[71] The idea of introducing one from

[69] The Conference was due to close on 17 July and the Bureau's proposal for an additional threshold was only discussed before the Committee of the Whole on 13 July 1998.

[70] See Chapter 4, at section 4.2.2.

[71] See section 5.2.3.1.

Additional Protocol II for section D was unacceptable.[72] As noted by Theodor Meron, if the proposal had succeeded it would have made this part of Article 8 'virtually ineffectual'.[73] Sierra Leone's amendment was incorporated as a means of fixing this problem. However, as the language contained in Sierra Leone's proposal had never been used before in an international treaty, it has thus been vulnerable to divergent interpretations, as noted earlier.

If the intention of the Statute's drafters is to be adhered to, the interpretation of the thresholds contained in Article 8 should not be coloured by division of offences relating to armed conflict not of an international character into sections 2(c) and 2(e). Prior to the Bureau's initiative both sections had been covered by the one *chapeau*. The fact that each section is now covered by a different *chapeau* should not necessarily be taken to imply different fields of application. Indeed, it will be argued in the section that follows that Article 8(2)(f) must be read as a development of the threshold contained in Article 8(2)(d), implying uniformity of applicability for both sections.

5.3.2 Textual interpretation of Article 8(2)(f)

The structure of Article 8 reflects the fact that the Statute was formulated through a process of negotiation. The awkward composition of this provision dealing with war crimes is commented on by Professor William Schabas, who states that 'not only are the specific acts set out in excruciating detail, but the actual categories impose a difficult exercise of assessment of the type of armed conflict involved'.[74] The divergent interpretations of the threshold contained in Article 8(2)(f) reflect an ambiguity in the text. Stated in full, the provision reads:

> Paragraph 2 (e) applies to armed conflicts not of an international character and thus does not apply to situations of internal disturbances and tensions, such as riots, isolated and sporadic acts of violence or other acts of a similar nature. It applies to armed conflicts that take place in the territory of a State when there is protracted armed conflict between governmental authorities and organized armed groups or between such groups.

The first sentence of Article 8(2)(f), reproduced from Article 1(2) of Additional Protocol II, provides an uncontroversial, negative formulation of the lower threshold of non-international armed conflict. Referring

[72] *Ibid.*
[73] Meron, *War Crimes Law*, p. 309.
[74] Schabas, *International Criminal Court*, p. 116.

to the exclusion of internal disturbances and tensions, the text is also included in Article 8(2)(d) of the Rome Statute. The second sentence of Article 8(2)(f) states a positive formulation of the same threshold. In doing so, it provides a source of contention for scholars of international law. The question as to whether the sentence represents a new threshold or the reformulation of an existing one is critically important for determining the applicability of the provisions contained in Article 8(2)(e). If interpreted as a new threshold, it would also imply the existence of a new category of non-international armed conflict. In order to apply the provisions contained in Article 8(2)(e), the Court would have to distinguish a situation's status according to how it interprets the characteristics of this as yet undefined, new category of armed conflict. If interpreted as a reformulation of an existing threshold, i.e. the threshold for the application of common Article 3, Article 8(2)(f) would correspond to the previously existing concept of non-international armed conflict in international humanitarian law. According to Marco Sassoli and Antoine Bouvier, however, the threshold contained in Article 8(2)(f) is distinct from that of common Article 3:

> The Statute of the International Criminal Court provides an intermediary threshold of application. There is no longer a requirement for the conflict to take place between governmental forces and rebel forces, for the latter to control part of territory, nor for there to be a responsible command. The conflict must however be protracted and the armed groups must be organized.[75]

Professor William Schabas also allows for the interpretation of an additional category of non-international armed conflict in Article 8(2)(f):

> As it now stands, Article 8 consists of four categories of war crimes, two of them addressing international armed conflict and two of them non-international armed conflict ... Courts will be required to distinguish between international and non-international armed conflicts, and this is further complicated by the fact that within the subset of non-international conflicts there are two distinct categories.[76]

While acknowledging the existence of diverging views on the interpretation of the thresholds contained in Article 8(2)(f) and Article 8(2)(d), Schabas further states that the 'better view would seem to be that there are no material distinctions between them'.[77]

[75] Sassoli and Bouvier (eds.), *How Does Law Protect in War?*, vol. I, p. 110. See also Provost, *International Human Rights*, pp. 268–9.

[76] Schabas, *International Criminal Court*, p. 54.

[77] Schabas, *International Criminal Court*, p. 131.

Judge Theodor Meron, however, insists that Article 8(2)(f) 'should not be considered as creating yet another threshold of applicability'.[78] Recalling the drafting of the Rome Statute, he states that:

> The reference to protracted armed conflict was designed to give some satisfaction to those delegations that insisted on the incorporation of the higher threshold of applicability of Article 1(1) of Additional Protocol II. It may be noted that this language tracks language contained in paragraph 70 of the *Tadić* decision on interlocutory appeal on jurisdiction of the ICTY (2 October 1995). Attempts to interpret protracted armed conflict as recognizing an additional high threshold of application should be resisted.[79]

Michael Bothe supports a position similar to that of Judge Meron. Describing Article 8(2)(f) as a 'replica' of the definition propounded in the *Tadić* Jurisdiction Decision, Bothe interprets a uniform threshold of application for situations of non-international armed conflict in the Rome Statute.[80] In doing so he maintains that there are only two distinct thresholds of applicability in Article 8: one relating to the distinction between international armed conflict and non-international armed conflict, and one relating to the distinction between non-international armed conflict and situations of internal disturbances and tensions that by definition do not constitute armed conflict.[81]

This position is favoured here. In supporting one uniform threshold of application for situations of non-international armed conflict, the section that follows examines the significance of the term 'armed conflict not of an international character' in Article 8(2)(c), (d), (e) and (f).

[78] Meron, 'Humanitarian Law', at 260.

[79] Meron, 'Crimes under the Jurisdiction of the International Criminal Court', in Herman A.M. von Hebel *et. al.*, *Reflections*, p. 54.

[80] Bothe, 'War Crimes', p. 423.

[81] Bothe states that:

> The systematic order of Article 8 (crimes in connection with an international armed conflict/crimes in connection with non-international armed conflict) involves the need to determine two different thresholds: that between an international and non-international armed conflict and that between an armed conflict and a situation which does not at all constitute an armed conflict within the meaning of subparagraphs (c) or (e). The latter threshold is regulated by subparagraphs (e) and (f) for subparagraphs (c) and (e), respectively.

Ibid., p. 418.

5.3.2.1 Applicability of Article 8(2)(c) and Article 8(2)(e) to 'armed conflicts not of an international character'

If understood as a development of the threshold contained in Article 8(2)(d), the text of Article 8(2)(f) would possess the same field of application as common Article 3. The first line of Article 8(2)(d) states the context of its application as 'armed conflict not of an international character'. This term is taken directly from the first line of common Article 3. Referred to in the Commentary of the ICRC as the field of application of this provision,[82] 'armed conflict not of an international character' indicates the established lower threshold for the application for international humanitarian law in all situations of non-international armed conflict. The use of this phrase in the Rome Statute is significant because of the meaning it has acquired in international humanitarian law. The exact wording has been reproduced in a number of instruments to indicate applicability to situations of non-international armed conflict falling within the scope of common Article 3. Examples include the Convention for the Protection of Cultural Property in the Event of Armed Conflict;[83] the Protocol on Prohibitions or Restrictions on the Use of Mines, Booby-Traps and Other Devices;[84] the Convention on Prohibitions or Restrictions on the Use of Certain Conventional Weapons Which may be Deemed to be Excessively Injurious or to Have Indiscriminate Effects;[85] and the Second Protocol to the Hague Convention of 1954 for the Protection of Cultural Property in the Event of Armed Conflict.[86]

It is significant that among instruments of international law there are no exceptions to this practice. It is worth noting that the term 'armed conflict not of an international character' is not used in the main text of Additional Protocol II and that this is consistent with the meaning of the term. As explained in Chapter 4, the Protocol has a much higher threshold of application. While Additional Protocol II

[82] Pictet (ed.), *Commentary I*, p. 49.

[83] Convention for the Protection of Cultural Property in the Event of Armed Conflict, 1954, Article 19(1).

[84] Protocol on Prohibitions or Restrictions on the Use of Mines, Booby-Traps and Other Devices as amended on 3 May 1996 (Protocol II to the 1980 Convention as amended on 3 May 1996), Article 1(3).

[85] Convention on Prohibitions or Restrictions on the Use of Certain Conventional Weapons Which may be Deemed to be Excessively Injurious or to Have Indiscriminate Effects, 2001, Article 1(3).

[86] Second Protocol to the Hague Convention of 1954 for the Protection of Cultural Property in the Event of Armed Conflict, 1999, Article 22.

relates to situations of non-international armed conflict, its application is limited to conflicts 'which take place in the territory of a High Contracting Party between its armed forces and dissident armed forces or other organized armed groups which, under responsible command, exercise such control over a part of its territory as to enable them to carry out sustained and concerted military operations and to implement this Protocol'.[87] The only usage of 'armed conflict not of an international character' in this instrument is in the preamble, where the context is a specific reference to common Article 3.[88] While there is no record of discussion relating to the meaning of the term in the *travaux préparatoires* of Additional Protocol II, there is evidence to suggest that its omission from the main text followed as a logical consequence of how the threshold of application associated with common Article 3 differed distinctly from that of the Protocol. According to the Commentary of the ICRC, the approach adopted:

> endeavoured to keep intact the achievements of common Article 3 by providing that the conditions of application of that article would not be modified. Keeping the conditions of application of common Article 3 as they are, and stipulating that the proposed definition will not apply to that article, meant that the Protocol was conceived as a self-contained instrument, additional to the four Conventions and applicable to all armed conflicts which comply with the definition and are not covered by common Article 2. Keeping the Protocol separate from common Article 3 was intended to prevent undercutting the scope of Article 3 itself by laying down precise rules. In this way common Article 3 retains an independent existence.[89]

To safeguard the scope of 'armed conflict not of an international character', Article 1(1) of the Protocol states that it develops and supplements common Article 3 'without modifying its existing conditions or application'. The ICRC Commentary on Article 1(1) explains this reference to the distinct field of application for common Article 3 constituted:

> one of the bases of the compromise which made the adoption of Article 1 possible ... [C]ommon Article 3 retains an autonomous existence, i.e., its

[87] Protocol Additional to the Geneva Conventions of 12 August 1949 and Relating to the Protection of Victims of Non-International Armed Conflicts, 12 December 1977, art. 1, 1125 UNTS 609.

[88] 'The High Contracting Parties, Recalling that the humanitarian principles enshrined in Article 3 common to the Geneva Conventions of 12 August 1949, constitute the foundation of respect for the human person in cases of armed conflict not of an international character.'

[89] Pilloud *et al.*, *Commentary*, p. 1350.

applicability is neither limited nor affected by the material field of application of the Protocol. This formula, though legally rather complicated, has the advantage of furnishing a guarantee against any reduction of the level of protection long since provided by common Article 3.[90]

While the title of the Additional Protocol states that it relates to 'the protection of victims of non-international armed conflicts', its scope is clearly limited to internal hostilities possessing certain characteristics, e.g. the conduct of sustained and concerted military operations, control of territory, the existence of responsible command, and so on. The term 'armed conflict not of an international character' relates to all situations of non-international armed conflict irrespective of whether such conditions are met. Its omission from the Protocol is thus consistent with the practice of using the term to distinguish the lower threshold for the application of international humanitarian law in situations of non-international armed conflict.

Given the threshold of application associated with 'armed conflict not of an international character', it is significant to note the common usage of the term in the first lines of paragraphs 2(c) and 2(e). Interpreted according to its conventional usage, the term would imply equivalent fields of application for these provisions. In addition to its usage in paragraphs 2(c) and 2(e) 'armed conflict not of an international character' is also used in paragraphs (d) and (f) in explicitly demarcating their scope of applicability. As conventional usage of the term indicates the lower threshold for the existence of armed conflict, it would appear peculiar for the utilisation of 'armed conflict not of an international character' in the Statute to be interpreted differently. The distinctive threshold of application associated with 'armed conflict not of an international character' suggests uniformity of application for sections 2(c) and 2(e) of Article 8. This supposition of uniformity is furthermore supported by a literal interpretation of the first line of 8(2)(e), which is examined in the section that follows.

5.3.2.2 The significance of the determiner 'other' in Article 8(2)(e)

The opening sentence of Article 8(2)(e) describes the provisions contained therein as '*other* serious violations of the laws and customs applicable to armed conflicts not of an international character'.[91] The

[90] *Ibid.*
[91] Emphasis added.

use of the word 'other' is significant in this context because it situates the offences listed in the same category of armed conflict as that of common Article 3. It follows by rule of logic in the use of this determiner that the 'serious violations of article 3 common to the four Geneva Conventions' listed in Article 8(2)(c) form a subset of 'serious violations of the laws and customs applicable to armed conflicts not of an international character'. If a plain reading of these clauses is adhered to, the use of 'other' would imply the same material field of application for Article 8(2)(e) as for 8(2)(c).

The drafting history of the Rome Statute is consistent on the use of the determiner mentioned above which allows specified war crimes to be situated in the same category of non-international armed conflict as common Article 3.[92] There is no record of this usage of 'other' being questioned in either the reports of the Preparatory Committee or Summary Records of the Rome Conference. The consistency of this formulation suggests an assumption that provisions relating to non-international armed conflict would apply uniformly to the category of situations constituting 'armed conflict not of an international character'.

If the approach adopted in the Statute's drafting history is adhered to, it follows that the provisions listed in Article 8(2)(c) and 8(2)(e) relate to only one category of non-international armed conflict. The determiner 'other' acts as a bridge between these two sections by explicitly situating the offences listed in one category of war crimes, i.e. 'serious violations of the laws and customs applicable to armed conflicts not of an international character'. Following this interpretation, the logical consequence is a shared threshold of application.

5.3.3 The customary status of provisions relating to non-international armed conflict and the interpretation of the threshold contained in Article 8(2)(f)

The interpretation of a shared threshold of application between 2(c) and 2(e) is supported by the customary status of the offences in these sections. It is arguable that their recognition as norms of customary

[92] See A/CONF.183/2/Add.1, p. 26; Report of the Inter-Session Meeting from 19 to 30 January 1998 in Zutphen, the Netherlands; A/AC.249/1998/L.13, 1998, p. 28; Decisions Taken by the Preparatory Committee at its Session Held 1 to 12 December 1997, A/AC.249/1997/L.9/Rev. 1, 1997, p. 12; Decisions Taken by the Preparatory Committee at its Session Held 11 to 21 February 1997, A/AC.249/1997/L.5, 1997, p. 12; and Report of the Preparatory Committee on the Establishment of an International Criminal Court, vol. II (Compilation of Proposals), GA, 51st Sess., Supp. No. 22, A/51/22, 1996, p. 62.

international law (applicable in all situations of armed conflict) makes the interpretation of a new category of non-international armed conflict in 8(2)(f) superfluous. Given that the *chapeau* of 2(e) states that all offences in this section stand 'within the established framework of international law', it would seem unusual to place the interpretation of 8(2)(f) outside this framework. According to Philippe Kirsch, there was a 'general agreement that the definitions of crimes in the ICC Statute were to reflect existing customary international law, and not to create new law'.[93] While not all provisions in Article 8 correspond to customary international law, it is clear that the offences listed relating to non-international armed conflict do have customary status.

Evidence of the customary status of 2(c) and 2(e) is provided by the ICRC study entitled *Customary International Humanitarian Law*.[94] The study details customary rules applicable to situations of international and non-international armed conflict. The offences listed in Article 8(2)(c) and 8(2)(e) are covered in these rules.[95] Their status as customary international law is illustrated in the study through the reproduction of the relevant state practice.[96] No distinction is made between different categories of non-international armed conflict or different thresholds for the application of international humanitarian law to situations of non-international armed conflict. This would suggest that no such differentiation is warranted for the application of customary rules to non-international armed conflicts, irrespective of their intensity. Given that the study does not distinguish different thresholds of applicability for non-international armed conflicts, and that the prohibitions listed in 2(c) and 2(e) are covered in rules applicable to both international and non-international armed conflict, it is evident that the interpretation of an additional threshold of applicability in 8(2)(f) would restrict the scope of the rules contained in 2(e) contrary to customary international law. If interpreted as a threshold distinct from that of 2(d), paragraph 2(f) would clearly confine the applicability of the norms contained in section 2(e) to a more limited category of situation. In order to situate offences 'within the established framework of the international law',[97] it would appear rational to interpret paragraphs 2(d) and 2(f) as

[93] Cited in Dormann, *Elements of War Crimes*, p. xiii.

[94] Henckaerts and Doswald-Beck (eds.), *Customary International Humanitarian Law*, vols. I and II.

[95] See Cullen, 'Definition of Non-International Armed Conflict', at 444, fn 105.

[96] *Ibid.*, fn 106.

[97] Article 8(2)(e).

stipulating the same threshold of application.[98] If not, then a departure from the existing standard of customary international law would be clearly evident.

5.4 Concluding observations

Considering the foregoing analysis of Article 8(2)(f), there exist clear grounds for the interpretation of one uniform concept of non-international armed conflict in the Rome Statute. The interpretation of an additional threshold of application creates a separate category of armed conflict and is not favoured here for a number of reasons. First, as illustrated earlier, there is evidence to suggest that such an interpretation would be contrary to the intention of the Statute's drafters. Second, the use of the term 'armed conflict not of an international character', interpreted in line with its conventional usage, indicates a threshold of application equivalent to that of common Article 3. Third, a plain reading of Article 8(2)(e) itself supports an interpretation of one threshold relating to non-international armed conflict, situating all crimes in this section in the same category of situation as 8(2)(c). The customary status of the Statute's non-international armed conflict provisions also supports the supposition of a common threshold of application.

It is useful also to consider the teleological aspect of this interpretation. If one of the cardinal functions of the Court is to provide a source of redress for war crimes committed in non-international armed conflict, it would arguably better serve the interests of the victims to avoid the introduction of distinctions that could unnecessarily complicate the application of war crimes provisions. As noted in the conclusion that follows, it is important to bear in mind the object and purpose of international humanitarian law when interpreting the concept of non-international armed conflict.

98 This would also be consistent with the Elements of Crimes, which state that the war crimes listed in 8(2) 'shall be interpreted within the established framework of the law of armed conflict'.

6 Conclusion

The aim of this study has been twofold: first, to highlight misconceptions surrounding the threshold of non-international armed conflict and, second, to present an argument for a particular approach to its interpretation. The approach adopted was to examine the development of the threshold and then to provide an analysis its contemporary formulation. It is hoped that by doing so, the content of this work may prove useful for the characterisation of non-international armed conflict.

Before elaborating on particular themes common to each of the chapters included above, it is beneficial first to provide an overview of the route taken in this work. The first chapter provided a starting point for the study in the international legal regime which preceded the Geneva Conventions of 1949. Here the relevant concepts of traditional international law were examined: rebellion, insurgency and belligerency. The mandatory application of international humanitarian standards in situations of civil war, achieved through recognition of belligerency, was viewed to be a significant development of international law. This practice of belligerent recognition emerged as a means of preserving the interests of states in the conduct of their international relations. While governed by restrictive criteria and limited to situations akin to conventional international war, the recognition of belligerency nevertheless introduced a practice allowing international legal concern for situations of armed conflict that were distinctly non-international in character. Although clearly a significant influence in the formulation of common Article 3, the doctrine of belligerency has now fallen into disuse.

The intended threshold for the application of common Article 3 was examined in Chapter 2. Here the drafting history of the provision was probed to illustrate how its scope, characterised by the term 'armed conflicts not of an international character', was understood by the drafters of the Geneva Conventions as being limited to situations of civil war. This intended threshold of applicability, evidenced in the *travaux préparatoires* of the Geneva Conventions, was similar to that required for the recognition of belligerency. This was confirmed in the Commentary of the International Committee of the Red Cross (ICRC) which interpreted the meaning of 'armed conflict not of an international character' in terms similar to civil war.

As the first codification specific to situations of non-international armed conflict, common Article 3 represented a turning point in the development of international humanitarian law. While the drafters of common Article 3 foresaw its application to situations akin to conventional international war, the use of the term 'armed conflict not of an international character' has allowed the concept scope to evolve. The absence of a formula determining the applicability of common Article 3 has, however, also had the effect of weakening its implementation. This is illustrated by the tendency of states engaged in non-international armed conflict not to recognise the applicability of this provision.

The field of application associated with common Article 3, framed in the term 'armed conflict not of an international character', has come to be recognised as the lower threshold for the application of international humanitarian law in all situations of non-international armed conflict. Two other thresholds for the application of international humanitarian law were examined in Chapter 3 in order to assess their impact on the concept of non-international armed conflict. This chapter focused on the Additional Protocols of 1977. Additional Protocol I internationalised wars of national liberation while Additional Protocol II created a new category of non-international armed conflict.

The internationalisation of wars of national liberation was brought about through Article 1(4) of Additional Protocol I. This provision extended the scope of international armed conflict to cover 'armed conflicts which peoples are fighting against colonial domination and alien occupation and against racist regimes in the exercise of their right of self-determination'. While much of the Protocol's content reflects customary international law, it was argued that Article 1(4) does not possess such status. Having considered that Article 1(4) has never been positively applied, and that no state whose interests are specially affected by the provision has ever recognised its applicability, the impact of this development on the characterisation of non-international armed conflict was deemed not significant.

The new category of non-international armed conflict introduced by Additional Protocol II was created through Article 1(1) of the instrument. This provision states that the Protocol shall apply to armed conflicts which 'take place in the territory of a High Contracting Party between its armed forces and dissident armed forces or other organized armed groups which, under responsible command, exercise such control over a part of its territory as to enable them to carry out sustained and concerted military operations and to implement this Protocol'. The threshold of application embodied in Article 1(1) was regarded as a regressive development for narrowing the scope of the Protocol's applicability using conditions similar in certain respects to those required for the recognition of belligerency. However, this is a threshold peculiar to Additional Protocol II and does not reflect customary international law. As most of the rules contained in the Protocol have crystallised into norms of customary international law applicable in all situations of non-international armed conflict, the relevance of the threshold contained in Article 1(1) to the applicability of these rules was questioned.

After establishing the status of the thresholds created by the Additional Protocols of 1977, and having examined their standing in relation to the threshold of common Article 3, the study then moved on to investigate the lower threshold for the application of international humanitarian law to situations of non-international armed conflict in Chapter 4. Here the definition of non-international armed conflict provided by the International Criminal Tribunal for the former Yugoslavia (ICTY) ('protracted armed violence between governmental authorities and organized armed groups or between such groups within a State') was explored in detail. Held as the most authoritative contemporary standard indicating the lower threshold for the application of international humanitarian law, the elements of the definition were probed to highlight its composition as a formula for determining the existence of armed conflict. In doing so, it was contended that the threshold associated with common Article 3 does not require the existence of responsible command and should not be interpreted using the Commentary of the ICRC.

The analysis of the threshold of non-international armed conflict in Chapter 4 informed the analysis of the Rome Statute of the International Criminal Court in Chapter 5. This chapter focuses in particular on the interpretation of the threshold of application contained in Article 8(2)(f) of the Statute. After probing the *travaux préparatoires* of this instrument, an argument was advanced for the interpretation of the threshold contained in Article 8(2)(f) as a development of Article 8(2)(d). In doing so it was maintained that both provisions share the same threshold of application, a threshold identical to that of common Article 3. This position was supported by an analysis of the debate that took place at the Rome Conference, the customary status of norms contained in Article 8(2)(c) and 8(2)(e) and a plain reading of the text informed by the Elements of Crimes for the Rome Statute. It was furthermore held that the interpretation of separate thresholds would not serve the interests of victims and that it would be best to avoid unwarranted distinctions between different categories of non-international armed conflict.

6.1 On the interpretation of non-international armed conflict

In terms of chronology, Chapters 1 to 3 provided an overview of the origins of the non-international armed conflict concept and its development prior to the establishment of the international criminal tribunals for Rwanda and the Former Yugoslavia while Chapters 4 and 5 examined developments of more recent significance to the interpretation of the threshold of non-international armed conflict in international humanitarian law. The analysis contained in the latter half of the study is informed by the findings of the former. Given that the contemporary concept of non-international armed conflict bears little resemblance to that intended by the drafters of common Article 3, it is not unforeseeable that the associated threshold of applicability may in the future be subject to further development. As noted by the Nuremburg Tribunal, the laws that govern armed conflict 'are not static, but by continual adaptation follow the needs of a changing world'.[1] The interpretation of international humanitarian law should be guided, among other things, by its object and purpose.[2] The object and purpose of this body of law is the protection of victims of armed conflict.[3] Any further development of the threshold of application

[1] *Trial of Major War Criminals before the International Military Tribunal*, Nuremburg, 14 November 1945–1 October 1946, vol. I, p. 221.

[2] Vienna Convention on the Law of Treaties, 1155 UNTS 331, 8 ILM 679, Article 31(1).

[3] Protocol Additional to the Geneva Conventions of 12 August 1949, and Relating to the Protection of Victims of International Armed Conflicts, 1125 UNTS 3, 1977,

associated with non-international armed conflict should be guided by this as the *raison d'être* of international humanitarian law.

In the context of protecting the victims of armed conflict, it is worth bearing in mind the maxim of *hominum causa omne jus constitutum est* (all law is created for the benefit of human beings). This maxim was used by the Appeals Chamber of the ICTY in the *Tadić* Jurisdiction Decision to highlight the influence of international human rights standards in the development of international humanitarian law.[4] It is important to recognise that there exists a tendency in state practice to a view that international human rights law and international humanitarian law are complementary and mutually reinforcing.[5] While considerations of reciprocity have been central to the historical development of the laws of war, it is notable that this is no longer the case. The humanisation of the law governing non-international armed conflict serves to limit, to the greatest possible extent, its consequences in terms of the human suffering. *Hominum causa omne jus constitutum est* serves as a reminder that the interpretation of the threshold for the application of international humanitarian law should be guided by an appropriate understanding of the purpose of this body of law. It should always in principle seek to provide the highest degree of protection to the victims of non-international armed conflict.

6.2 On the significance of the *Tadić* definition

The most authoritative contemporary formulation of the lower threshold for the application of international humanitarian law to

preambular para. 3; Protocol Additional to the Geneva Conventions of 12 August 1949 and Relating to the Protection of Victims of Non-International Armed Conflicts, 1125 UNTS 609, 1977, preambular para. 3. See Prosecutor v. Akayesu, Judgment, Appeals Chamber, 1 June 2001, Case No. ICTR 96-4, para. 630.

[4] *Tadić* Jurisdiction Decision, para. 97.

[5] See Resolution 2005/63 of the 61st session of the UNCHR, 'Protection of the Human Rights of Civilians in Armed Conflicts', 20 April 2005. For a survey of state practice related to the continued applicability of international human rights law in armed conflict, see Henckaerts and Doswald-Beck (eds.), *Humanitarian Law*, pp. 299–306. See also Hampson and Salama, 'Working Paper on the Relationship between Human Rights Law and International Humanitarian Law', UN Doc. E/CN.4/Sub.2/2005/14, 21 June 2005; Sassoli and Bouvier (eds.), *How Does Law Protect in War?*, vol. I pp. 342–53; Clapham, 'Human Rights Obligations'; HRC, General Comment No. 31, Nature of the General Legal Obligation Imposed on States Parties to the Covenant, CCPR/C/21/Rev.1/Add. 13, 26 May 2004, para. 11.

situations of non-international armed conflict is arguably the definition put forward in the *Tadić* Jurisdiction Decision: 'protracted armed violence between governmental authorities and organized armed groups or between such groups within a State'. The characterisation of situations using this definition is determined by two related criteria: the organisation of insurgents and the intensity of hostilities. It is important that these criteria should be applied carefully and not be interpreted according to the originally intended threshold of common Article 3 or the thresholds of application associated with Additional Protocols I or II. As illustrated in Chapter 2, the threshold intended by the drafters of common Article 3 was one similar to that of civil war. As explained in Chapter 4, the threshold of 'armed conflict not of an international character' now covers a variety of other situations, including cases of hostilities between organised armed groups without the involvement of governmental authorities. It also covers armed conflicts where insurgents lack control over territory. When referring to the field of application for common Article 3 it is important to recognise that the use of the term 'internal armed conflict' can sometimes be misleading. As the scope of this provision includes situations other than internal armed conflict, the term 'non-international armed conflict' is arguably more appropriate. This term mirrors more accurately the meaning of 'armed conflict not of an international character'. It also allows for the application of common Article 3 to situations that are neither internal nor international in nature and thus ensures there are no gaps in the scope of protection provided by international humanitarian law.

In order to avoid a lacuna in the application of the fundamental humanitarian guarantees provided by international humanitarian law, it essential that the threshold associated with common Article 3 is interpreted according to what would best serve the interests of victims. It is important in this regard not to introduce rigid or formalistic conditions into the applicability of international humanitarian law. The introduction of additional thresholds of application should be discouraged, as they can serve to complicate unnecessarily its implementation. Responsible command should not be treated as a requirement for the characterisation of non-international armed conflict. To do so would be to heighten the threshold for the application of international humanitarian law beyond that established for 'armed conflict not of an international character'.

6.3 The characterisation of non-international armed conflict and its effect on the legal status of parties

The characterisation of a situation as non-international armed conflict should also not be interpreted as implying a change in the legal status of non-state actors. Although there is nothing in international humanitarian law which would affect the legal status of organised armed groups engaged in non-international armed conflict, states are generally reluctant to recognise the applicability of international humanitarian law in such situations. While the practice of recognising the belligerency of warring parties is now obsolete, some authors still consider that it may have some influence on the behaviour of states.[6] As illustrated in Chapter 1, the practices of insurgent and belligerent recognition are from a different era of international relations. For a state to interpret a change in the legal status of an organised armed group as a result of the characterisation of non-international armed conflict would be to misconstrue the current regime of international humanitarian law with that which preceded it. While the doctrines of belligerency and insurgency served a purpose in defining relations between states prior to the formulation of the Geneva Conventions, they have now fallen into disuse and no longer have any bearing on the applicability of international humanitarian law to situations of non-international armed conflict. According to one author, they 'derail intelligent commentators and statesmen from the more productive pursuit of a genuine consensus on minimal humanitarian principles applicable in such domestic settings'.[7]

The concept of non-international armed conflict has evolved considerably over the past sixty years. It is important to recognise that the distinctions between different categories of armed conflict were not created as a means of streamlining the implementation of international humanitarian law. Indeed, it has been suggested by many experts that in principle one body of law should apply to all situations of armed conflict irrespective of their characterisation. The reproduction of the distinction contained in the Geneva Conventions between international and non-international armed conflict in the Rome Statute was viewed as a setback by many who had strived for its eradication to lessen complications in the implementation of international humanitarian

[6] See, for example, Stewart, 'Towards a Single Definition' at 348.
[7] Elder, 'Historical Background' at 40.

norms. Nevertheless, the terms of Article 8(2)(f) provide the Statute with the broadest scope possessed by any instrument concerned with the prohibition of war crimes. It should thus be viewed as a favourable development, providing an additional measure of protection for the victims of non-international armed conflict.

Bibliography

MONOGRAPHS

Alley, Roderic, *Internal Conflict and the International Community: Wars Without End?* (Dartmouth: Ashgate, 2004).

Altiparmak, Kerem, 'Responsibility for the Violation of Human Rights by Non-State Armed Groups', Ph.D. dissertation (Leeds: University of Leeds, 2002).

Arnold, Roberta, *The ICC as a New Instrument for Repressing Terrorism* (New York: Transnational Publishers, 2004).

Ayala, Balthazar, *On the Law of War* (Washington, DC: Carnegie Institution, 1912).

Ballentine, Karen and Sherman, Jake (eds.), *The Political Economy of Armed Conflict: Beyond Greed and Grievance* (Boulder, CO: Lynne Rienner Publishers, 2003).

Ballis, William B., *The Legal Position of War: Changes in its Practice and Theory from Plato to Vattel* (The Hague: Martinus Nijhoff Publishers, 1937).

Bassiouni, Cherif M., *Introduction to International Criminal Law* (New York: Transnational Publishers Inc., 2003).

Belli, Pierino, *A Treatise on Military Matters and Warfare in Eleven Parts*, H.C. Nuting (trans.) (Oxford: Clarendon Press, 1936).

Berdal, Mats R. and Malone, David M. (eds.), *Greed and Grievance: Economic Agendas in Civil Wars* (Boulder, CO: Lynne Rienner Publishers, 2000).

Best, Geoffrey Francis Andrew, *War and Law since 1945* (Oxford: Clarendon Press, 1994).

Black, C.E. and Falk, R.A. (eds.), *The Future of the International Legal Order* (Princeton, NJ: Princeton University Press, 1971).

Bond, James E., *The Rules of Riot: Internal Conflict and the Law of War* (Princeton: Princeton University Press, 1974).

Boot, Machteld, *Nullum Crimen Sine Lege and the Subject Matter Jurisdiction of the International Criminal Court: Genocide, Crimes against Humanity, War Crimes* (Oxford: Intersentia, 2002).

Borchard, Edwin M., *The Legal Evolution of Peace* (St. Louis, MO: Nixon Jones, 1911).

Bothe, M., Partsch, K.-J. and Solf, W.A., *New Rules for Victims of Armed Conflicts: Commentary on the Two 1977 Protocols Additional to the Geneva Conventions of 1949* (London: Martinus Nijhoff, 1982).
Brown Scott, James, *The Proceedings of the Hague Peace Conferences: Translation of the Official Texts*, vols. 1–5 (New York: Oxford University Press, 1920–1).
Brown Scott, J. (ed.), *Prize Cases Decided in the United States Supreme Court: 1789–1918, vol. III* (Oxford: Clarendon Press, 1923), pp. 1413–60.
Brownlie, Ian, *International Law and the Use of Force by States* (Oxford: Clarendon Press, 1981).
Principles of Public International Law, 4th edn (Oxford: Oxford University Press, 1990).
Buchheit, Lee C., *Secession: The Legitimacy of Self-Determination* (New Haven: Yale University Press, 1978).
Bynkershoek, Cornelius, *On the Law of War and Peace* (Oxford: Oxford University Press, 1923).
Cassese, Antonio (ed.), *Current Legal Problems of International Law and the Law of Armed Conflict* (Milan: Dott. A. Guiffre, 1975).
The New Humanitarian Law of Armed Conflict: Proceedings of the 1976 and 1977 Conferences, vols. I and II (Naples: Editoriale Scientifica, 1979).
The Current Legal Regulation of the Use of Force (Lancaster: Martinus Nijhoff Publishers, 1986).
Cassese, Antonio, Gaeta, Paola, and Jones, John R.W.D. (eds.), *The Rome Statute of the International Criminal Court: A Commentary* (Oxford: Oxford University Press, 2002).
Castrén, Erik, *Civil War* (Helsinki: Suomalainen Tiedeakatemia, 1966).
Chadwick, Elizabeth, *Self-Determination, Terrorism and International Humanitarian Law of Armed Conflict* (The Hague: Martinus Nijhoff Publishers, 1996).
Cho, Sihyun, 'Applicability of International Humanitarian Law to Internal Armed Conflicts', Ph.D. dissertation (Cambridge: University of Cambridge, 1996).
Clapham, Andrew, *Human Rights in the Private Sphere* (Oxford: Oxford University Press, 1993).
Human Rights Obligations of Non-State Actors (Oxford: Oxford University Press, 2006).
Damrosch, Lori F., *Enforcing Restraint: Collective Intervention in Internal Conflicts* (New York: Council on Foreign Relations Press, 1993).
Detter de Lupis, Ingrid, *The Law of War* (Cambridge: Cambridge University Press, 1987).
Dinstein, Yoram and Tabory, Mala, *War Crimes in International Law* (The Hague: Martinus Nijhoff Publishers, 1996).
Dörmann, Knut, Doswald-Beck, Louise and Kolb, Robert, *Elements of War Crimes under the Rome Statute of the International Criminal Court: Sources and Commentary* (Cambridge: Cambridge University Press, 2003).

Durham, H. and McCormack, T.L.H. (eds.), *The Changing Face of Conflict and the Efficacy of International Humanitarian Law* (The Hague: Martinus Nijhoff Publishers, 1999).

Dymond, Jonathan, *War: Its Causes, Lawfulness* (London: Peace Committee of the Society of Friends, 1915).

Erskine Holland, Thomas, *The Law of War on Land* (Oxford: Oxford University Press, 1908).

Falk, Richard A., *Law, Morality and War in the Contemporary World* (New York: Praeger, 1963).

The International Law of Civil War (Balimore, MD and London: Johns Hopkins University Press, 1971).

Fleck, Dieter (ed.), *The Handbook of Humanitarian Law in Armed Conflict* (Oxford: Oxford University Press, 1995).

Goor, Luc van de, Rupesinghe, Kumar and Sciarone, Paul, *Between Development and Destruction: An Enquiry into the Causes of Conflict in Post-Colonial States* (New York: St. Martin's Press, 1996).

Green, Leslie C., *Essays on the Modern Law of War*, 2nd edn (New York: Transnational Publishers, 1999).

The Contemporary Law of Armed Conflict, 2nd edn (Manchester: Manchester University Press, 2000).

Grotius, Hugo, *The Law of War and Peace*, L.R. Loomis (trans.) (New York: Classic Club, 1949).

Gutman, Roy and Rieff, David, *Crimes of War: What the Public Should Know* (London: W.W. Norton & Company, 1999).

Hartigan, Richard Shelly, *Lieber's Code and the Law of War* (Chicago: Precedent, 1983).

Hebel, H.A.M. von, Lammers, J.G. and Schukking, J., *Reflections on the ICC* (The Hague: T.M.C. Asser Press and Cambridge, MA: Kluwer Law International, 1999).

Henckaerts, Jean-Marie and Doswald-Beck, Louise, *Customary International Humanitarian Law*, vols. I and II (Cambridge: Cambridge University Press, 2004).

Howard, Michael, *Restraints on War: Studies in the Limitation of Armed Conflict* (Oxford: Oxford University Press, 1979).

International Commission on Kosovo, *The Kosovo Report: Conflict, International Response, Lessons Learned* (Oxford: Oxford University Press, 2000).

International Committee of the Red Cross, *Commentary on the Additional Protocols of 8 June 1977 to the Geneva Conventions of 12 August 1949* (Geneva: Martinus Nijhoff Publishers, 1987).

International Committee of the Red Cross, *Commentary on the Geneva Conventions I, II, III, IV of 12 August 1949*, vols. 1–4 (Geneva: ICRC, 1995).

International Committee of the Red Cross, *Respect for International Humanitarian Law* (Geneva: ICRC, 1999).

International Committee of the Red Cross, *Customary Rules of International Humanitarian Law* (Cambridge: Cambridge University Press, 2004).

International Committee of the Red Cross, *The International Criminal Court and Enlarging the Scope of International Humanitarian Law* (Damascus: ICRC, 2004).
Johnson, James Turner, *Morality and Contemporary Warfare* (New Haven, CT and London: Yale University Press, 1999).
Kalshoven, Frits and Zegveld, Liesbeth, *Constraints on the Waging of War: An Introduction to International Humanitarian Law* (Geneva: ICRC, 2001).
Khadduri, Majid, *War and Peace in the Law of Islam* (New York: Ams Press, 1979).
Khairallah, Daoud L., *Insurrection under International Law: With Emphasis on the Rights and Duties of Insurgents* (Beirut: Lebanese University, 1973).
Kotzsch, Lothar, *The Concept of War in Contemporary History and International Law* (Geneva: Librairie E. Droz, 1956).
Kwakwa, Edward K., *The International Law of Armed Conflict: Personal and Material Fields of Application* (Dordrecht: Kluwer, 1992).
Lattanzi, Flavia (ed.), *The International Criminal Court: Comments on the Draft Statute* (Naples: Editoriale Scientifica, 1998).
Lauterpacht, Hersh, *Recognition in International Law* (Cambridge: Cambridge University Press, 1947).
Lee, Roy S., *The International Criminal Court: The Making of the Rome Statute, Issues, Negotiations, Results* (London: Kluwer Law International, 1999).
Levie, Howard S. (ed.), *The Law of Non-International Armed Conflict: Protocol II to the 1949 Geneva Conventions* (Dordrecht: Martinus Nijhoff, 1987).
Luard, Evan (ed.), *The International Regulation of Civil Wars* (London: Thames & Hudson, 1972).
McCoubrey, H., *International Humanitarian Law. The Regulation of Armed Conflicts* (Aldershot: Dartmouth, 1990).
International Humanitarian Law: Modern Developments in the Limitation of Warfare, 2nd edn (Aldershot: Dartmouth, 1998).
McCoubrey, H. and White, N.D., *International Law and Armed Conflict* (Aldershot and Brookfield, VT: Ashgate, 1992).
International Organisations and Civil Wars (Aldershot and Brookfield, VT: Dartmouth Publishing Company Limited, 1995).
McGoldrick, Dominic, Rowe, Peter and Donnelly, Eric, *The Permanent International Criminal Court: Legal and Policy Issues* (Oxford: Hart publishing, 2004).
Meron, Theodor, *Human Rights in Internal Strife: Their International Protection* (Cambridge: Grotius, 1987).
Human Rights and Humanitarian Norms as Customary Law (Oxford: Clarendon Press, 1991).
War Crimes Law Comes of Age: Essays (Oxford: Oxford University Press, 1998).
The Humanization of International Law (The Hague: Brill, 2006).
Meyer, Michael A. and McCoubrey, Hilaire, *Reflections on the Law of Armed Conflict* (The Hague: Kluwer, 1998).
Moir, Lindsay, *The Law of Internal Armed Conflict* (Cambridge: Cambridge University Press, 2002).

Moore, John Norton (ed.), *Law and Civil War in the Modern World* (Baltimore: John Hopkins University Press, 1974).

Mulinen, F. de, *Handbook on the Law of War for Armed Forces* (Geneva: ICRC, 1987).

Murphy, Ray, *UN Peacekeeping in Lebanon, Somalia and Kosovo: Legal and Operational Issues in Practice* (Cambridge: Cambridge University Press, 2007).

Nabulsi, Karma, *Traditions of War: Occupation, Resistance and the Law* (Oxford: Oxford University Press, 1999).

Ní Aoláin, Fionnuala, *The Politics of Force: Conflict Management and State Violence in Northern Ireland* (Belfast: Blackstaff Press, 2000).

Nussbaum, Arthur, *A Concise History of the Law of Nations*, revised edn (New York: MacMillan Company, 1954).

Oppenheim, Lassa and Lauterpacht, Hersch, *International Law: A Treatise*, vol. II, 6th edn (London: Longmans, Green & Co., 1947).

Perna, Laura, *The Formation of the Treaty Law of Non-International Armed Conflicts* (Leiden: Martinus Nijhoff Publishers, 2006).

Pfankuchen, Llewellyn, *A Documentary Textbook in International Law* (New York: Rinehart & Company Inc., 1940).

Phillipson, Coleman, *The International Law and Custom of Ancient Greece and Rome*, 2 vols., (London: Macmillan and Co. Ltd., 1911).

Pictet, Jean S. (ed.), *Commentary I Geneva Convention for the Amelioration of the Condition of the Wounded and Sick in Armed Forces in the Field* (Geneva: ICRC, 1952).

Commentary IV Geneva Convention Relative to the Protection of Civilian Persons in Time of War (Geneva: ICRC, 1958).

Commentary II Geneva Convention for the Amelioration of the Condition of Wounded, Sick and Shipwrecked Members of Armed Forces at Sea (Geneva: ICRC, 1960).

Commentary III Geneva Convention Relative to the Treatment of Prisoners of War (Geneva: ICRC, 1960).

Pictet, Jean S., *Development and Principles of International Humanitarian Law* (Lancaster: Martinus Nijhoff Publishers, 1985).

Pilloud, Claude, Sandoz, Yves, Swinarski, Christophe and Zimmermann, Bruno (eds.), *Commentary on the Additional Protocols of 8 June to the Geneva Conventions of 12 August 1949* (Geneva: Martinus Nijhoff Publishers, 1987).

Provost, René, *International Human Rights and International Humanitarian Law* (Cambridge: Cambridge University Press, 2002).

Przetacznik, Frank, *The Philosophical and Legal Concept of War* (Lewiston, NY: Edwin Mellen Press, 1994).

Reed, Kary B., 'The Law and Internal Armed Conflict Past, Present and Future', LLM thesis (Buffalo, NY: Judge Advocate General's School, 1999).

Roberts, Adam and Guelff, Richard, *Documents on the Laws of War*, 3rd edn (Oxford: Oxford University Press, 2000).

Rogers, A.P.V., *Law on the Battlefield*, 2nd edn (New York: Juris Publishing, 2004).

Rosenau, James N. (ed.), *International Aspects of Civil Strife* (New Jersey: Princeton University Press, 1964).
Rowe, Peter, *The Impact of Human Rights Law on Armed Forces* (Cambridge: Cambridge University Press, 2006).
Sandoz, Yves, Swinarski, Christophe and Zimmerman, Bruno (eds.), *Commentary on the Additional Protocols of 8 June to the Geneva Conventions of 12 August 1949* (Geneva: Martinus Nijhoff Publishers, 1987).
Sassoli, Marco and Bouvier, A. (eds.), *How Does Law Protect in War?* (Geneva: ICRC, 1999).
Schabas, William A., *An Introduction to the International Criminal Court*, 3rd edn (Cambridge: Cambridge University Press, 2007).
The UN International Criminal Tribunals: The Former Yugoslavia, Rwanda and Sierra Leone (Cambridge: Cambridge University Press, 2006).
Schabas, William A. and Lattanzi, Flavia, (eds.), *Essays on the Rome Statute of the International Criminal Court* (Ripa Fagnano Alto: Editrice Il Sirente, 1999).
Smith, Dan, *Atlas of War and Peace* (London: Earthscan Publications Ltd., 2003).
Soitis, Jean, *Le droit de la guerre et les conflits armés d'un caractère non international* (Paris: LGDJ, 1958).
Stockholm International Peace Research Institute, *SIPRI Yearbook 2006: Armaments, Disarmament and International Security* (Oxford: Oxford University Press, 2006).
Suter, Keith, *An International Law of Guerrilla Warfare* (London: Frances Pinter, 1984).
Swinarski, Christophe (ed.), *Études et essais sur le droit international humanitaire et sur les principes de la Croix-Rouge, en honneur de Jean Pictet* (the Netherlands: Martinus Nijhoff Publishers, 1984).
Tanca, Antonio, *Foreign Armed Intervention in Internal Conflict* (Boston: M. Nijhoff Publishers, 1993).
UK Ministry of Defence, *The Manual of the Law of Armed Conflict* (Oxford: Oxford University Press, 2004).
United Nations Educational, Scientific and Cultural Organization, *International Dimensions of Humanitarian Law* (London: Martinus Nijhoff Publishers, 1988).
Vitoria, Franciscus de, *On the Law of War* (Washington, DC: Carnegie Institution, 1917).
Weiss, Thomas George, *The United Nations and Civil Wars: Emerging Global Issues* (Boulder, CO: L. Rienner Publishers, 1995).
Wells, Donald A., *War Crimes and Laws of War* (Lanham, MD: University Press of America, 1984).
Wilson, Heather A., *International Law and the Use of Force by Liberation Movements* (Oxford: Clarendon Press, 1988).
Zegveld, Liesbeth, *Accountability of Armed Opposition Groups in International Law* (Cambridge: Cambridge University Press, 2002).

ARTICLES AND CHAPTERS IN BOOKS

Abbott, Kenneth W., 'International Relations Theory, International Law and the Regime Governing Atrocities in Internal Conflicts' (1999) 93 *AJIL* 361.

Abi-Saab, Georges, 'Wars of National Liberation and the Laws of War' (1972) 3 *Annales d'Études Internationales* 93.

'Non-International Armed Conflict', in UNESCO, *International Dimensions of Humanitarian Law* (London: Martinus Nijhoff Publishers, 1988), p. 217.

Abi-Saab, Rosemary, 'Humanitarian Law and Internal Conflicts: The Evolution of Legal Concern', in Astrid J.M. Delissen and Gerard J. Tanja (eds.), *Humanitarian Law of Armed Conflict: Challenges Ahead Essays in Honour of Frits Kalshoven* (Dordrecht: Martinus Nijhoff Publishers, 1991), p. 209.

Aldrich, George H., 'Protocols to the Geneva Conventions on the Laws of War' (1980) 72 *Annual Survey of International and Comparative Law* 191.

'New Life for the Laws of War' (1981) 75 *AJIL* 764.

'Prospects for United States Ratification of Additional Protocol I to the 1949 Geneva Conventions' (1991) 85 *AJIL* 1.

'Jurisdiction of the International Criminal Tribunal for the Former Yugoslavia' (1996) 90 *AJIL* 64.

'The Laws of War on Land' (2000) 94 *AJIL* 42.

Arsanjani, Mahnoush H., 'Developments in International Criminal Law: The Rome Statute of the International Criminal Court' (1999) 93 *AJIL* 22.

Baltes, Aaron K., '*Prosecutor* v. *Tadić*: Legitimizing the Establishment of the International Criminal Tribunal for the Former Yugoslavia' (1997) 49 *University of Maine Law Review* 577.

Baxter, Richard R., 'The Privy Council on the Qualification of Belligerents' (1969) 6 *AJIL* 290.

'The Geneva Conventions of 1949 and Wars of National Liberation' (1974) 57 *Rivista di Diritto Internazionale* 193.

'*Ius in bello interno*: The Present and Future Law' in John Norton Moore (ed.), *Law and Civil War in the Modern World* (Baltimore: Johns Hopkins University Press, 1974), p. 518.

Baxter, R.R., 'Some Existing Problems of Humanitarian Law', in *The Concept of International Armed Conflict: Further Outlook* (Proceedings of the International Symposium on Humanitarian Law, Brussels, 1974).

Boelaert-Suominen, Sonja, 'Grave Breaches, Universal Jurisdiction and Internal Armed Conflict: Is Customary International Law Moving Towards a Uniform Enforcement Mechanism for all Armed Conflicts?' (2000) 5(1) *JCSL* 63.

'The Yugoslav Tribunal and the Common Core of Humanitarian Law Applicable to All Armed Conflicts' (2000) 13 *Leiden Journal of International Law* 619.

Bond, James E., 'Internal Conflict and Article 3 of the Geneva Conventions' (1971) 48 *Denver Law Journal* 263.

Boot, Machteld, 'Commentary', in André Klip and Göran Sluiter (eds.), *Annotated Leading Cases of International Criminal Tribunals: The International*

Criminal Tribunal for the Former Yugoslavia 1997–1999 (Oxford: Intersentia, 2001), p. 452.

Bos, Adriaan, 'The Universal Declaration of Human Rights and the Statute of the International Criminal Court' (1998) 22 *Fordham International Law Journal* 229.

Bothe, M., 'Article 3 and Additional Protocol II: Case Studies of Nigeria and El Salvador' (1982) 31 *American University Law Review* 889.

Bruch, Carl E., 'Criminal Liability for Environmental Damage in Internal Armed Conflict' (2001) 25 *Vermont Law Review* 695.

Byron, Christine, 'Armed Conflicts: International or Non-International?' (2001) 6(1) *JCSL* 63.

Carnahan, Burrus M., 'Lincoln, Lieber and the Laws of War: The Origins and Limits of the Principle of Military Necessity' (1998) 92 *AJIL* 213.

Carrillo-Suarez, Arturo, '*Hors de logique*: Contemporary Issues in International Humanitarian Law as Applied to Internal Armed Conflict' (1999) 15 *American University International Law Review* 1.

Cassese, Antonio, 'The Status of Rebels under the 1977 Geneva Protocol on Non-International Armed Conflicts' (1981) 30 *ICLQ* 416.

'The Geneva Protocols of 1977 and Customary International Law' (1984) 3 *UCLA Pacific Basin Law Journal* 55.

'Respect for Humanitarian Norms in Non-International Armed Conflict', in ICIHI, *Modern Wars* (London: Zed Books, 1986), p. 86.

'The Spanish Civil War and the Development of Customary Law Concerning Internal Armed Conflict', in Antonio Cassese (ed.), *The Current Legal Regulation of the Use of Force* (Lancaster: Martinus Nijhoff Publishers, 1986), p. 313.

Cayci, Sadi, 'Countering Terrorism and the Law of Armed Conflict: The Turkish Experience' (2004) 8 *International Peacekeeping* 333.

Chifflet, Pascale, 'The First Trial of Former Members of the Kosovo Liberation Army: *Prosecutor* v. *Fatmir Limaj, Haradin Bala and Isak Musliu*' (2006) 19 *Leiden Journal of International Law* 459.

Chip, William, 'A United Nations Role in Ending Civil Wars' (1981) 19 *Columbia Journal of Transnational Law* 15.

Ciobanu, D., 'The Concept and the Determination of the Existence of Armed Conflict not of an International Character' (1975) 48 *Rivista di Diritto Internazionale* 43.

Clapham, Andrew, 'Human Rights Obligations of Non-State Actors in Conflict Situations' (2006) 88(863) *IRRC* 491.

Corey, Ian G., 'The Fine Line between Policy and Custom: *Prosecutor* v. *Tadić* and the Customary International Law of Internal Armed Conflict' (2000) 166 *Military Law Review* 145.

Crawford, Emily, 'Unequal Before the Law: The Case for the Elimination of the Distribution between International and Non-International Armed Conflicts' (2007) 20 *Leiden Journal of International Law* 441.

Crook, John R., 'Strengthening Legal Protection in Internal Conflicts' (1997) 3 *ILSA Journal of International & Comparative Law* 491.

Cullen, Anthony, 'The Parameters of Internal Armed Conflict in International Humanitarian Law' (2004) 12 *University of Miami International and Comparative Law Review* 189.

'Chechnya: A Forgotten Conflict' (2005) 7(1) *Human Rights Features* 7.

'Key Developments Affecting the Scope of Internal Armed Conflict in International Humanitarian Law' (2005) 183 *Military Law Review* 65.

'The Definition of Non-International Armed Conflict in the Rome Statute of the International Criminal Court: An Analysis of the Threshold of Application Contained in Article 8(2)(f)' (2007) 12(3) *JCSL* 419.

Dhokalia, R.P., 'Civil Wars and International Law' (1971) 11 *Indian Journal of International Law* 219.

Dinstein, Yorham, 'Terrorism and Wars of Liberation Applied to the Arab–Israeli Conflict: An Israeli Persrective' (1973) 3 *IYBHR* 78.

'The New Geneva Protocols: A Step Forward or Backward?' (1979) 33 *Yearbook of World Affairs* 265.

Draper, G.I.A.D., 'The Geneva Conventions of 1949' (1965) 1 *Recueil des cours* 82.

'The Implementation and Enforcement of the Geneva Conventions of 1949 and of the Two Additional Protocols of 1979' (1979) 164(3) *Recueil des cours* 1.

'Humanitarian Law and Internal Armed Conflicts' (1983) 13 *Georgia Journal of International and Comparative Law* 253.

Egorov, Sergey Alexeyevich, 'The Kosovo Crisis and the Law of Armed Conflicts' (2000) 837 *IRRC* 183.

Eide, Asbjörn, 'The New Humanitarian Law in Non-International Armed Conflict', in Antonio Cassese (ed.) *The New Humanitarian Law of Armed Conflict* (Naples: Editoriale Scientifica, 1979).

'Internal Disturbances and Tensions', in UNESCO, *International Dimensions of Humanitarian Law* (London: Martinus Nijhoff Publishers, 1988).

Elder, David A., 'The Historical Background of Common Article 3 of the Geneva Conventions of 1949' (1979) 11 *Case Western Reserve Journal of International Law* 37.

Falk, Richard A., 'Janus Tormented: The International Law of Internal War', in James N. Rosnau (ed.), *International Aspects of Civil Strife* (New York: Princeton University Press, 1964), p. 185.

Farer, Tom J., 'Humanitarian Law and Armed Conflicts: Towards the Definition of "International Armed Conflict"' (1971) 71 *Columbia Law Review* 37.

Fenrick, William J., 'The Development of the Law of Armed Conflict through the Jurisprudence of the International Criminal Tribunal for the Former Yugoslavia' (1998) 2 *JACL* 197.

'The Application of the Geneva Conventions by the International Criminal Tribunal for the Former Yugoslavia' (1999) 834 *IRRC*, 317.

Fenwick, C.G., 'Can Civil Wars Be Brought under the Control of International Law?' (1938) 32 *AJIL* 538.

Fleck, Dieter, 'Humanitarian Protection against Non-State Actors', in Jochen Abr. Frowein, Klaus Scharioth and Indo Winkelmann (eds.), *Verhandeln für den Frieden* (London: Springer, 2003).

Forsythe, David P.,'The 1974 Diplomatic Conference on Humanitarian Law: Some Observations' (1975) 69 *AJIL* 77.

'Support for a Humanitarian *Jus in bello*' (1977) 11 *International Lawyer* 723.

'The Legal Management of Internal War: The 1977 Protocol of Non-International Armed Conflicts' (1978) 72 *AJIL* 272.

Franco, Andrés, 'Armed Nonstate actors', in David M. Malone (ed.), *The UN Security Council: From the Cold War to the Twenty-First Century* (London: Lynne Rienner, 2004).

Freeman, Mark, 'International Law and Internal Armed Conflicts: Clarifying the Interplay between Human Rights and Humanitarian Protections' (2000) *Journal of Humanitarian Assistance*. Available at: www.jha.ac/articles/a059.htm.

Fryer, Eugene D., 'Applicability of International Law to Internal Armed Conflicts: Old Problems, Current Endeavors' (1977) 11 *International Law* 567.

Gaparayi, I. 'The Milošević Trial at Halfway Stage: Judgement for the Motion of Acquittal' (2004) 17 *Leiden Journal of International Law* 737.

Gardam, Judith, 'Protocol I to the Geneva Conventions: A Victim of Short Sighted Political Considerations?' (1990) 17 *Melbourne University Law Review* 107.

Gardam, Judith (ed.), *Humanitarian Law* (Aldershot: Dartmouth, 1999).

Garner, James W., 'Recognition of Belligerency' (1938) 32 *AJIL* 106.

Gasser, Hans-Peter, 'Internationalized Non-International Armed Conflicts: Case Studies of Afghanistan, Kampuchea and Lebanon' (1983) 33 *American University Law Review* 145.

'Code of Conduct in the Event of Internal Disturbances and Tensions' (1998) 262 *IRRC* 51–3.

Ginsburgs, George, ' "Wars of National Liberation" and the Modern Law of Nations – The Soviet Thesis' (1964) 29 *Law and Contemporary Problems* 911.

Goldman, Robert K., 'The Applicable Law: Angola: An Internationalized Internal Armed Conflict' in *Angola: Violations of the Laws of War by Both Sides* (New York: Africa's Watch, 1989).

'International Humanitarian Law: Americas Watch's Experience in Monitoring Internal Armed Conflicts' (1993) 9 *American University Journal of International Law and Policy* 49.

Gomulkiewicz, Robert W., 'International Law Governing Aid to Opposition Groups in Civil War: Resurrecting the Standards of Belligerency' (1988) 63 *Washington Law Review* 43.

Gorbiel, Andrzej, 'A New Achievement in the Codification of the International Law Applicable in Armed Conflicts' (1984) 18(4) *Revue Roumaine d'Études Internationales* 4.

Gordadzé, Thorniké, 'Chechnya: Eradication of the Enemy Within', in Fabrice Weissmann (ed.), *In the Shadow of 'Just Wars'* (New York: Cornell University Press, 2004).

Graditzky, Thomas, 'Individual Criminal Responsibility for Violations of International Humanitarian Law Committed in Non-International Conflicts' (1998) 322 *IRRC* 29.

'War Crime Issues Before the Rome Diplomatic Conference on the Establishment of an International Criminal Court' (1999) 5 *UC Davis Journal of International Law & Policy* 199.

Gray, C., 'Bosnia and Herzegovina: Civil War or Interstate Conflict? Characterisation and Consequences' (1996) 6 *BYBIL* 155.

Green, Leslie C., 'Terrorism and Armed Conflict: The Plea and the Verdict' (1989) 19 *IYBHR* 131.

'Enforcement of the Law in International and Non-International Conflicts – The Way Ahead' (1996) 24 *Denver Journal of International Law and Policy* 285.

'Strengthening Legal Protection in Internal Conflicts: Low-Intensity Conflict and the Law' (1997) 3 *ILSA Journal of International & Comparative Law* 493.

Greenberg, E. van C., 'Law and the Conduct of the Algerian Revolution' (1970) 11 *HILJ* 37, at 70–1.

Greenspan, Morris, 'Civil and Colonial War', in Greenspan, Morris, *The Modern Law of Land Warfare* (Berkeley and Los Angeles: University of California Press, 1959), pp. 619–27.

Greenwood, Christopher, 'A Critique of the Additional Protocols to the Geneva Conventions of 1949', in Helen Durham and Timothy L.H. McCormack (eds.), *The Changing Face of Conflict and the Efficacy of International Humanitarian Law* (The Hague: Martinus Nijhoff Publishers, 1999), p. 3.

'International Humanitarian Law and the *Tadić Case*' (1996) 7 *EJIL* 265.

'The Development of International Law by the International Criminal Tribunal for the Former Yugoslavia' (1998) 2 *Max Planck Yearbook of United Nations Law* 114.

'Command Responsibility and the *Hadžihasanović* Decision' (2004) 2 *Journal of International Criminal Justice* 598.

Grotius, Hugo, *The Law of War and Peace*, L.R. Loomis (trans.) (New York: Classic Club, 1949).

Gutteridge, 'The Geneva Conventions of 1949' (1949) *BYBIL*, 300–1.

Hadden, Tom, 'Legal Controls on the Use of Lethal Force: Options for Reform', in *Standing Advisory Commission on Human Rights, 18th Annual Report*, 1992–3, p. 128.

Hadden, Tom and Harvey, Colin, 'The Law of Internal Crisis and Conflict' (1999) 833 *IRRC* 119.

Hampson, F. 'Human Rights and Humanitarian Law in Internal Conflicts', in Michael Meyer (ed.), *Armed Conflict and the New Law: Aspects of the 1977 Protocols and 1981 Weapons Convention* (London: British Institute of International and Comparative Law, 1989), p. 55

Harroff-Tavel, Marion, 'Promoting Norms to Limit Violence in Crisis Situations: Challenges, Strategies and Alliances' (1998) 322 *IRRC* 5.

Hayden, R., 'Bosnia's Internal War and the International Criminal Tribunal' (1998) 22(1) *Fletcher Forum of World Affairs* 45.

Hayden, William, 'Seeds of Unrest: The Political Genesis of the Conflict in Chechnya (1990–1994)' (2000) 24 *Fletcher Forum of World Affairs* 49.

Higgins, Noelle, 'The Application of International Humanitarian Law to Wars of National Liberation' (2004) *Journal of Humanitarian Assistance*. Available at www.jha.ac/articles/a132.pdf.

Higgins, Rosalyn, 'Internal War and International Law', in Cyril E. Black and Richard A. Falk (eds.) *The Future of the International Legal Order* (Princeton: Princeton University Press, 1971), p. 81.

'International Law and Civil Conflict', in Evan Luard (ed.), *The International Regulation of Civil Wars* (London: Thames & Hudson, 1972), p. 169.

Hollis, Duncan B., 'Accountability in Chechnya – Addressing Internal Matters with Legal and Political International Norms' (1995) 36 *Boston College Law Review* 793.

International Committee of the Red Cross, 'Armed Conflicts Linked to the Disintegration of State Structures: Preparatory Document Drafted by the International Committee of the Red Cross for the First Periodical Meeting on International Humanitarian Law', Geneva, 19–23 January 1998. Available at www.icrc.org.

Jaramillo, Daniel García-Pena, 'Humanitarian Protection in Non-International Armed Conflicts: A Case Study of Colombia' (2000) 30 *IYBHR* 179.

Jessup, Phillip C., 'Should International Law Recognize an Intermediate Status Between Peace and War?' 48 *AJIL* 1954.

Jinks, Derek, 'The Temporal Scope of Application of International Humanitarian Law in Contemporary Conflicts' (2003) Harvard Program on Humanitarian Policy and Conflict Research Policy Brief. Available at www.oejc.or.at/oejc/recht/Session31.pdf.

'State Responsibility for the Acts of Private Armed Groups' (2003) 4(1) *Chicago Journal of International Law* 83.

'September 11 and the Laws of War' (2003) 28 *Yale Journal of International Law* 1.

Junod, Sylvie, 'Additional Protocol II: History and Scope' (1983) 33 *American University Law Review* 29.

Kalshoven, Frits, 'Applicability of Customary International Law in Non-International Armed Conflicts', in Antonio Cassese (ed.), *Current Problems of International Law* (Milan: Giuffrè, 1975), p. 267.

'"Guerrilla" and "Terrorism" in Internal Armed Conflict' (1983) 33 *American University Law Review* 67.

'The Undertaking to Respect and Ensure Respect in All Circumstances: From Tiny Seed to Ripening Fruit' (1999) 2 *Yearbook of International Humanitarian Law* 3.

Kooijmans, Peter H., 'In the Shadowland between Civil War and Civil Strife: Some Reflections on the Standard-Setting Process', in Astrid J. M. Delissen and Gerard J. Tanja (eds.), *Humanitarian Law of Armed Conflict: Challenges Ahead. Essays in Honour of Frits Kalshoven* (Dordrecht: Martinus Nijhoff Publishers, 1991), p. 225.

'The Security Council and Non-State Entities as Parties to Conflicts', in Karel Wellens (ed.), *International Law* (Boston, MA and London: Martinus Nijhoff Publishers, 1998), pp. 333–46.

Kress, Claus, 'War Crimes Committed in Non-International Armed Conflict and the Emerging System of International Criminal Justice' (2000) 30 *IYBHR* 103.

Kritsiotis, Dino, 'International Humanitarian Law and the Disintegration of States' (2000) 30 *IYBHR* 17.

Lauterpacht, Hersh, 'The Problem of the Revision of the Law of War' (1952) 39 *BYBIL* 139.

Lee, Luke T., 'Strengthening Legal Protection in Internal Conflicts: Protection of Internally Displaced Persons in Internal Conflicts' (1997) 3 *ILSA Journal of International & Comparative Law* 529.

Lootsteen, Yair M., 'The Concept of Belligerency in International Law' (2000) 166 *Military Law Review* 109.

Lopez, Laura, 'Uncivil Wars: The Challenge of Applying International Humanitarian Law to Internal Armed Conflicts' (1994) 69 *NYUL Rev.* 916.

Luard, Evan, 'Civil Conflicts in Modern International Relations', in Luard (ed.), *International Regulation*, p. 7.

Mangu, Andre Mbata B., 'Conflict in the Democratic Republic of Congo: An International Legal Perspective' (2003) 28 *South African Yearbook of International Law* 82.

Matheson, Michael J., 'The United States Position on the Relation of Customary International Law to the 1977 Protocols Additional to the 1949 Geneva Conventions' (1987) 2 *American University Journal of International Law and Policy* 419.

'Strengthening Legal Protection in Internal Conflicts' (1997) 3 *ILSA Journal of International & Comparative Law* 523.

McDonald, G. K., 'The Eleventh Annual Waldemar A. Solf Lecture: The Changing Nature of the Laws of War' (1998) 156 *Military Law Review* 30.

Meindersma, C., 'Violations of Common Article 3 of the Geneva Conventions as Violations of the Laws or Customs of War under Article 3 of the Statute of the International Criminal Tribunal for the Former Yugoslavia' (1995) *Netherlands International Law Review* 375.

Menon, P. K., 'Recognition of Belligerency and Insurgency', in P. K. Menon, *The Law of Recognition in International Law: Basic Principles* (New York: Edwin Mellen Press, 1994), pp. 109–37.

Meron, Theodor, 'On the Inadequate Reach of Humanitarian and Human Rights Law and the Need for a New Instrument' (1983) 77 *AJIL* 589.

'Towards a Humanitarian Decision on Internal Strife' (1984) 78 *AJIL* 859.

'The Geneva Conventions as Customary Law' (1987) 81 *AJIL* 348.
'Draft Model Declaration on Internal Strife' (1988) 262 *IRRC* 59.
'Internal Strife: Applicable Norms and a Proposed Instrument', in Astrid J. M. Delissen and Gerard J. Tanja (eds.), *Humanitarian Law of Armed Conflict: Challenges Ahead. Essays in Honour of Frits Kalshoven* (Dordrecht: Martinus Nijhoff Publishers, 1991), p. 249.
'Shakespeare's Henry the Fifth and the Law of War' (1992) 86 *AJIL* 1–45.
'War Crimes in Yugoslavia and the Development of International Law' (1994) 88 *AJIL* 78.
'International Criminalisation of Internal Atrocities' (1995) 89 *AJIL* 554.
'The Continuing Role of Custom in the Formation of International Humanitarian Law' (1996) 90 *AJIL* 238.
'Francis Lieber's Code and Principles of Humanity' (1997) 36 *Columbia Journal of Transnational Law* 269.
'Classification of the Conflict in the Former Yugoslavia: Nicaragua's Fallout' (1998) 92 *AJIL* 236.
'Customary Law', in Gutman and Rieff, *Crimes of War.*
'The Humanization of Humanitarian Law' (2000) 94 *AJIL* 239.
'The Marten's Clause, Principles of Humanity and Dictates of Public Conscience' (2000) 94 *AJIL* 78.
'Cassese's "*Tadić*" and the Law of Non-International Armed Conflicts', in Lal Chand Vohrah (ed.), *Man's Inhumanity to Man: Essays in Honour of Antonio Cassese* (The Hague and London: Kluwer Law International, 2003) pp. 533–8.
Meron, Theodor and Rosas, Allan, 'A Declaration of Minimum Humanitarian Standards' (1991) 85 *AJIL* 375.
Meron, Theodor, Eide, Asbjörn and Rosas, Allan, 'Combating Lawlessness in Gray Zone Conflicts through Minimum Humanitarian Standards' (1995) 89 *AJIL* 215.
Miller, David M., 'Non-International Armed Conflicts' (1982) 31 *AJIL* 897.
Moir, Lindsay, 'The Historical Development of the Application of Humanitarian Law in Non-International Armed Conflicts to 1949' (1998) 47 *ICLQ* 337.
Momtaz, Djamchid, 'The Minimum Humanitarian Rules Applicable in Periods of Internal Tension and Strife' (1998) 324 *IRRC* 455.
'War Crimes in Non-International Armed Conflicts under the Statute of the International Criminal Court' (2000) 13 *Leiden Journal of International Law* 177.
Moore, John Norton, 'A Theoretical Overview of the Laws of War in a Post-Charter World, with Emphasis on the Challenge of Civil Wars, "Wars of National Liberation", Mixed Civil–International Wars and Terrorism' (1982) 31 *American University Law Review* 841.
Müllerson, Rein, 'International Humanitarian Law in Internal Conflicts' (1997) 2 *JACL* 109.

Murphy, Sean D., 'Progress and Jurisprudence of the International Criminal Tribunal for the Former Yugoslavia' (1999) 93 *AJIL* 57.

Obradovíc, Konstantin, 'International Humanitarian Law and the Kosovo Crisis' (2000) 839 *IRRC* 699.

O'Brien, James C., 'The International Tribunal for Violations of International Humanitarian Law in the Former Yugoslavia' (1993) 87 *AJIL* 639.

O'Brien, William V., '*The Jus in bello* in Revolutionary War and Counter-Insurgency' (1978) 18 *Virginia Journal of International Law* 193.

Oglesby, Roscoe R., 'The Decline of Belligerent Recognition: Desuetude in International Law', in Roscoe Ralph Oglesby, *Internal War and the Search for Normative Order* (The Hague: Martinus Nijhoff, 1971), p. 100.

O'Rourke, V.A., 'The Recognition of Belligerency in the Spanish Civil War' (1937) 31 *AJIL* 398.

Paust, Jordan J., 'Law in a Guerrilla Conflict: Myths, Norms and Human Rights' (1973) 3 *IYBHR*.

Peterson, Alex G., 'Order out of Chaos, Domestic Enforcement of the Law of Internal Armed Conflict' (2002) 171 *Military Law Review* 1.

Petrasek, David, 'Moving Forward on the Development of Minimum Humanitarian Standards' (1998) 92 *AJIL* 557.

Pictet, Jean, 'La Croix-Rouge et les Conventions de Genève' (1950) *Recueil des cours* 45–6.

Plattner, Denise, 'The Penal Repression of Violations of International Humanitarian Law Applicable to Non-International Armed Conflict' (1990) *IRRC* 409.

Quénivet, Noëlle, 'The Moscow Hostage Crisis in the Light of the Armed Conflict in Chechnya' (2001) 4 *Yearbook of International Humanitarian Law* 348.

Reydams, Luc, '*Niyonteze* v. *Public Prosecutor*' (2002) 96 *AJIL* 231.

Robinson, Darryl and Hebel, Herman von, 'War Crimes in Internal Conflicts: Article 8 of the ICC Statute' (1999) 2 *Yearbook of International Humanitarian Law* 193.

Rosenne, Shabtai, 'Participation in the Geneva Conventions (1864–1949) and the Additional Protocols of 1977', in Christophe Swinarski (ed.), *Études*, p. 803.

Rover, Cees de, 'No War, No Enemy: Low Intensity Operations: LOAC and Human Rights Law', Seminar on the Law of Armed Conflict (SLAC), Chavannes-de-Bogis/Geneva, October 1998.

Rowe, Peter, 'The International Criminal Tribunal for the Former Yugoslavia: The Decision of the Appeals Chamber on the Interlocutory Appeal on Jurisdiction in the *Tadić* Case' (1996) 45 *ICLQ* 691.

Rowe, Peter and Meyer, Michael A., 'Ratification by the United Kingdom of the 1977 Protocols Additional to the Geneva Conventions of 1949: Selected Problems of Implementation' (1994) 45(4) *Northern Ireland Legal Quarterly* 343.

Rumpf, Helmut, 'The Concept of Peace and War in International Law' 27 *German Yearbook of International Law* 1984.

Rwelamira, M.R., 'The Significance and Contribution of the Protocols Additional to the Geneva Conventions of August 1949' in Christophe Swinarski (ed.), *Études et essais sur le droit international humanitaire et sur les principes de la Croix-Rouge, en honneur de Jean Pictet* (The Netherlands: Martinus Nijhoff Publishers, 1984), pp. 234–5.

Sassoli, Marco, 'The Legal Qualification of the Conflicts in the Former Yugoslavia: Double Standards or New Horizons for International Humanitarian Law', in Sienho Yee and Wang Tieya, *International Law in the Post-Cold War World* (Routledge: London, 2001), p. 307.

Sassoli, Marco and Olsen, Laura, 'International Decisions: *Prosecutor* v. *Tadić*' (2000) 94 *AJIL* 571.

'The Judgment of the ICTY Appeals Chamber on the Merits of the *Tadić* Case' (2000) 839 *IRRC* 733.

Schabas, William A., 'Theorical and International Framework: Punishment of Non-State Actors in Non-International Armed Conflict' (2003) 26 *Fordham International Law Journal* 907.

Schachter, Oscar, 'The United Nations and Internal Conflict', in John Norton Moore (ed.), *Law and Civil War in the Modern World* (Baltimore: Johns Hopkins University Press, 1974), p. 401.

Scharf, M.P., '*Prosecutor* v. *Tadić*' (1997) 91 *AJIL* 718.

Scheffer, David J., 'A Negotiator's Perspective on the International Criminal Court' (2001) 167 *Military Law Review* 1.

'The Future of Atrocity Law' (2002) 25 *Suffolk Transnational Law Review* 389.

Scherbich, Yury, 'What Law Applies to the Conflict in Chechnya?' (2005) 2(1) *Eastern European Humanitarian Law Journal* 19.

Schindler, Dietrich, 'The Different Types of Armed Conflicts According to the Geneva Conventions and Protocols' (1979) 163 *Recueil des cours* 117.

'State of War, Belligerency, Armed Conflict', in Cassese (ed.), *New Humanitarian Law.*

'Significance of the Geneva Conventions for the Contemporary World' (1999) 836 *IRRC* 715.

Schindler, Dietrich and Toman, Jiří (ed.), *The Laws of Armed Conflicts*, 3rd edn (Dordecht: Martinus Nijhoff Publishers, 1988).

Schlögel, Anton, 'Civil War' (1970) 108 *IRRC* 123.

Schutter, Bart de and van de Wyngaet, Christine 'Coping with Non-International Armed Conflicts: The Borderline Between National and International War' (1983) 13 *Georgia Journal of International and Comparative Law* 279.

Sepulveda, Cesar, 'Interrelationships in the Implementation and Enforcement of International Humanitarian Law and Human Rights Law' (1983) 33 *American University Law Review* 117.

Simma, Bruno and Paulus, Andreas L., 'The Responsibility of Individuals for Human Rights Abuses in Internal Conflicts: A Positivist View' (1999) 93 *AJIL* 302.

Siordet, Fédéric, 'Les Conventions de Genève et la guerre civile' (1950) *Revue internationale de la Croix-Rouge* 104.
'The Geneva Conventions and Civil War' (1950) Supplement to the *Revue internationale de la Croix-Rouge*, vol. III, nos. 8, 9 and 11, Geneva, August, September and November 1950.
Solf, Waldemar A., 'Problems with the Application of Norms Governing Interstate Armed Conflict to Non-International Armed Conflict' (1983) 13 *Georgia Journal of International and Comparative Law* 279.
'The Status of Combatants in Non-International Armed Conflicts under Domestic Law and Transnational Practice' (1983) 33 *American University Law Review* 53.
Spieker, Heike, 'The International Criminal Court and Non-International Armed Conflicts' (2000) 13 *Leiden Journal of International Law* 395.
'Twenty-Fifth Anniversary of Additional Protocol II' (2001) 4 *Yearbook of International Humanitarian Law* 129.
Sternberg, Mark R. von, 'Yugoslavian War Crimes and the Search for a New Humanitarian Order: The Case of Duško Tadić' (1997) 12 *St John's Journal of Legal Commentary* 351.
Stewart, James G., 'Towards a Single Definition of Armed Conflict in International Humanitarian Law: A Critique of Internationalized Armed Conflict' (2003) 85 *IRRC* 313.
Taubenfeld, Howard J., 'The Applicability of the Laws of War in Civil War' in John Norton Moore (ed.), *Law and Civil War in the Modern World* (Baltimore: Johns Hopkins University Press, 1974), p. 499.
Thahzib-lie, Bahia and Swaak-Goldman, Olivia, 'Determining the Threshold for the Application of International Humanitarian Law', in Liesbeth Lijnzaad, Johanna Van Sambeek and Bahia Tahzib-lie (eds.), *Making the Voice of Humanity Heard* (Leiden and Boston, MA: Martinus Nijhoff Publishers, 2004), pp. 239–53.
Thornberry, Cedric, 'Peacekeepers, Humanitarian Aid and Civil Conflicts' (2000) *Journal of Humanitarian Assistance*. Available at: www.jha.ac/articles/a002.htm.
Thürer, Daniel, 'The "Failed State" and International Law' (1999) 836 *IRRC* 731.
Veuthey, Les, 'Conflits armés de charactère non-internationals', in Antonio Cassese (ed.), *Current Legal Problems of International Law and the Law of Armed Conflict* (Milan: Dott. A. Guiffre, 1975).
Veuthey, Michel, 'Implementation and Enforcement of Humanitarian Law and Human Rights Law in Non-International Armed Conflicts: The Role of the International Committee of the Red Cross' (1993) 33 *American University Law Review* 83.
'Remedies to Promote the Respect of Fundamental Human Values in Non-International Armed Conflict' (2000) 30 *IYBHR* 37.
Walker, George K., 'Responses to Humanitarian Law Violations in Non-International Armed Conflicts: Historical Perspectives and Considerations on Conflicts of Jurisdiction' (2000) 30 *IYBHR* 79.

Wallensteen, P. and Sollenberg, M., 'Armed Conflict 1989–2000' (2001) 38(5) *Journal of Peace Research* 629.

Watson, 'The Humanitarian Law of the Yugoslavia War Crimes Tribunal: Jurisdiction in *Prosecutor* v. *Tadić*' (1996) 36 *Virginia Journal of International Law* 687.

Wells, Sarah L., 'Crimes against Child Soldiers in Armed Conflict Situations: Application and Limits of International Humanitarian Law' (2004) 12 *Tulane Journal of International and Comparative Law* 287.

Wilson, George Grafton, 'Insurgency and International Maritime Law' (1907) 1 *AJIL* 46.

Wippman, David, 'Change and Continuity in Legal Justifications for Military Intervention in Internal Conflict' (1996) 27 *Columbia Human Rights Law Review* 435.

Wright, Quincy, 'International Law and the American Civil War' (1967) 61 *American Society of International Law Proceedings* 50.

Zimmermann, Andreas, 'War Crimes Committed in an Armed Conflict not of an International Character', in Otto Triffterer (ed.), *Commentary on Statute of the International Criminal Court* (Baden-Baden: Verlagsgesellschaft, 1999), p. 233.

Index

CAMBRIDGE STUDIES IN INTERNATIONAL AND COMPARATIVE LAW

Books in the series

The Concept of Non-International Armed Conflict in International Humanitarian Law
Anthony Cullen

The Challenge of Child Labour in International Law
Franziska Humbert

Shipping Interdiction and the Law of the Sea
Douglas Guilfoyle

International Courts and Environmental Protection
Tim Stephens

Legal Principles in WTO Disputes
Andrew D. Mitchell

War Crimes in Internal Armed Conflicts
Eve La Haye

Humanitarian Occupation
Gregory H . Fox

The International Law of Environmental Impact Assessment: Process, Substance and Integration
Neil Craik

The Law and Practice of International Territorial Administration: Versailles, Iraq and Beyond
Carsten Stahn

Cultural Products and the World Trade Organization
Tania Voon

United Nations Sanctions and the Rule of Law
Jeremy Farrall

National Law in WTO Law Effectiveness and Good Governance in the World Trading System
Sharif Bhuiyan

The Threat of Force in International Law
Nikolas Stürchler

Indigenous Rights and United Nations Standards
Alexandra Xanthaki

International Refugee Law and Socio-Economic Rights
Michelle Foster

The Protection of Cultural Property in Armed Conflict
Roger O'Keefe

Interpretation and Revision of International Boundary Decisions
Kaiyan Homi Kaikobad

Multinationals and Corporate Social Responsibility
Limitations and Opportunities in International Law
Jennifer A. Zerk

Judiciaries within Europe
A Comparative Review
John Bell

Law in Times of Crisis
Emergency Powers in Theory and Practice
Oren Gross and Fionnuala Ní Aoláin

Vessel-Source Marine Pollution
The Law and Politics of International Regulation
Alan Tan

Enforcing Obligations Erga Omnes *in International Law*
Christian J. Tams

Non-Governmental Organisations in International Law
Anna-Karin Lindblom

Democracy, Minorities and International Law
Steven Wheatley

Prosecuting International Crimes
Selectivity and the International Law Regime
Robert Cryer

Compensation for Personal Injury in English, German and Italian Law
A Comparative Outline
Basil Markesinis, Michael Coester, Guido Alpa, Augustus Ullstein

Dispute Settlement in the UN Convention on the Law of the Sea
Natalie Klein

The International Protection of Internally Displaced Persons
Catherine Phuong

Imperialism, Sovereignty and the Making of International Law
Antony Anghie

Necessity, Proportionality and the Use of Force by States
Judith Gardam

International Legal Argument in the Permanent Court of International Justice
The Rise of the International Judiciary
Ole Spiermann

Great Powers and Outlaw States
Unequal Sovereigns in the International Legal Order
Gerry Simpson

Local Remedies in International Law
C. F. Amerasinghe

Reading Humanitarian Intervention
Human Rights and the Use of Force in International Law
Anne Orford

Conflict of Norms in Public International Law
How WTO Law Relates to Other Rules of Law
Joost Pauwelyn

Transboundary Damage in International Law
Hanqin Xue

European Criminal Procedures
Edited by Mireille Delmas-Marty and John Spencer

The Accountability of Armed Opposition Groups in International Law
Liesbeth Zegveld

Sharing Transboundary Resources
International Law and Optimal Resource Use
Eyal Benvenisti

International Human Rights and Humanitarian Law
René Provost

Remedies Against International Organisations
Karel Wellens

Diversity and Self-Determination in International Law
Karen Knop

The Law of Internal Armed Conflict
Lindsay Moir

International Commercial Arbitration and African States
Practice, Participation and Institutional Development
Amazu A. Asouzu

The Enforceability of Promises in European Contract Law
James Gordley

International Law in Antiquity
David J. Bederman

Money Laundering
A New International Law Enforcement Model
Guy Stessens

Good Faith in European Contract Law
Reinhard Zimmermann and Simon Whittaker

On Civil Procedure
J.A. Jolowicz

Trusts
A Comparative Study
Maurizio Lupoi

The Right to Property in Commonwealth Constitutions
Tom Allen

International Organizations Before National Courts
August Reinisch

The Changing International Law of High Seas Fisheries
Francisco Orrego Vicuña

Trade and the Environment
A Comparative Study of EC and US Law
Damien Geradin

Unjust Enrichment
A Study of Private Law and Public Values
Hanoch Dagan

Religious Liberty and International Law in Europe
Malcolm D. Evans

Ethics and Authority in International Law
Alfred P. Rubin

Sovereignty Over Natural Resources
Balancing Rights and Duties
Nico Schrijver

The Polar Regions and the Development of International Law
Donald R. Rothwell

Fragmentation and the International Relations of Micro-States
Self-Determination and Statehood
Jorri Duursma

Principles of the Institutional Law of International Organizations
C.F. Amerasinghe

Lightning Source UK Ltd.
Milton Keynes UK
UKOW050225030312

188243UK00001B/30/P

9 780521 760485